A Muslim Woman's GUIDE TO MENSTRUATION RULINGS

WRITTEN & COMPILED BY

NAIELAH ACKBARALI

A Muslim Woman's Guide to Menstruation Rulings

Author Email: help@muslimacoaching.com

ISBN: 978-1-7395999-1-1 *Paperback*

Published in England by
Inspired Muslim Women Ltd
Romford, United Kingdom
Tel: +44 7 915 765 815
Email: info@inspiredmuslimwomen.com
Website: www.inspiredmuslimwomen.com

British Library Cataloguing in Publication Data.
A catalogue record for this book is also available from the British Library.

بسم الله الرحمن الرحيم

To my husband,
who supported me throughout my journey.

Transliteration Table

ARABIC LETTER	ENGLISH TRANSLITERATION	ARABIC LETTER	ENGLISH TRANSLITERATION
ء	ʾ	ض	ḍ
ا	a, ā	ط	ṭ
ب	b	ظ	ẓ
ت	t	ع	ʿ, ʿa, ʿi, ʿu
ث	th	غ	gh
ج	j	ف	f
ح	ḥ	ق	q
خ	kh	ك	k
د	d	ل	l
ذ	dh	م	m
ر	r	ن	n
ز	z	و	w, ū, u
س	s	ه	h
ش	sh	ي	y, ī, i
ص	ṣ		

ARABIC SYMBOL	ENGLISH TRANSLITERATION	ENGLISH TRANSLATION
ﷺ	*ṣalla ʾLlāhu ʿalayhi wa sallam*	Allāh bless him and give him peace.
عليه السلام	*ʿalahī as-salām*	Peace be upon him.
رضي الله عنهم	*raḍiya ʾLlāhu ʿanhum*	May Allāh be pleased with them.
رضي الله عنها	*raḍiya ʾLlāhu ʿanhā*	May Allāh be pleased with her.
رضي الله عنه	*raḍiya ʾLlāhu ʿanhu*	May Allāh be pleased with him.

Contents

Introduction **13**

Part One: Adopting the Right Mindset **19**

Chapter 1. Written for the Daughters of Adam 21
Chapter 2. What You Weren't Told Growing Up 34
Chapter 3. Colors, Flows & Discharges 46

Part Two: Menstruation Rulings **63**

Chapter 4. Menstruation 101 65
Chapter 5. Rulings in Practice 83
Chapter 6. The *Ghusl* & Related Questions 101
Chapter 7. Blood Exceeding Ten Days 120
Chapter 8. The *Kursuf* 128
Chapter 9. Prohibited & Permitted Acts 138

Part Three: Lochia Rulings **165**

Chapter 10. Pregnancy & Birth 167
Chapter 11. Lochia 101 176
Chapter 12. Rulings in Practice 188
Chapter 13. Blood Exceeding Forty Days 203
Chapter 14. Miscarriages 211

Part Four: Purity Rulings **221**

Chapter 15. The Sound Purity 223
Chapter 16. Abnormal Uterine Bleeding (*Istiḥāḍa*) 237
Chapter 17. Praying While Bleeding 245
Chapter 18. Early Blood Formula 257

Part Five: Concluding Topics **267**

Chapter 19. Menopause 269
Chapter 20. Most Popular Questions 277

Appendix **293**

Contents In Detail

Introduction **13**

About This Book 14

Advice to the Reader 15

PART ONE: ADOPTING THE RIGHT MINDSET

Chapter 1. Written for the Daughters of Adam **21**

Menstruation Is a Blessing, Not a Punishment 24

How The Prophet ﷺ Treated Menstruating Women 25

Dos & Don'ts During Menstruation 28

1.1 Definition of Ritual Impurity 30

1.2 Types of Ritual Impurity 30

1.3 Menstruation & Major Ritual Impurity 31

1.4 Impermissible Acts During Menstruation 31

1.5 Permissible Acts During Menstruation 32

Review Questions 33

Chapter 2. What You Weren't Told Growing Up **34**

2.1 Female-Only Parts 35

2.2 Menstruation According to Doctors 38

2.3 Menstruation According to Islamic Law 40

2.4 Top Ten Mistakes Women Make 42

Review Questions 45

Chapter 3. Colors, Flows & Discharges **46**

3.1 Definition of Blood 46

3.2 Colors of Blood 47

3.3 Color Mixed in Clear or White Discharge 48

3.4 Three Types of Blood 48

3.5 Differing Colors & Flows 48

3.6 The Habit 49

3.7 Obligation to Record 51

3.8 Sound Blood vs. Unsound Blood 53

3.9 Normal Vaginal Discharge 55
3.10 Normal Vaginal Discharge & *Wuḍū*ʾ 56
3.11 Yellow Vaginal Discharge 56
3.12 Normal Vaginal Discharge Drying Yellow 57
3.13 Other Vaginal Discharges 57
Review Questions 61

PART TWO: MENSTRUATION RULINGS

Chapter 4. Menstruation 101 **65**
4.1 Definition of Menstruation 67
4.2 Conditions of Menstruation 69
4.3 First Condition: The Menstrual Minimum 69
4.4 Second Condition: The Menstrual Maximum 72
4.5 Third Condition: Purity Span Between Two Menses 74
4.6 Establishing a Menses Habit 76
4.7 Recording the Menses Habit 77
4.8 Types of Habits 77
4.9 Habit in Place & Habit in Number 80
Review Questions 82

Chapter 5. Rulings in Practice **83**
5.1 Ruling in the Moment vs. Ruling in Retrospect 84
5.2 Possible Days of Menses (PDM) 85
5.3 Rulings for the Possible Days of Menses (PDM) 87
5.4 First PDM Ruling: Whenever Blood Is Seen 88
5.5 Second PDM Ruling: When Blood Stops Before 72 Hours 90
5.6 Process for Blood Stopping Before 72 Hours 91
5.7 Third PDM Ruling: When Blood Stops At or After 72 Hours 92
5.8 Bleeding Exceeding the Menses Habit in PDM 95
5.9 Bleeding Returning After It Previously Stopped in PDM 95
5.10 Worship Performed During Gaps of Purity in PDM 96
5.11 Change in the Habit 98
5.12 Bleeding Exceeding the Menstrual Maximum 99
5.13 Abnormal Bleeding Scenarios 100
Review Questions 100

Chapter 6. The Ghusl & Related Questions 101

6.1 Ruling for the Purificatory Shower (*Ghusl*) 102
6.2 Obligatory Actions of the *Ghusl* 102
6.3 Complete *Ghusl* With *Sunna* Actions 103
6.4 Definition of the *Ghusl* Time 104
6.5 *Ghusl* Time & the Habit 104
6.6 Blood Ending Before the Maximum 107
6.7 Before the Habit Rulings 108
6.8 At or After the Habit Rulings 112
6.9 Blood Ending at the Maximum 114
6.10 Preferred Prayer Time 118
Review Questions 119

Chapter 7. Blood Exceeding Ten Days 120

7.1 Rulings for Possible Days of Menses (PDM) 121
7.2 Blood Reaching the Maximum 122
7.3 Blood Exceeding the Maximum 123
7.4 Returning to the Habit 124
Review Questions 127

Chapter 8. The Kursuf 128

8.1 Definition of the *Kursuf* 128
8.2 Pads & Pantyliners 129
8.3 Wearing the *Kursuf* 129
8.4 Ruling of Discharge Found on the *Kursuf* 131
8.5 Discharge Exits Yellow 131
8.6 Discharge Exits White 131
8.7 Avoiding Multiple *Ghusls* 132
8.8 Using the *Kursuf* to Check the End of Bleeding 132
8.9 Who Wears the *Kursuf* 134
8.10 Stopping the Onset of Menses 134
8.11 Using the *Kursuf* for Abnormal Bleeding 137
Review Questions 137

Chapter 9. Prohibited & Permitted Acts 138

9.1 Performing the Ritual Prayer During Menses 140
9.2 Recommended Forms of Worship 140

9.3 Bleeding Starts During the Prayer 140
9.4 Bleeding Starts After the Prayer Time Entered 141
9.5 Call to Prayer 142
9.6 Prostration of Recitation or Gratitude 142
9.7 Fasting During Menses 143
9.8 Menstrual Bleeding Starts During the Fast 143
9.9 Missing *Ramaḍān* Fasts 144
9.10 Eating During the Day in *Ramaḍān* 144
9.11 Menses Stops During the Day in *Ramaḍān* 145
9.12 Menses Stops During the Night in *Ramaḍān* 145
9.13 *ʿItikāf* 146
9.14 *Kaffārat Al-Fiṭr* 146
9.15 Touching the Qurʾān During Menses 147
9.16 Touching the Qurʾān With a Barrier 147
9.17 Translations of the Qurʾān 147
9.18 *Tafsīr* Books 148
9.19 Books of Sacred Knowledge 148
9.20 Objects With Qurʾān Inscribed on Them 148
9.21 Phones & Electronic Devices 148
9.22 Reading With Eyes Only 149
9.23 Reciting the Qurʾān During Menses 150
9.24 Reciting for Reward 150
9.25 Qurʾānic Supplications 150
9.26 Other Forms of *Dhikr* 151
9.27 Reading the Qurʾān With the Heart 151
9.28 Listening to the Qurʾān 151
9.29 Entering a Mosque During Menses 152
9.30 Menstruation Starts in the Mosque 153
9.31 Entering Islamic Centers 153
9.32 Courtyards in Makkah & Madīna 153
9.33 *ʿĪd* Prayer Area 153
9.34 Graveyards 153
9.35 Making *Ṭawāf* During Menses 154
9.36 Menstruation Starts Before or During *Ṭawāf* 154
9.37 *Ṭawāf* Penalties 155
9.38 Dropping *Ṭawāf* Penalties 156

9.39 Permissible Acts During *Ḥajj* & *ʿUmra* 157
9.40 Performing the *Saʿī* 158
9.41 Farewell *Ṭawāf* & Menses 158
9.42 Sexual Intercourse During Menses 159
9.43 Knowing the Time of Menses 159
9.44 Touching Between the Navel to Knee During Menses 160
9.45 Permissible Touching 160
9.46 Being Divorced During Menses 161
9.47 *Khulʿ* During Menses 162
9.48 Related Rulings During Impure States 162
Review Questions 163

PART THREE: LOCHIA RULINGS

Chapter 10. Pregnancy & Birth **167**

10.1 Menstruation During Pregnancy 168
10.2 Bleeding During Pregnancy 168
10.3 Obligation to Pray 169
10.4 Obligation to Fast 169
10.5 Vaginal Exams 170
10.6 Colored Discharge Exiting Before Childbirth 171
10.7 Removing Filth Before Praying 172
10.8 Praying During Labor 172
10.9 Making *Duʿāʾ* During Childbirth 174
10.10 Owing the Prayer 175
10.11 Post-Marital Waiting Period 175
Review Questions 175

Chapter 11. Lochia 101 **176**

11.1 Definition of Lochia 178
11.2 Conditions of Lochia 179
11.3 First Condition: The Lochia Minimum 179
11.4 Second Condition: The Lochia Maximum 180
11.5 Third Condition: Purity Span Between Lochia & Menses 182
11.6 Fourth Condition: Six-Month Span Between Two Lochia 184
11.7 Establishing a Lochia Habit 185
11.8 Recording the Lochia Habit 186

11.9 Lochia Beginner 186
11.10 Woman With a Lochia Habit 187
Review Questions 187

Chapter 12. Rulings in Practice **188**

12.1 Possible Days of Lochia (PDL) 189
12.2 Rulings for the Possible Days of Lochia (PDL) 190
12.3 First PDL Ruling: Whenever Blood Is Seen 191
12.4 Second PDL Ruling: When Blood Stops 192
12.5 Bleeding Exceeding the Lochia Habit in PDL 194
12.6 Bleeding Returning After It Previously Stopped in PDL 195
12.7 Worship Performed During Gaps of Purity in PDL 195
12.8 Change in the Habit 196
12.9 Bleeding Exceeding the Lochia Maximum 197
12.10 Ruling for the Purificatory Shower (*Ghusl*) 198
12.11 *Ghusl* Time & the Habit 199
12.12 Lochia Beginner & the *Ghusl* Time 199
12.13 Lochia Beginner & the Habit 200
12.14 Menstruation After Lochia 201
Review Questions 202

Chapter 13. Blood Exceeding Forty Days **203**

13.1 Rulings for Possible Days of Lochia (PDL) 204
13.2 Blood Reaching the Maximum 204
13.3 Ruling for a Lochia Beginner 205
13.4 Ruling for a Woman With a Lochia Habit 206
13.5 Returning to the Lochia Habit 208
13.6 Menstruation After Lochia 209
Review Questions 210

Chapter 14. Miscarriages **211**

14.1 Types of Miscarriages 212
14.2 Definition of a Developed Fetus 212
14.3 Definition of an Undeveloped Embryo 212
14.4 Development by Number of Months or Weeks 212
14.5 Blood During Pregnancy 213
14.6 Miscarriage of a Developed Fetus 214

14.7 Burial Rulings for a Developed Fetus 215
14.8 Miscarriage & Burial of a Still Birth 215
14.9 Miscarriage of an Undeveloped Embryo 215
14.10 Burial Rulings for an Undeveloped Embryo 218
14.11 Post-Marital Waiting Period 219
Review Questions 219

PART FOUR: PURITY RULINGS

Chapter 15. The Sound Purity **223**
15.1 Definition of Purity 224
15.2 Need for a Purity Span Between Bloods 224
15.3 Purity Span Minimum 224
15.4 Purity Span Maximum 225
15.5 Sound Purity vs. Unsound Purity 225
15.6 Sound Purity Conditions 226
15.7 First Condition: At Least 15 Days (360 Hours) or More 226
15.8 Second Condition: Free From Blood for the Entire Span 228
15.9 Third Condition: Situated Between Two Sound Bloods 229
15.10 Establishing a Purity Habit 230
15.11 Recording the Purity Habit 231
15.12 Types of Unsound Purity 232
15.13 Incomplete Purity 232
15.14 Unsound Complete Purity 233
15.15 Intervening Purity 235
15.16 Bleeding During Purity 236
Review Questions 236

Chapter 16. Abnormal Uterine Bleeding (*Istiḥāḍa*) **237**
16.1 Definition of Abnormal Uterine Bleeding 239
16.2 Examples of Abnormal Bleeding 239
16.3 All Forms of Worship Permitted 240
16.4 Praying While Bleeding 240
16.5 Praying With Blood on Clothes 240
16.6 How to Remove Blood from Clothes 241
16.7 Intimacy During Abnormal Bleeding 241
16.8 Comparison to Menstruation & Lochia 242

Review Questions 244

Chapter 17. Praying While Bleeding **245**

17.1 Ruling of Praying With Abnormal Bleeding 246
17.2 Praying With Spotting 247
17.3 Praying With a Constant Flow 248
17.4 Blocking Blood Flow 248
17.5 Blood Leaking After Blocking 250
17.6 Exceptions to Blocking 250
17.7 Excused Person's Rulings 252
17.8 Establishing the Excused Person Status 252
17.9 Maintaining the Excused Person Status 253
17.10 Forms of Worship Permitted 253
17.11 *Wuḍū*ʾ Nullifiers for the Excused Person 254
17.12 Losing the Excused Person Status 254
17.13 Excused Person Praying With Blood on Clothes 255
Review Questions 256

Chapter 18. Early Blood Formula **257**

18.1 Blood Starts Before a Purity Span of 15 Days 257
18.2 Blood Starts After a Purity Span of 15 Days 259
18.3 Early Blood Formula 260
18.4 Rulings in Retrospect 263
18.5 Long Purity Exception 264
Review Questions 265

PART FIVE: CONCLUDING TOPICS

Chapter 19. Menopause **269**

19.1 Menopause According to Doctors 270
19.2 Menopause According to *Ḥanafī* Scholars 270
19.3 Bleeding After 55 Lunar Years 271
19.4 Black or Red Blood 271
19.5 Like Her Premenopausal Period 272
19.6 Post-Marital Waiting Period 274
19.7 Early Menopause 275
Review Questions 276

Chapter 20. Most Popular Questions **277**

20.1 I went to the bathroom and saw blood, but I do not know when it came out. When do I consider my menses to have started? 277

20.2 If I wake up at *Fajr* and do not see blood, do I make up the *ʿĪshaʾ* prayer? 277

20.3 How do I know if I am really seeing yellow discharge? 277

20.4 I heard that the colors yellow and turbid are not menses. Is that true? 278

20.5 Can I remove body hair during menstruation? 279

20.6 Are marital relations permitted when bleeding stops before 3 days during the possible days of menses? 279

20.7 Can I delay taking my *ghusl* after my bleeding ends? What if I know my bleeding will return? 279

20.8 My menses is going to end while I am in an airplane. What do I do? 280

20.9 I am spotting during *ʿumra* or after inserting an IUD. Is it menstruation? 280

20.10 Where did the concept of the habit come from? Why not consider colors and flow? 281

20.11 Can I take medication to delay my period in *Ramaḍān*? 282

20.12 If I wake up for *suḥūr* and do not see blood, do I intend to fast *Ramaḍān* if I haven't taken a *ghusl* yet? 282

20.13 Can I take medication to delay my period for *ḥajj* or *ʿumra*? 283

20.14 What if my menses starts before I do the *ṭawāf* and will only finish after my group leaves? 284

20.15 Can a married women wear a tampon? 284

20.16 What is the ruling for bleeding after sex? 285

20.17 What is the ruling for bleeding after vaginal exams? 285

20.18 Is withdrawal blood from birth control and Primolut N menses? 286

20.19 What is legal blood? Why am I being told that I menstruated when I did not see any blood on those days? 286

20.20 Why am I experiencing abnormal bleeding? 288

APPENDIX

Menses in a Nutshell 295
Lochia in a Nutshell 297
Purity in a Nutshell 299
Glossary of Terms 301
Bibliography 311

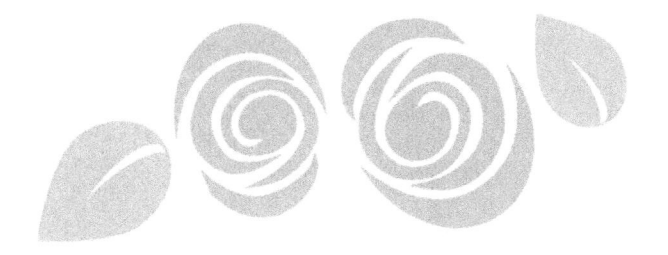

Introduction

I was lost. I had pressing questions related to my menstrual cycle, but no one could help me.

I asked my friends, their mothers, and the women in my local community. Some attempted to give answers, which confused me more, while others shrugged their shoulders saying they did not know what to say.

I remember crying several times over my situation, feeling like I could not win. I hated my period. I felt hopeless with the rulings.

After several years of living in ignorance and sheer guessing, I finally met learned people who could answer my questions. I was relieved from one perspective but overwhelmed from another.

I had to learn the rulings from century-old *fiqh* books. I had to ask embarrassing questions to male teachers. I had to spend years of my life trying to seek this knowledge from several scholars. I even studied the rulings from different schools of law (*madhāhib*) searching for answers. It has been a long twenty-year journey.

Over the years, I began to meet more women like myself. Women who had urgent questions but could not always find someone to give them the answer they needed. They had other obstacles in their path that stopped them from learning the rulings in detail. Many times, they could not grasp the foundational principles to take their studies further.

I wrote this book with the intention to help women understand the rulings related to menstruation and how to practice them. I do not want women to struggle the way that I did in trying to put the puzzle pieces together. I want to make learning this subject easy and accessible to as many women as possible.

When menstruation is taught, it is usually one of two extremes. It is either oversimplified so that women do not gain the full picture of what the rulings entail, or it is overly complicated so that women leave feeling hopeless in grasping what is taught.

I intended to produce a work that was the middle way. This book is not a beginner's book, but it is not advanced either. I pray that every woman who reads it will understand its details, even if it takes a few times to digest certain points. The basis of studying knowledge is repetition, and hopefully with it being in a book format, it will make revision of the concepts easier.

Menstruation is known to be one of the most difficult chapters to master in the books of Islamic law (*fiqh*) due to its fine details, terse definitions, and numerous rulings that are connected to other chapters of *fiqh*. However, at the same time, its practical application in a woman's life cannot be ignored.

God-fearingness (*taqwā*) is the key to success in this Life and the Next. Allāh Most High tells us that He loves those who are God-fearing (*Āli ʿImrān*, 3:76). Thus, it is imperative to learn the rulings of menstruation and make the effort to apply them in one's life. Learning and practicing this knowledge are for Allāh Most High's sake. With His assistance, anything is possible.

ABOUT THIS BOOK

This guide is designed to be practical, engaging, and easy to read.

- ✧ Inspirational content based on verses of the Qurʾān and stories from the lives of the female Companions ﷺ introduces each chapter.
- ✧ Core topics and their related rulings are organized into structured chapters.
- ✧ Legal rulings are broken down into simplified portions and categorized by numbered headings.
- ✧ Bullet point lists, tables, charts, and picture diagrams are utilized to consolidate the knowledge shared.
- ✧ Tables, charts, and picture diagrams are labeled for easy referencing.
- ✧ Blurbs that highlight concepts to remember are included in relevant places.
- ✧ Icons are used to direct and help the reader. A list of the icons along with their meanings can be found in Table i.

- ✧ Review questions are provided at the end of each chapter to test the reader's comprehension.
- ✧ Answers to the most popular questions that women ask are detailed in the final chapter.
- ✧ Relevant medical information is mentioned.
- ✧ A summary of the rulings related to menstruation, lochia, and purity spans is given in the Appendix section for a quick overview.
- ✧ A glossary of terms is provided for any words that are unfamiliar to the reader.

Table i: Key for Icons

ICONS	MEANING
	Represents the start of a chapter along with its contents.
	Points out an associated ruling or important detail.
	Describes the topic further.
	Alerts the reader to a must-know issue.
	Indicates that a related diagram, table, or chart is available.
	Directs the reader to another relevant section or chapter.
	Signifies a common question with its answer.
	Draws attention to important things to remember.

ADVICE TO THE READER

Before beginning, there are a few things to note about this book.

Firstly, the rulings in this guide are based on the *Ḥanafī madhhab*. Each school of law (*madhhab*) has developed its own specific methodology to understand what has been conveyed about menstruation from the Qurʾān and the *Sunna*. This may lead to notable differences of opinion amongst scholars. As such, women should not be surprised if they come across rulings different from the ones mentioned in this book.

The reason this guide focuses on teaching one *madhhab* is because it is easier to learn the rulings from one *madhhab* instead of the rulings across the various schools of law in one go. Sometimes it can cause more confusion than good.

However, the *Ḥanafī madhhab*'s way of resolving menstruation issues may not be practical for every person's circumstance. Consequently, each woman should choose the *madhhab* that works best for her situation, providing that she has access to a teacher who can help her.

The differences of opinion are a mercy for the *ummah*, especially when there is a need to take them. As long as a woman is following the Prophet's ﷺ way, this is what matters.

? What is a *madhhab*? What is the *Ḥanafī madhhab*?

The Sacred Law rulings are derived primarily from the Qurʾān, the *Sunna*, scholarly consensus (*ijmāʿ*), and legal analogy (*qiyās*). A *madhhab* is a school of law that unites scholars upon a common methodology concerning how to understand, interpret, and derive legal rulings from the guidance of Allāh Most High and His beloved Messenger ﷺ.

There are four main schools of law (*madhāhib*) in Sunni Islam: the *Ḥanafī*, *Mālikī*, *Shāfiʿī*, and *Ḥanbalī madhhab*. A very common misconception is that following a *madhhab* means following the opinion of the founder instead of the Qurʾān and the *Sunna*. This is not true. Rather it is about following a legal methodology to understand and apply the Qurʾān and the *Sunna*. The system of law provided by each *madhhab* was further developed and refined by scholars throughout each century up to today's times.

The *Ḥanafī madhhab* is one of the four traditional schools. Its eponym is the 8th-century Kufan scholar, Abū Ḥanīfa an-Nuʿmān ibn Thābit, whose legal views were preserved primarily by his two disciples, Imām Abū Yūsuf and Imām Muḥammad ibn al-Ḥasan ash-Shaybānī. May Allāh have mercy on them.

Secondly, although this guide will give a strong foundation for menstruation rulings, reading it with a teacher – or asking one's questions to a teacher – must be a priority.

Finally, each chapter of this guide is a layer of knowledge that builds upon the previous chapters. Therefore, it is not recommended to skip sections.

Before starting, test your current knowledge of the rulings with the quiz below. The answer key is given on the following page, and detailed answers are explained throughout the guide.

TRUE OR FALSE QUESTIONS

❶ Only red blood can be considered menstruation.

❷ The least amount of days menstruation can be is different for each woman, and it is based on her body's cycle.

❸ The spotting of blood is not menstruation. Menstruation starts when bleeding becomes a constant flow.

❹ Every time bleeding stops, a woman is obliged to take a purificatory shower (*ghusl*).

❺ The maximum amount of days menstruation can be is 10 days (240 hours). Any bleeding that exceeds this amount will be ruled as abnormal bleeding (*istiḥāḍa*).

❻ If the bleeding exceeds 10 days, all 10 days are menstruation. Thereafter, a woman uses 10 days as her menstrual habit and 15 days as her purity habit until her situation normalizes.

❼ A purity span of at least 15 days (360 hours) free of blood must follow menstruation.

❽ If a woman starts bleeding before 15 days of purity elapses, she keeps praying until she reaches the completion of day 15.

❾ Bleeding during labor is considered lochia (*nifās)*.

❿ If a woman's lochia (*nifās)* stops before 40 days, she waits until 40 days finishes before taking a purificatory shower (*ghusl*).

ANSWER KEY: All false except numbers 5 and 7.

PART ONE:

Adopting The Right Mindset

Chapter 1

WRITTEN FOR THE DAUGHTERS OF ADAM

Chapter 2

WHAT YOU WEREN'T TOLD GROWING UP

Chapter 3

COLORS, FLOWS, AND DISCHARGES

This is a thing **which Allāh has** written for the **daughters of** Adam عليه السلام

Bukhārī

Chapter 1

Written for the Daughters of Adam عليه السلام

IN THIS CHAPTER

- ✧ The Prophet's ﷺ explanation of menstruation
- ✧ The Islamic view on menstruation
- ✧ How the Prophet ﷺ treated menstruating women

It was the tenth year after the *hijra*, the last year of the Prophet Muḥammad's ﷺ life. Yet, no one knew that his ﷺ demise was to come. The Prophet ﷺ intended to undertake *ḥajj* during this year. It was the only *ḥajj* that the Prophet ﷺ performed after it became compulsory. Less than three months later, he ﷺ would suddenly fall sick and pass away.

Thousands of the Companions رضي الله عنهم came from various parts of the Arabian Peninsula to complete the *ḥajj* with the Prophet ﷺ. As for his wives رضي الله عنهن, all of them accompanied him to Makkah during his final pilgrimage.

The Prophet ﷺ and his Companions رضي الله عنهم left Madīna when there were only five days remaining of the month of *Dhū ʾl Qaʿda*. They entered into a state of pilgrim sanctity (*iḥrām*) just a few miles outside of Madīna at Dhūl Ḥulayfah, which is known as Masjid ash-Shajara in today's times.

The Prophet ﷺ ordered those with him to intend what they wanted. There are different intentions that a pilgrim can make for *ḥajj*. A pilgrim can intend to do *ḥajj* only (*ifrād*), or a *ḥajj* and an *ʿumra* together with the same intention (*qirān*), or an *ʿumra* by itself and a *ḥajj* by itself (*tamattuʿ*). The Prophet's ﷺ beloved wife Lady ʿĀʾisha رضي الله عنها intended to do the latter type, which is an *ʿumra* and a *ḥajj* with separate intentions.

The Companions ﷺ were so excited to perform the *ḥajj*. They chanted the *talbiya* throughout their trip down to Makkah. One can only dream of how elated their spirits were and the immense honor that they must have felt to be part of the Prophet's pilgrimage ﷺ.

The Prophet ﷺ and his Companions ﷺ entered Makkah on the fourth of *Dhū 'l Ḥijjah*, prepared to complete the sacred rites due upon them. However, Lady ʿĀʾisha ﷺ started to menstruate before that at Sarif, a location that is approximately ten miles outside of Makkah.

She was already in the state of pilgrim sanctity, and not knowing what was to come, she became deeply saddened by the thought that she could not do *ḥajj* at all.

In her own narration, she describes what happened and says:

> "We set out with the Prophet ﷺ for *ḥajj*, and we were not making mention of anything except *ḥajj*. When we reached Sarif, I got my menses. When the Prophet ﷺ came to me, I was crying. He ﷺ asked, 'Why are you weeping?' I said, 'I wish – by Allāh! - that I had not performed *ḥajj* this year.' He asked, 'Perhaps you got your menses?' I replied, 'Yes.' He then said, 'This is a thing which Allāh has written for the daughters of Adam. So do what all the pilgrims do except that you do not perform the *ṭawāf* around the Kaʿba until you are (ritually) pure.'"
>
> (*Bukhārī*, 305)

Lady ʿĀʾisha ﷺ was crying out of disappointment. She did not want to miss the momentous experience of *ḥajj*, but what could she do? In those days, there were no hormonal medications that existed to stop her menstrual flow.

She had to submit to Allāh Most High's will, but it was nevertheless a heartbreaking moment for her – even to the extent that she wished that she had not performed *ḥajj* that year! Little did she know that this would be the only *ḥajj* that her beloved husband ﷺ would perform, and he ﷺ would die only a few months later in her own arms.

The Prophet's ﷺ response to Lady ʿĀʾisha's crying was exemplary in many ways. Firstly, he ﷺ knew why she was crying. This is the type of loving relationship that they had with each other. He ﷺ could sense his wife's emotional state.

Secondly, he was gentle in his approach. He ﷺ saw that she was in pain and reached out to her in a caring way. His words comforted and consoled her worries. And what were his words? That women are the daughters of Prophet Adam عليه السلام.

Sometimes people think that menstruation is dirty and disgusting, but the Prophet ﷺ elevated women to the lofty status of being the progeny of the first Prophet to mankind because of their monthly cycles.

This *ḥadīth* also proves that menstruation is not a punishment. Rather, menstruation is natural and normal – something which Allāh Most High has ordained for all women until the end of time.

In fact, Allāh Most High honored women with their monthly cycles. If it were not for menstruation, Muslim women could not get pregnant, have children, and continue to uphold the lifeline of the *ummah*.

The Prophet ﷺ informed Lady ʿĀʾisha رضي الله عنها that she could perform *ḥajj*, but she could not do the *ṭawāf*. This is the only *ḥajj* ritual that a menstruating women must avoid until her menstruation ceases.

She can do everything else: camp at Minā, stand at ʿArafat, sleep at Muzdalifa, stone the *jamarāt*, carry out the slaughtering, make *dhikr*, supplicate, engage in repentance, make *ṣalawāt*, and much more.

Lady ʿĀʾisha رضي الله عنها followed through with the Prophetic instruction. She exited her pilgrim state for *ʿumra* and entered into a new pilgrim state for *ḥajj*. She completed the standing at ʿArafat, and when her menstruation ended she performed the *ṭawāf* on *ʿĪd* day.

She accepted that this is what Allāh Most High had willed for her. Furthermore, she was still able to benefit and have a spiritual experience despite her circumstance.

In another narration, Lady ʿĀʾisha رضي الله عنها told the Prophet ﷺ that everyone else had completed a *ḥajj* and an *ʿumra* but she had only done a *ḥajj*. The Prophet ﷺ ordered her brother, ʿAbdur Raḥmān ibn Abī Bakr 🌸, to take her to Tanʿīm so that she could enter into a state of pilgrim sanctity for ʿumra. (*Muslim*, 1213)

In today's times, this location is demarcated by a mosque known as Masjid ʿĀʾisha. It is where everyone goes nowadays to enter into pilgrim sanctity (*iḥrām*) for ʿumra once they are in Makkah.

Because of Lady ʿĀʾisha's situation 🌸, Muslim women know what to do when they experience menstruation during *ḥajj*. More than this, all Muslims know where to go if they want to perform another ʿumra. Her trial, her pain, and her worry over her menstruation became a symbol of Islam – landmarked by a *masjid* that people will use until the end of time.

MENSTRUATION IS A BLESSING, NOT A PUNISHMENT

It is quite common for women to complain about their period woes. The cramping, the headaches, and the messy bleeding on a monthly basis could be viewed as inconvenient.

However, believing women must overlook the emotional highs and lows of their menstrual cycle and direct their focus upon what the religion of Islam says about menstruation.

Islam does not consider menstruation to be a punishment. Rather, menstruation is viewed as a natural process that normal, healthy women experience throughout their lifetime.

A menstruating woman is not dirty, but rather from a legal perspective she is ritually impure for the duration that she is menstruating. This classification has legal consequences and not spiritual consequences.

As such, a menstruating woman is instructed by Allāh Most High to stop certain forms of worship, and every second that she obeys these commands, it is worship if done for Allāh Most High's sake.

The rulings of menstruation have other benefits. They make a woman aware of her body, so that she takes care of it. They instill a longing for her to perform certain acts of worship, so she is keen to pray and fast once her bleeding ends. They compel her to learn the Islamic sciences, so she increases in love for her religion. They keep her conscious of her Lord's commands, so she is avid to obey His orders throughout her days and nights.

Menstruation is not a barrier to a woman's spirituality. Instead, it is an opportunity to learn how to devote herself to Allāh Most High in a different way. Following the rulings and living them out in her daily life is a means for reward.

Medically speaking, it is impossible for a woman to become pregnant if she cannot menstruate, which is the case for young children and postmenopausal women. The blessing of being able to menstruate is quite clear for the one who reflects.

The first time a girl sees menstrual blood, her body is signaling to her that she is growing into a young woman. She is now physically able to start conceiving. In fact, only by the occurrence of menstruation is a woman given the opportunity to begin and nurture a righteous family.

For most women, Allāh Most High gives them this chance once a month for a series of decades to attempt conception and enjoy the blessing of raising pious children. Surely, the wondrous joys experienced during parenthood would never be possible without first experiencing menstruation.

HOW THE PROPHET ﷺ TREATED MENSTRUATING WOMEN

The Prophet ﷺ instructed the Companions ﷺ with how to interact with menstruating women, and he ﷺ also demonstrated the best of ways through his own noble behavior. The following are a few notable examples from the Prophet's ﷺ life.

> Anas ibn Malik ﷺ relates, "Among the Jews at the time of the Prophet ﷺ when one of their women would menstruate, they would not eat with her, and they would not remain in the same houses with menstruating women. So, the Companions ﷺ of the Prophet asked the Prophet ﷺ (about how to interact with them) and thereafter Allāh revealed the verse, 'And they ask you about menstruation. Say: It is an impurity. So, keep away from women during menstruation...' to the end of the verse. The Prophet ﷺ then said, 'Do everything with her except sexual intercourse.'"
>
> (*Muslim*, 302)

> The Mother of the Believers Maymūna ﷺ said, "The Messenger of Allāh ﷺ touched his wives over the *izār* (lower garment) when they were menstruating."
>
> (*Muslim*, 294)

These *aḥādīth* demonstrate that a husband must still act favorably and lovingly towards his wife even while she is menstruating. A man should not ignore his menstruating wife but continue to live with her as companions for the sake of Allāh Most High. He can eat with her, drink with her, and dwell in the same house as her.

Additionally, the given responses indicate that it is permissible to touch her, and even to sexually stimulate her, providing that the husband does not directly touch the skin between her navel and knee.

> The Mother of the Believers ʿĀʾisha ﷺ said, "The Prophet ﷺ would recline on my lap while I was menstruating, and he ﷺ would recite the Qurʾān."
>
> (*Bukhārī*, 297)
>
> In another *ḥadīth* ʿĀʾisha ﷺ also said, "I would drink while menstruating, then pass the vessel to the Prophet ﷺ. He would place his mouth on the (same) place as my mouth and drink...."
>
> (*Muslim*, 300)

The Prophet ﷺ continued to be intimately affectionate with his wives even while they were menstruating. He ﷺ did not act repulsed by them or turn away from being in their company. Rather, he ﷺ sought their comfort by laying in their laps and sharing their food.

These *aḥādīth* also prove that a menstruating woman is physically pure. Her limbs, skin, and sweat are not filthy. Moreover, when she drinks from a container, her saliva does not render the water impure. This shows that menstruation is merely an intangible state of ritual impurity and nothing more.

> The Mother of the Believers Umm Salama ﵂ said, "I was lying down with the Prophet ﷺ under a black, wool cover. Suddenly, I started to menstruate. I left quietly to put on clothing worn for menstruation. He ﷺ said, 'Did you get your menses?' I said, 'Yes.' He ﷺ called out to me to lie down again with him under the cover."
>
> (*Bukhārī*, 322)

This *ḥadīth* illustrates the permissibility of sleeping next to a menstruating woman and lying with her under the same cover. Women wore different clothing during menstruation to avoid soiling their everyday garments with filth, which is similar to what women do in today's times.

What is interesting is that the Prophet ﷺ specifically requested for Lady Umm Salama ﵂ to return and lay by his side so that he could enjoy her companionship. This is another proof that a menstruating woman is not of a lower status in Islam. She remains under the protection and care of those who love her.

> The Mother of the Believers ʿĀʾisha ﵂ said, "The Messenger of Allāh ﷺ said to me, 'Get me the prayer mat from the prayer area.' I replied, 'I am menstruating.' He said, 'Verily, your menstruation is not in your hand.'"
>
> (*Muslim*, 298)
>
> In another *ḥadīth* she ﵂ said, "I used to wash the head of the Messenger of Allāh ﷺ while I was in a state of menstruation."
>
> (*Muslim*, 297)

The meaning of the phrase 'not in your hand' in the first ḥadīth shows that only the place where menstrual blood exits needs to be avoided. As for the rest of a menstruating woman's body, it is pure.

Both reports indicate that a menstruating woman can still live her life and carry on with her regular worldly routine, even while in this state. Menstruation does not prevent her from being of service to others, like her family or her community.

> The Mother of the Believers Maymūna ﵂ related that she would be menstruating and not praying. She would lie next to the Prophet's ﷺ prayer area while he would pray on a prayer mat. She said, "When he prostrated, some of his clothing would touch me."
>
> (*Bukhārī*, 333)

One can only imagine how close Lady Maymūna ﵂ must have been to the Prophet ﷺ for his clothes to touch her while in prayer. He ﷺ never shunned his menstruating wives or pushed them away.

Thus, what is understood from the previously mentioned *aḥādīth* is that menstruation is natural, healthy, and normal. It is a matter which Allāh Most High has willed for women until the end of time. Therefore, a woman who experiences it should be treated with the same amount of honor, dignity, and love that she would receive if she was not in a state of menstruation.

It is through the Prophet's ﷺ teachings that one learns the right mindset to adopt when approaching menstruation rulings and understanding their details.

DOS & DON'TS DURING MENSTRUATION

Sometimes it is hard to accept the list of dos and don'ts that apply to a menstruating woman. It is doubly difficult during *Ramaḍān* when everyone is fasting, and even more so during ʿ*umra* and *ḥajj*. It is a common complaint from menstruating ladies that they feel left out.

Allāh Most High says:

> "But perhaps you hate a thing and it is good for you; and perhaps you love a thing and it is bad for you. And Allāh Knows, while you know not."
>
> (*al-Baqara*, 2:216)

Scholars unanimously agree that all Sacred Law rulings have a benefit in them, even if humans cannot rationally deduce it. Allāh Most High loves His creation, and He will always decree what is best for them.

It is true that during a woman's menstruation certain acts of worship cannot be performed. Yet, one must keep in mind that they are only a select number, and many more acts remain permissible. Allāh Most High is not closing the doors of worship during the time of menstruation.

Allāh Most High clearly says in the Qur'ān:

> "I did not create the *jinn* and humans except to worship Me."
>
> (*al-Dhāriyāt*, 51:56)

Furthermore, if a menstruating woman avoids certain actions with the intention to submit to Allāh Most High's command, she is actually worshiping Allāh the entire time that she refrains from these acts.

It has been said, "Her praying while pure is worship and her refraining from prayer while menstruating is worship. All of it is worship." Thus, a menstruating woman is rewarded for submitting to Allāh Most High's command, and in reality, she is not losing out on anything.

1.1 DEFINITION OF RITUAL IMPURITY

According to the Sacred Law, ritual impurity is an intangible state that prevents the performance of certain acts of worship, like praying. The state of ritual impurity is lifted by ablution (*wuḍūʾ*), the purificatory shower (*ghusl*), or dry ablution (*tayammum*).

☑ These are ritual acts of cleanliness that were revealed by Allāh Most High and taught to the believers through the Prophet ﷺ.

⚠ The Arabic words *wuḍūʾ* and *ghusl* will be used throughout this guide, rather than their English translations.

Chart 1a: Types of Ritual Impurity

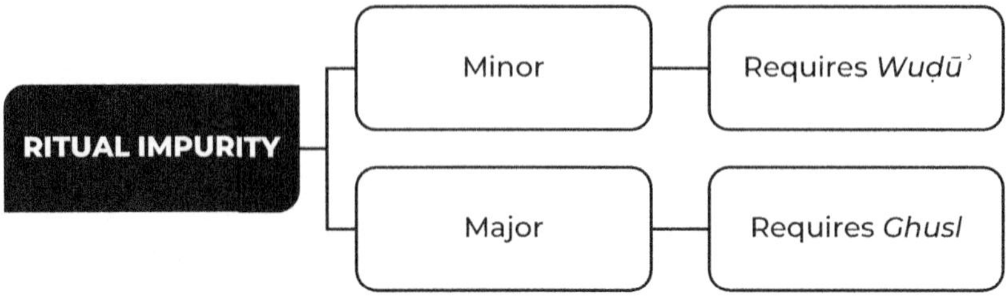

1.2 TYPES OF RITUAL IMPURITY

There are two types of ritual impurity: minor and major.

- **Minor ritual impurity** (*al-ḥadath al-aṣghar*) is a state that necessitates *wuḍūʾ*, like after sleeping, urinating, or flatulence.
- **Major ritual impurity** (*al-ḥadath al-akbar*) is a state that necessitates *ghusl*, like the state of sexual impurity (*janāba*) after engaging in sexual intercourse or ejaculating.

➔ The *ghusl* is described in Sections 6.2 to 6.3.

🔍 Compare the classifications of ritual impurity in Chart 1a.

1.3 MENSTRUATION & MAJOR RITUAL IMPURITY

Based on sound scholarship and clear evidence from the Qur'ān and the *Sunna*, a menstruating woman follows similar rulings to a person in major ritual impurity.

Thus, the only way a menstruating woman can lift her state of ritual impurity is by performing a *ghusl*. However, the *ghusl* is not valid until she stops bleeding within the possible days of menses, or her bleeding reaches the menstrual maximum.

Consequently, she will need to refrain from a handful of actions until her time comes to take a *ghusl*.

✔ The same ruling applies to a woman who is in a state of lochia (*nifās*).

1.4 IMPERMISSIBLE ACTS DURING MENSTRUATION

According to the *Ḥanafī madhhab*, there are nine actions that a woman in a state of menstruation (*ḥayḍ*) or lochia (*nifās*) needs to avoid:

1. Performing the ritual prayer or prostrating.
2. Fasting.
3. Touching the Qur'ān.
4. Reciting the Qur'ān.
5. Entering any mosque.
6. Making *ṭawāf*.
7. Engaging in sexual intercourse.
8. Being directly touched between the navel to the knee.
9. Being divorced.

➔ Each of these prohibitions are discussed in detail in Chapter 9.

> ﴾ Whoever does good, whether male or female, and is a believer, We will surely bless them with a good life, and We will certainly reward them according to the best of their deeds. ﴿
>
> (*an-Naḥl*, 16:97)

1.5 PERMISSIBLE ACTS DURING MENSTRUATION

Even though the list in Section 1.4 may seem limiting, there are numerous acts of worship that remain permissible.

In the *Ḥanafī madhhab*, it is an overall recommendation that a menstruating woman make *wuḍū*ʾ for each prayer time, sit in her usual place of worship, and make remembrance (*dhikr*) for the time it takes her to normally pray so that she does not lose her habit of worship.

A menstruating woman can also:

- ✧ Supplicate for whatever she wishes.
- ✧ Make remembrance (*dhikr*) of Allāh Most High.
- ✧ Repent (make *tawba*) to Allāh Most High.
- ✧ Listen to the Qurʾān.
- ✧ Make *ṣalawāt* on the Prophet ﷺ.
- ✧ Beg for forgiveness (*istighfār*) and the pardon of her sins (ʿ*afū*).
- ✧ Demonstrate good character towards her spouse, parents, children, and fellow Muslims.
- ✧ Memorize any Prophetic *du*ʿ*ā*ʾ.
- ✧ Teach, study, and review sacred knowledge.
- ✧ Give in charity.
- ✧ Perform acts of service to others.
- ✧ Read the *sīra* and stories about the Companions (*ṣaḥāba*) or righteous people (*ṣalīhīn*).

- Practice gratitude for her blessings.
- Practice patience and contentment with her trials.
- Forgive those who wronged her.
- Reflect about Allāh Most High's great signs.
- Read *ḥadīth*, like *Riyāḍ aṣ-Ṣalīhīn* or Imam al-Nawawī's forty *ḥadīth* collection.
- Listen to religious lectures.

The feeling of being limited only increases when a woman focuses on what she cannot do while menstruating. However, if she focuses on what she can do in the circumstance that Allāh Most High placed her in, her heart will be filled with contentment.

Thus, there is nothing dreadful or awful about the prohibitions or rulings related to menstruation. Rather, what matters is a person's attitude towards them.

REVIEW QUESTIONS

1. Why was the Mother of the Believers ʿĀʾisha ﵂ disappointed when she started menstruating during *ḥajj*?
2. What did the Prophet ﷺ tell her in response?
3. Is menstruation a punishment? Why or why not?
4. How did the Prophet ﷺ treat menstruating women?
5. What is the difference between major and minor ritual impurity? Which category does menstruation fall under?
6. Which acts must a menstruating woman avoid?
7. Which acts are permissible for her to perform?

Chapter 2

What You Weren't Told Growing Up

IN THIS CHAPTER

- ✧ Names of female body parts
- ✧ Medical definition of menstruation
- ✧ Sacred Law definition of menstruation
- ✧ Ten common mistakes women make

Many women were not educated about how their bodies function when they were growing up. Perhaps it was against the cultural norm to speak about their periods, so menstruation issues were never mentioned.

However, this is contrary to what has been conveyed about how the female Companions رضي الله عنهن learned knowledge. The Mother of the Believers Umm Salama رضي الله عنها reported that Umm Sulaym رضي الله عنها came to the Messenger of Allāh ﷺ and said:

> "O Messenger of Allāh! Verily Allāh is not shy of the truth! If a woman has a wet dream, is she required to take a purificatory shower (*ghusl*)?" He ﷺ replied, "Yes if she sees discharge (from sexual fluid)."
>
> (*Bukhārī*, 6121)

Despite the nature of the topic, Umm Sulaym رضي الله عنها asked the Prophet ﷺ about her private matter. Scholars often use this *ḥadīth* as proof that every Muslim must seek the knowledge that is needed for their personal affairs, no matter how embarrassing the question may be. In fact, not asking out of shyness is blameworthy.

In another *ḥadīth*, a female companion asked the Prophet ﷺ about the details of how to take a *ghusl* after menstruation finishes. The Mother of the Believers ʿĀʾisha ؓ was present and said in response:

> "How excellent are the women of the Ansār! They did not allow shyness to prevent them from learning their religion."
>
> (*Muslim*, 332; *Abū Dāwūd*, 316)

Sometimes women cringe when hearing the names of their lady parts. There is nothing to be ashamed of. In fact, it is essential to be aware of a woman's basic anatomy to comprehend the definition of menstruation and the rulings related to it. With the intention to educate women about their bodies, this section will give insight into the things that are a must-know for any Muslim woman.

2.1 FEMALE-ONLY PARTS

There are eight female-only body parts that women should be aware of:

1. The Uterus
2. The Cervix
3. The Fallopian Tubes and Fimbriae
4. The Ovaries
5. The Vagina
6. The Labia Majora
7. The Labia Minora
8. The Clitoris

> 🔍 Examine the various organs in Diagram 2a and 2b.

Diagram 2a: Internal Female Reproductive Organs

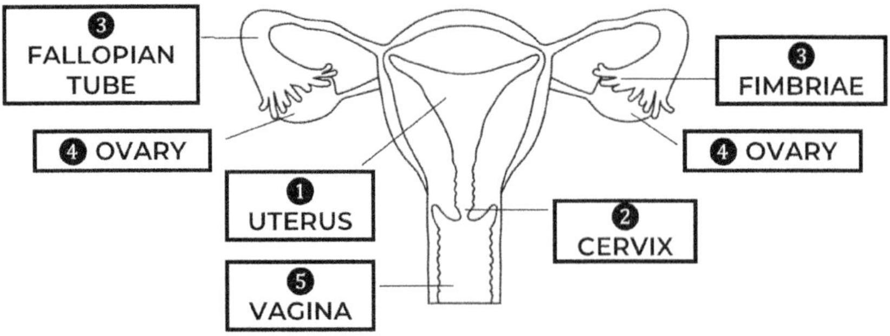

❶ The Uterus

The uterus, also known as the womb, is a hollow muscular organ that is responsible for the development of the embryo and fetus during pregnancy. The uterus is approximately the shape and size of a pear and sits in an inverted position within the pelvis. The narrow region of the uterus, which is known as the cervix, connects the uterus to the vagina.

❷ The Cervix

The cervix is located at the end of the uterus, and it is also known as the 'neck' of the uterus. The cervix plays vital roles in the control of substances moving in and out of the uterus, protection of the fetus during pregnancy, and the delivery of the fetus during childbirth.

During pregnancy, the cervix and its mucus plug protect the developing fetus by sealing the uterus from possible contamination by external pathogens. During menstruation, the cervix dilates to allow the passage of menstrual flow.

❸ The Fallopian Tubes and Fimbriae

The fallopian tubes are a pair of 4-inch (10 cm) long narrow tubes located in the pelvis extending from the upper corners of the uterus to the ovaries. Ova (egg cells) are carried to the uterus through the fallopian tubes following ovulation. Many finger-like projections known as fimbriae extend from its end to reach the surface of the ovary.

❹ The Ovaries

The ovaries produce the female sex hormones that control reproduction. They are where ova (egg cells) are stored, developed, and released. Each ovary is about the shape and size of an almond. The ovaries are located on opposite sides of the uterus and are attached to the uterus by the ovarian ligament. The open ends of the fallopian tubes rest just beyond the surface of the ovaries to transport ova to the uterus.

❺ The Vagina

The vagina is an elastic, muscular tube connecting the cervix of the uterus to the external female genitalia. Measuring around three to four inches in length and an inch in diameter, the vagina stretches to become several inches longer and many inches wider during child delivery.

Watery secretions lubricate the vagina and have an acidic pH to prevent the growth of bacteria and yeast. During childbirth, the vagina acts as the birth canal to transport the fetus from the uterus and out of the mother's body. The vagina provides a passageway for menstrual flow to exit the body.

Diagram 2b: External Female Genital Structure

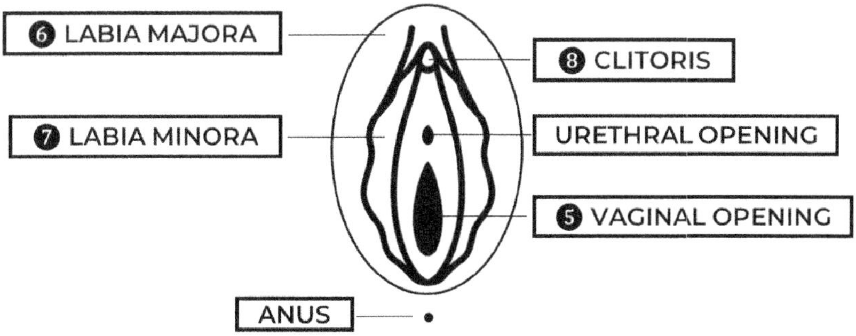

❻ The Labia Majora

The labia majora (outer lips) are a pair of fleshy folds of skin and fatty tissue that are part of the external female genitalia (vulva). Their function is to cover and protect the inner structures of vulva, such as the labia minora, clitoris, urinary orifice, and vaginal orifice. The labia majora contain many pubic hairs that help to protect the rest of the vulva from friction.

❼ The Labia Minora

The labia minora (inner lips) are a pair of thin folds that lie just inside the labia majora. The labia minora surround the openings to the vagina and urethra, serving to protect them from dryness, irritation, and infections.

❽ The Clitoris

The clitoris is located where the inner lips meet towards the top of the vulva. The clitoris is made up of erectile tissue that contains thousands of nerve endings, which make it an extremely sensitive organ. Stimulating it produces sensations of sexual pleasure that can result in an orgasm. Although it looks like a small pea, its internal structure is much larger. The prepuce of the clitoris, or the clitoral hood, is a fold of skin that covers and protects the clitoris.

2.2 MENSTRUATION ACCORDING TO DOCTORS

Medically speaking, menstruation is the shedding of the thickened lining of the uterus (endometrium) through the vagina when pregnancy does not occur. It is part of the menstrual cycle, which includes the days of menstruation and the days of purity.

The menstrual cycle begins with the first day of a woman's period and ends just before the next menstrual period. A normal cycle lasts between 21 and 35 days. Each woman's cycle will differ.

How the menstrual cycle works:

- The menstrual cycle is controlled by various hormones.

- After menstruation, rising levels of the follicle stimulating hormone (FHS) cause the ovary to develop follicles. One of the follicles will form a fully matured egg. As this occurs, the hormone estrogen rises, causing the uterine lining to grow.
- Ovulation is when the ovary releases the matured egg. The egg then moves into the fallopian tube.
- As the egg travels down the fallopian tube towards the uterus, the hormone progesterone rises, preparing the thickened uterine lining for a possible pregnancy.
- If the egg becomes fertilized by sperm and attaches itself to the uterine wall, a woman will become pregnant. The hormones will then keep the uterine lining from shedding.
- If pregnancy does not occur, the egg is reabsorbed into the body. Levels of estrogen and progesterone then fall, and the uterine lining begins to pull away.
- The uterine lining leaves the body from the uterus through the cervix, and it passes out of the vagina as menstrual blood. This marks the beginning of a new cycle.

> The end of menstruation is called menopause. Refer to Chapter 19 for more information.
>
> View the stages of the menstrual cycle in Diagram 2c.

Diagram 2c: How the Menstrual Cycle Works

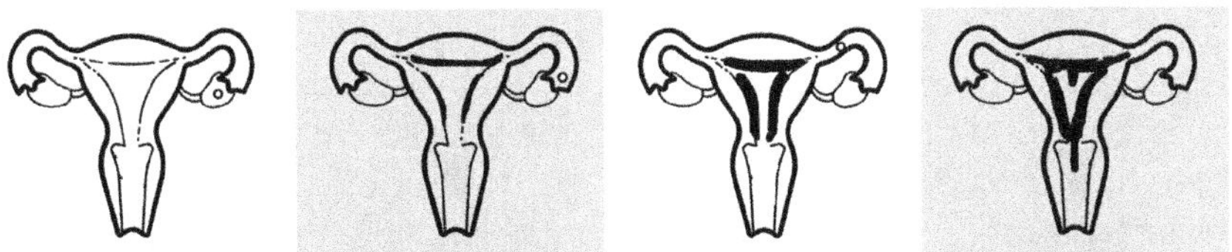

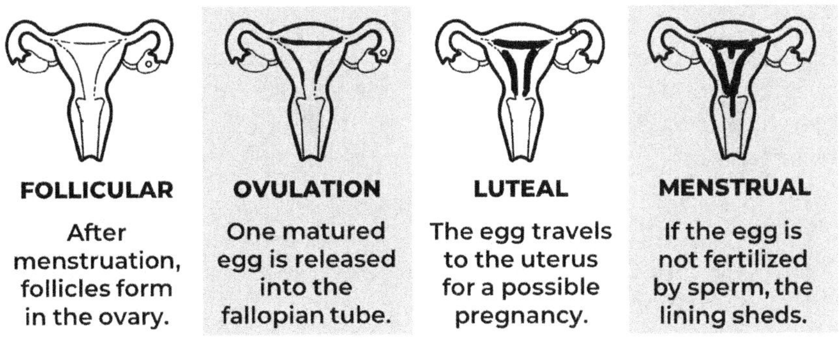

FOLLICULAR	**OVULATION**	**LUTEAL**	**MENSTRUAL**
After menstruation, follicles form in the ovary.	One matured egg is released into the fallopian tube.	The egg travels to the uterus for a possible pregnancy.	If the egg is not fertilized by sperm, the lining sheds.

What is menstrual blood? What is normal?

Menstrual fluid contains a mixture of blood, cervical mucus, and cells from the lining of the uterus.

A healthy menstrual flow resembles the color of cranberry juice. The bleeding lasts for 3 to 7 days, averaging 5 days. Under normal conditions, menstrual blood loss only constitutes 2 to 3 tablespoons of blood each month (approximately 30 to 50 milliliters).

It is normal to have heavier and lighter flow days. Heavier flow days usually occur at the beginning of a woman's menstruation, and the flow tends to lighten as the days go by. Expelling small clots of blood is also considered normal.

2.3 MENSTRUATION ACCORDING TO ISLAMIC LAW

From a Sacred Law perspective, menstruation (*ḥayḍ*) is:

- Blood that originates from the uterus and comes out of the vagina of a female who is at least 9 lunar years old (approximately 8 solar years and 9 months).
- It is not blood due to an illness or injury.
- It is not blood that is seen during pregnancy or after childbirth.
- The menstrual minimum is three complete days (72 hours), and the menstrual maximum is 10 complete days (240 hours).

Islamically, a woman's vaginal bleeding must first abide by this specific definition for it to be considered menstruation. Any bleeding that does not stand by this definition will not be called menstruation.

> Refer to Chapter 4 for a detailed explanation of the definition of menstruation.

A point of contention can arise between what is medically viewed as menstruation and what is Islamically viewed as menstruation. Women may find themselves confused about what to do when their doctor tells them that they are menstruating, but at the same time, a Muslim teacher says that they are not menstruating.

Who to follow when a conflict occurs between doctors and teachers:

- Muslims must always act upon what the Sacred Law says with concerns related to the validity of their prayers, fasts, permissibility of sexual intercourse, and anything connected to the Islamic sphere of their lives.

- The advice of doctors can be followed when their prognosis is used to determine if a person's body is physically healthy or if proper medical attention is needed to address a problem, such as abnormal bleeding or vaginal infections.

KEY TERMINIOLOGY

◆ **Menstruation** (*ḥayḍ*) is the normal, healthy blood that a woman expels when she does not get pregnant.

◆ **Lochia** (*nifās*) is the normal, healthy blood that a pregnant woman expels after childbirth or after the miscarriage of a developed fetus.

◆ **Abnormal uterine bleeding** (*istiḥāḍa*) is any blood that is not considered menstruation or lochia.

◆ A **purity span** (*ṭuhr*) is a duration of time that must separate between a menstruation and menstruation, or a lochia and menstruation, or a lochia and a lochia.

◆ The **habit** (*ʿāda*) is the last sound menses, sound lochia, or sound purity span that a woman experienced.

2.4 TOP TEN MISTAKES WOMEN MAKE

Unfortunately, the rulings related to menstruation are often misunderstood. This can result in mistakes arising with how to practice the rulings.

As such, it is vital that women are informed and educated about prevalent errors so that they are not repeated. The following are a list of common mistakes conveyed by women over the years.

Mistake #1: Not recording their bleeding.

It may come as a surprise, but it is obligatory for a woman to record the dates and timings of her menses, lochia, and purity habits. Additionally, she must record any colored discharge that she experiences during her time of purity.

The reasons for this ruling are emphasized throughout this guide, and with each chapter that is read, hopefully an appreciation for why the scholars say this will develop.

Mistake #2: Not considering all colored discharge to be blood.

Sometimes women think that the rulings of menstruation only apply when they experience a heavy, red flow. However, menstrual blood is not just red. It can be brown or yellow too.

A woman cannot ignore these colors when she sees them during her time of menstruation or during her time of purity.

> ➔ The colors of blood are discussed in Chapter 3.

Mistake #3: Thinking that dried yellow takes the ruling of fresh yellow.

It is possible for discharge to exit clear or white, but dry into a yellowish color soon after. This will obviously impact when a woman considers her menses to start or end.

The ruling returns to what color the discharge was when it first exited the vagina – not the color that it changes into after drying.

Without knowing this, women may mistakenly judge the color of their discharge when they see it on their underwear or panty liner. Only fresh discharge is considered when determining the rulings, and a *kursuf* should be used to ascertain the exact color.

> ➔ How to wear a *kursuf* is explained in Chapter 8.

Mistake #4: Not using a *kursuf* to determine the end of bleeding.

Towards the end of menstruation, blood flow becomes lighter, and it may take a longer time for the bleeding to descend to the vaginal opening.

This can cause many women to take multiple showers if they wrongly assume that their menstruation has finished when in reality it has not.

The *kursuf* was used by the female Companions ﷺ to determine when bleeding ends, and it can help prevent further confusion.

> ➔ Using a *kursuf* for the end of bleeding is detailed in Chapter 8.

Mistake #5: Delaying the *ghusl* after menstruation or lochia ends.

Any time menstrual bleeding ends – or a woman reaches the menstrual maximum of 10 days (240 hours) – a *ghusl* is required. It is not permissible to unduly delay taking the *ghusl* and miss prayers when it is certain that the bleeding has ceased.

The same ruling applies to lochia. If the blood stopped before 40 days elapses, a woman is obliged to take a *ghusl* and begin praying. She cannot wait until she reaches the 40-day mark when there is an absence of blood.

> ➔ This issue is discussed in Chapter 5 for menstruation and Chapter 12 for lochia.

Mistake #6: Not making up missed *Ramaḍān* fasts.

A menstruating woman and woman in a state of lochia are excused from fasting the current *Ramaḍān*, but they must make up the missed fasts (*qaḍā*ʾ) after *Ramaḍān* finishes in a time when they are able.

> ➔ The ruling for making up fasts is mentioned in Chapter 9.

Mistake #7: Not knowing that a minimal 15-day purity span (360 hours) is required between two menstruations.

Bleeding that occurs before a purity span of 15 complete days (360 hours) free of blood will not be ruled as menstruation. A woman cannot stop praying and fasting *Ramaḍān* any time she experiences bleeding. There are conditions for the bleeding, as well as conditions for the purity span.

> ➔ These conditions are discussed in Chapters 15 and 18.

Mistake #8: Considering the first 10 days of abnormal bleeding to be menses and the next 15 days to be purity.

According to the *Ḥanafī madhhab*, a woman who experiences abnormal bleeding will return to her menstrual and purity habits. The habit is based upon what she actually saw during her previous cycles. A woman cannot give herself a habit of 10 days menses and 15 days purity.

Likewise, if she had previously given birth, she cannot give herself a lochia habit of 40 days when she bleeds over the 40 possible days of lochia in a subsequent birth. Rather, she must return to her habits.

> ➔ What to do when abnormal bleeding is seen is discussed in Chapter 7 for menstruation and Chapter 13 for lochia.

Mistake #9: Making ablution (*wuḍū*ʾ) at the beginning of each prayer time for abnormal bleeding.

There are various rulings related to praying with abnormal bleeding. Depending on how heavy the flow is will determine which ruling a woman uses before she prays.

> ➔ The relevant rulings are discussed in Chapter 17.

Mistake #10: Not studying the rulings or double checking one's understanding with a teacher.

The trickiest part about the science of menstruation and lochia is understanding how and when the rulings change in retrospect. This will be explained and demonstrated in Parts 2, 3, and 4.

As such, it is crucial that one takes their religion from scholars who took their religion from scholars. The Islamic tradition is rooted in seeking knowledge from qualified experts in each field who have been trained and equipped with how to answer questions.

This guide will give a foundation for menstruation rulings but reading it with a teacher – or asking one's questions to a teacher – must be a priority. Allāh Most High commands believers in the Qurʾān to ask those who know if one does not know. (*an-Naḥl*, 16:43)

> ➔ For a quick overview of the rulings, refer to Menses in a Nutshell, Lochia in a Nutshell, and Purity in a Nutshell in the Appendix.

REVIEW QUESTIONS

1. What is the uterus, the cervix, and the vagina?
2. Where are the labia minora located on a woman's body?
3. What does a woman do if her medical menses conflicts with the Sacred Law rulings?
4. What are common mistakes that women make regarding menstruation rulings?

Chapter 3

Colors, Flows & Discharges

IN THIS CHAPTER

- ✧ Colors of blood
- ✧ Normal vaginal discharge
- ✧ Yellow vaginal discharge
- ✧ Other possible vaginal discharges

Red. It is usually the color that comes to mind when menstrual blood is mentioned. However, the truth is that menstrual blood is not limited to one color.

A woman's menstrual period could consist of a spectrum of colors that range from dark red to brown to yellow. The colors seen during a woman's time of menstruation can also change over the course of her life as she experiences hormonal changes.

The scholars often mention six main colors of blood, but there is no stipulation that a woman must see all of these colors during her time of menses. Each woman's cycle is unique, and each woman should concern herself with what is relevant to her body.

3.1 DEFINITION OF BLOOD

The term blood (*dam*) refers to any vaginal discharge that is not completely white or clear.

> ☑ As for completely white or clear vaginal discharge, it is called normal vaginal discharge (*ruṭūbat ʾl-farj*) and it is not blood.

3.2 COLORS OF BLOOD

The six main colors of blood are: black, red, brown, yellow, turbid, and green.

- ✧ **Black:** Looks like a deep-colored, cherry jam or what is seen in glass tubes of withdrawn blood. It is an extremely dark red that looks closer to the color black or an eggplant purple.

- ✧ **Red:** Looks like the color of blood that is seen when a finger is cut. A healthy menstrual flow resembles the color of cranberry juice. Pink and orange are red blood watered down with cervical mucus.

- ✧ **Brown:** Looks like dirt or earth. Medically considered old blood discharged from the vagina.

- ✧ **Yellow:** Looks like the skin of a banana or the fruit itself. Any shade of yellow counts, providing that it originally exited the vagina as yellow.

- ✧ **Turbid:** Looks like cloudy pond water. Often an indication that brown blood is mixed in clear or white discharge.

- ✧ **Green:** There is a difference of opinion about it. Some scholars completely disregard it as a color of menstruation.

⚠ Medically, if a woman sees vaginal discharge that is light green, it is indicative of a vaginal infection, which is not counted as menstruation or lochia.

> **❓ Why are colors other than red considered to be menstrual blood?**
>
> The Mother of Believers ʿĀ'isha ؓ taught the female Companions ؓ that yellow is a color of menstrual blood. She told them that they should not rush to take a *ghusl* until white discharge is seen. What is understood from her statement is that any colored discharge takes the ruling of blood, and a woman's menstruation is not finished until she sees white or clear discharge.

3.3 COLOR MIXED IN CLEAR OR WHITE DISCHARGE

If any of the colors of blood are mixed within clear or white discharge, the entire discharge takes the ruling of blood.

For example, a woman sees a spot or streak of red blood within a glob of clear discharge. The entire discharge takes the ruling of blood. The same ruling applies if the color was black, brown, or yellow mixed within clear or white discharge.

> ☑ This highlights why the phrase 'not completely' is added to the definition of blood in Section 3.1.

3.4 THREE TYPES OF BLOOD

Whenever any colored vaginal discharge is seen, it will be classified into one of the three types of blood:

- ✧ **Menstruation** (*ḥayḍ*).
- ✧ **Lochia** (*nifās*), which is also known as postpartum bleeding.
- ✧ **Abnormal uterine bleeding** (*istiḥāḍa*), which is any blood that is not considered menstruation or lochia.

Each type has specific rulings related to it. Therefore, if a woman sees colored vaginal discharge at any point in her cycle, it matters.

She cannot disregard the colored discharge she sees, nor can she automatically assume that it is abnormal uterine bleeding (*istiḥāḍa*) just because it does not 'feel' or 'look' like her normal menstruation.

3.5 DIFFERING COLORS & FLOWS

The different colors of blood do not influence the *Ḥanafī madhhab* rulings for determining which days are menstruation. As a general principle, all colors are equal.

This means that one color is not stronger than the other such that it takes precedence in being ruled as menstruation. Red is the same as brown, and yellow is the same as black.

Furthermore, a heavy flow of bleeding is not given preference over a lighter flow. The same concept applies to physical symptoms. Even if the blood is accompanied with cramps or other physical changes to the body, it does not make it more likely to be menstruation.

Colors are mentioned because:

- ✧ It helps women identify which colors are normal to see during the days of menstruation or lochia.
- ✧ It informs women that brown, yellow, and turbid are colors of menstruation and lochia, and not only black or red. Thus, these colors should not be ignored when seen.

> ⚠ Women must take note of any blood seen during their cycle, as its presence may impact the rulings related to menstruation.

3.6 THE HABIT

Instead of the strengths of colors or the qualities of blood (*tamyīz),* the rulings of the *Ḥanafī madhhab* revolve around the habit.

What is a habit? Simply put, a woman's habit is her body's usual pattern of when blood and purity are seen during the month and for how many days.

For example, a woman menstruates for 5 days at the beginning of every month. After her menstruation, she sees 25 days without blood. Her menses habit is 5 days, and her purity habit is 25 days.

At a technical level, the habit (*ʿāda*) is any bleeding or purity span that fulfills the definitions and conditions for a sound menstruation, a sound lochia, or a sound purity.

Thus, a woman can have three habits: a menses habit, a lochia habit, or a purity habit. The details related to each type are discussed in Parts 2, 3, and 4.

The habit is needed for various reasons, and they will be mentioned throughout this guide. A few examples are:

- ✧ The habit is used when a woman experiences abnormal uterine bleeding (*istiḥāḍa*). It will distinguish between what is menses, lochia, or abnormal bleeding.

- ✧ The habit is used when blood is seen before the expected time of menses, which is known as early blood. It will help determine when a woman should stop praying.

- ✧ The habit is used to establish when sexual intercourse is permitted after menstruation ends.

? Where did the concept of the habit come from? Why not consider colors and flow?

The *Ḥanafī madhhab* does not rely upon the strengths of colors or qualities of blood (*tamyīz)* like other schools of law. The reason for this difference of opinion is based upon how the scholars interpreted certain *aḥādīth.*

The Mother of the Believers ʿĀʾisha ﷺ said:

> "Faṭima bint Abī Ḥubaysh ﷺ came to the Prophet ﷺ and said, 'O Messenger of Allāh, indeed I am a woman who experiences abnormal bleeding such that I never see any purity. Do I leave praying?' The Prophet ﷺ responded, 'No. Verily that is from a (ruptured) vein, and it is not menstruation. Leave the prayer for the number of days (*qadr al-ayyām*) you used to menstruate, then take a purificatory shower (*ghusl*) and pray.'" (*Bukhārī,* 325)

The Arabic phrase '*qadr al-ayyām*' means the number of days or the time of the month that the woman in question would usually menstruate. This is her habit. Thus, when a woman experiences abnormal bleeding, the way to resolve her problem is to return to her habit.

There are numerous *aḥādīth* that convey a similar meaning in other *ḥadīth* works. Based on these *aḥādīth*, the *Ḥanafī* scholars explain how to establish a habit and use it so that a woman with abnormal bleeding knows when she should pray or not pray.

3.7 OBLIGATION TO RECORD

It is obligatory for every woman to record her menses, lochia, and purity habits.

When problems with abnormal bleeding occur, the last menses, lochia, or purity habit a woman experienced is used to resolve her issue and distinguish between the types of bloods.

This methodology is based upon various statements transmitted from the Prophet ﷺ. When the female Companions رضي الله عنهن who experienced abnormal bleeding asked the Prophet ﷺ about how to deal with their circumstance, the Prophet ﷺ instructed them to stop praying for the amount of days that they used to menstruate, and to take a *ghusl* and resume praying after those days elapsed.

Thus, the way to resolve a woman's problem will be built upon what she saw in the past. Abnormal bleeding often occurs when a woman least expects it, and her habits are needed to clarify the rulings related to any bleeding that she is seeing.

A woman must record:

- The date and time any vaginal blood begins, including the spotting of blood.
- The date and time any vaginal blood ends.

Some women use a small notebook as a diary to record their dates. Others log their dates and times using an Excel sheet. By far, the most popular option is to use a period phone app. This is certainly a convenient option.

However, it must be mentioned that phones are not always reliable. When they crash or get lost, it poses problems for women who urgently need to know their dates of bleeding. Therefore, if a woman chooses to use an electronic device or program to keep track of her habits and dates of bleeding, it is best to create a backup copy and store it in a second place as a safeguard.

If possible, it is advisable for women to be aware of the colors of blood they see just in case another *madhhab* is used to resolve their problem.

View a sample record of a woman's dates of blood in Table 3a.

Table 3a: Sample Record of Dates of Bleeding

BLOOD STARTS	BLOOD ENDS	TOTAL DAYS OF BLOOD	TOTAL DAYS OF PURITY
January 5th 1 pm	*January 10th 2 pm + 15 mins GT (2:15pm)*	*5 days, 1 hour and 15 mins*	*22 days*
February 1st 2:15 pm	*February 8th 4 pm + 15 mins GT (4:15pm)*	*7 days and 2 hours*	*30 days, 4 hours and 45 mins*
March 10th 9 pm	*March 17th 10 pm + 15 mins GT (10:15pm)*	*7 days, 1 hour and 15 mins*	*22 days and 45 mins*
April 8th 11 pm	*April 12th 6 pm*	****Brown spots on April 25th 2 pm and April 27th 11 am*	

GT refers to *ghusl* time. Find out when to add it to the habit in Chapter 6.

What if a woman never recorded her dates of bleeding? What should she do?

It is obligatory upon every woman to record her habits. The habit is needed for various rulings related to her situation. If a woman never recorded her dates of bleeding but her cycle is normal, then she should start recording from this point forward.

If she is currently experiencing abnormal bleeding and did not record anything, she should try her hardest to remember when the last time was that she saw a normal menstrual cycle and how long it lasted. A reasoned guess is sufficient. Then, she should contact a teacher to help her work through her situation.

3.8 SOUND BLOOD VS. UNSOUND BLOOD

At a technical level, the types of blood can be classified into two main categories: sound blood (*ad-dam aṣ-ṣaḥīḥ*) and unsound blood (*ad-dam al-fāsid*).

- **Sound blood** is any blood that is deemed menstruation or lochia according to the Sacred Law.
- **Unsound blood** is any blood that is not deemed menstruation or lochia according to the Sacred Law. It is commonly termed abnormal uterine bleeding (*istiḥāḍa*).

> Compare the classifications of blood in Chart 3b.

Chart 3b: Sound & Unsound Blood

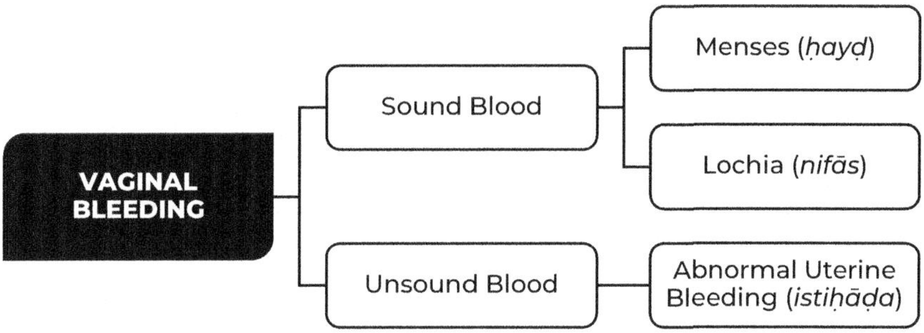

The classification of sound and unsound blood matters because:

1. Sound bloods are the only bloods that can be taken as a habit. Unsound blood cannot be taken as a habit.

❷ Sound bloods have designated time limits, meaning that they must adhere to a certain time range.

This means that there is a minimum and a maximum time limit for when menstruation or lochia can occur. Once the bleeding fails to meet the minimal duration or exceeds the maximum duration, a woman automatically knows that the ruling for her situation needs to be revised.

❸ Both sound and unsound bloods have specific daily rulings related to them, such as how a woman should act when she sees either of these bloods.

For example, when a woman sees sound blood, she will not pray or fast. However, when a woman sees unsound blood, she will pray and fast.

When teaching the Sacred Law rulings, many teachers focus on issues related to sound blood because unsound blood is not normal and its details can become complicated.

POINTS TO REMEMBER

- Blood is any colored vaginal discharge other than completely white or clear.
- Blood mixed in clear or white discharge takes the ruling of blood.
- A woman must not ignore or disregard any blood she sees, even if it is spotting.
- A woman's vaginal bleeding can be categorized as one of the three: menstruation (*ḥayḍ*), lochia (*nifās*), or abnormal uterine bleeding (*istiḥāḍa*).
- Menstruation and lochia are sound bloods, whereas abnormal uterine bleeding is unsound blood.
- The rulings differ for sound and unsound bloods.

3.9 NORMAL VAGINAL DISCHARGE

Normal vaginal discharge is the discharge that a woman sees during her cycle at the time when she is not menstruating or in a state of lochia. It is clear or white in color, and it may have a subtle scent that is not unpleasant or foul smelling.

It is healthy for the body to excrete this discharge. Its fluid keeps the vagina clean and moist, and it protects it from infections. Within the possible days of menstruation, seeing normal vaginal discharge marks the end of a woman's menstrual blood.

Normal vaginal discharge looks differently throughout a woman's cycle:

- After a woman finishes her menstruation, her vagina is often dry with hardly any discharge at all.
- When the discharge returns, it will be thick, pasty, and white in color like yogurt. As the days pass, its consistency slowly begins to thin out to be lotion-like, and cloudy in color.
- When her ovulation occurs, she will see a clear, stretchy, slippery, gooey discharge that is similar to raw egg whites. This can last for about two days. The timing of when ovulation occurs in the cycle differs from woman to woman. These are the optimal days for trying to become pregnant.
- If a woman does not become pregnant, about fourteen days later from ovulating, her new menstruation will begin. During those fourteen days, her discharge will increasingly become thick, white, and tacky. It will soon dry up upon approaching the days of menstruation.

> ⚠ Normal vaginal discharge can look off-white when it is pasty or tacky. Also, during ovulation, copious amounts of clear discharge can look like a very pale yellow. Thus, women should not worry about seeing discharge that looks like a faint yellow.
>
> Compare the way normal vaginal discharge looks before and during ovulation in Diagram 3c.

Diagram 3c: Normal Vaginal Discharge

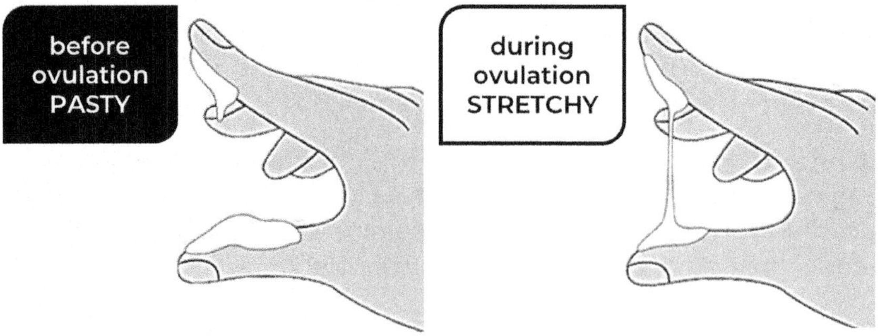

3.10 NORMAL VAGINAL DISCHARGE & WUḌŪʾ

As for if the exiting of normal vaginal discharge breaks *wuḍūʾ*, there is a difference of opinion amongst the Ḥanafī scholars.

- ✧ According to Imām Abū Ḥanīfa (Allāh have mercy on him), clear and white discharge is considered pure (*ṭāhir*), and its exiting does not break a woman's *wuḍūʾ*.
- ✧ According to Imām Abū Yūsuf and Muḥammad (Allāh have mercy on them), it is considered filthy (*najis*), and its exiting breaks a woman's *wuḍūʾ*.

Scholars will generally encourage women to follow the position of Imām Abū Yūsuf and Imām Muḥammad out of caution. This means that women must remake their *wuḍūʾ* after the discharge exits and remove it from their clothing before praying.

However, the position of Imām Abū Ḥanīfa is followable, especially in times of hardship and need.

3.11 YELLOW VAGINAL DISCHARGE

Yellow vaginal discharge is discharge that exits the vagina as yellow. It is commonly called 'fresh' yellow. The Mother of Believers ʿĀʾisha ﷺ taught the female Companions ﷺ that yellow is a color of menstrual blood.

In a *ḥadīth* found in the *Muwaṭṭa'* of Imām Mālik, the maid servant of the Mother of Believers 'Ā'isha ؓ said:

> "Women used to send small boxes to 'Ā'isha, the Mother of the Believers, that had a piece of cotton cloth (*kursuf*) contained in them in which there was a yellow discharge upon it from menstrual blood. They would ask her about the prayer. She would say to them, 'Do not be hasty (to take a *ghusl*) until you see a white discharge.'" By that she meant purity from menses.
>
> (*Muwaṭṭa'*, 85)

3.12 NORMAL VAGINAL DISCHARGE DRYING YELLOW

It is possible for normal vaginal discharge to exit the vagina as clear or white, but then dry into a yellowish color over time. Instead of depending on what is seen on a panty liner, women should use a *kursuf* to assist them in knowing what the color was when it exited.

- ✧ If the discharge exits white or clear on the *kursuf* and dries yellow, then the discharge is considered white or clear.

- ✧ If the discharge exits yellow on the *kursuf* and dries white, then the discharge is considered yellow.

> ➔ The *kursuf* and the rulings related to yellow discharge are discussed in Chapter 8.

3.13 OTHER VAGINAL DISCHARGES

A woman may experience other types of vaginal discharges that are not specifically related to the science of menstruation, like discharge from vaginal infections, childbirth, or sexual arousal.

The following is a breakdown of other possible vaginal discharges that a woman can see.

Vaginal Infections: Looks like white, green, or gray discharge.

Vaginal infections can be caused by a bacteria imbalance, a yeast overgrowth, or an irritation from chemicals in female products. The discharge is accompanied with obvious signs of an infection, like:

- The discharge is clumpy like cottage cheese.
- The discharge has a fish stench.
- The vagina itches or burns.
- The vulva is inflamed or swollen.
- Sex hurts.

☑ When discharge from vaginal infections exit, it breaks *wuḍūʾ* and the discharge is filthy (*najis*).

Bloody Show: Looks like pink, red, or brown discharge.

It is only experienced by pregnant women. A bloody show occurs because the cervix starts to soften, thin (efface), and dilate in preparation for labor.

☑ When the bloody show occurs or the mucus plug is dislodged, it breaks *wuḍūʾ* and the discharge is filthy (*najis*).

Arousal Fluid: Looks like clear discharge. It is wet, sticky, and slippery.

This fluid is produced in response to sexual stimulation by glands in and around the vagina to lubricate the vagina for the possibility of intercourse.

☑ When arousal fluid exits, it breaks *wuḍūʾ* and the discharge is filthy (*najis*).

Orgasmic Fluid: Looks like a thin, watery yellow.

It is experienced at the time of female ejaculation.

☑ When orgasmic fluid exits, it requires a *ghusl* and the discharge is filthy (*najis*).

Compare the different vaginal discharges in Table 3d.

Table 3d: Comparison of Different Vaginal Discharges

TYPE OF DISCHARGE	COLOR OF DISCHARGE	QUALITIES OF DISCHARGE	RULING OF DISCHARGE
Menstruation (*ḥayḍ*) or Lochia (*nifās*)	Any color other than white or clear	Possible to be thin, thick, mucus like, stretchy	*Ghusl* required upon ending & filthy
Abnormal Uterine Bleeding (*istiḥāda*)	Any color other than white or clear	Possible to be thin, thick, mucus like, stretchy	*Wuḍūʾ* required & filthy
Normal Vaginal Discharge	Completely white or clear	Cloudy, lotion-like, stretchy like egg whites, pasty, or tacky	Difference of opinion of if it breaks *wuḍūʾ* and is filthy
Discharge From Vaginal Infections	White, gray, or green	Clumpy, or fish stench, or vagina itches / burns, or vulva swollen, or sex hurts	*Wuḍūʾ* required & filthy
Bloody Show	Pink, brown or red	Mucus-like	*Wuḍūʾ* required & filthy
Arousal Fluid	Clear	Wet, sticky, and slippery - only exits upon arousal	*Wuḍūʾ* required & filthy
Orgasmic Fluid	Yellow	Thin and watery, at the time of orgasm	*Ghusl* required & filthy

CHANGE PADS REGULARLY
WASH WITH WATER ONLY
AVOID SCENTED PRODUCTS
AVOID BUBBLE BATHS
AVOID TIGHT CLOTHING
WIPE FROM FRONT TO BACK
WEAR 100% COTTON
CHANGE WET CLOTHING

TIPS TO AVOID VAGINAL INFECTIONS

Vaginal infections can be caused by douching, taking antibiotics, using tampons, and some types of contraception. Products like soap, bubble baths, detergents and fabric conditioners can also irritate the sensitive skin around the vulva and vagina – potentially triggering an infection. Try these tips to prevent vaginal infections.

- When menstruating, change pads, panty liners, and tampons regularly.
- When showering, wash the private parts with a gentle, mild soap and warm water. There is no need to put soap directly in the vagina.
- Avoid using scented soaps and feminine products around the vagina. It can cause irritation.
- Avoid douching and taking bubble baths. Cleansing the inside of the vagina will disrupt the vagina's natural bacteria balance.
- Avoid overly tight clothing, which can increase moisture around the private parts.
- After going to the bathroom, always wipe from front to back to prevent bacteria from getting into the vagina and causing an infection.
- Wear 100% cotton underwear.
- Do not sit in wet clothing. Change swimsuits and wet gym clothes to dry clothing as soon as possible.

REVIEW QUESTIONS

1. What is the definition of blood? What are its main colors?
2. What is the ruling of blood mixed in clear or white discharge?
3. What are the types of vaginal bleeding a woman can see?
4. What is the ruling for a woman recording her habits?
5. Which bloods are sound, and which are unsound? What does sound and unsound mean?
6. What is normal vaginal discharge? Is it filthy and does its exiting break *wuḍūʾ*?

PART TWO:

Menstruation Rulings

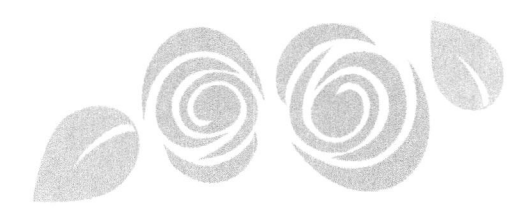

And they ask
you about
menstruation.
Say, ‘It is an
impurity...’

Qurʾān
2:222

Chapter 4

Menstruation 101

IN THIS CHAPTER

- ✧ Definition of menstruation
- ✧ Conditions of menstruation
- ✧ How to establish a menses habit
- ✧ Types of habits

Allāh Most High says:

﴿ ٱلْيَوْمَ أَكْمَلْتُ لَكُمْ دِينَكُمْ وَأَتْمَمْتُ عَلَيْكُمْ نِعْمَتِي وَرَضِيتُ لَكُمُ ٱلْإِسْلَٰمَ دِينًا ﴾

> Today I have perfected your religion for you and have completed My favor upon you and chosen Islam as the way for you.
>
> (*al-Māʾida,* 5:3)

Out of all the faiths in the world, Allāh Most High chose Islam to be the most upright way. He perfected its teachings, and He guaranteed His blessings upon the one who follows it.

Islam gives one purpose and direction. It also provides guidance of how to act in different types of situations so that one's awareness of Allāh Most High increases with each passing moment. Whether it be how to eat, or how to use the restroom, or how to act during the time of menstruation, Islam provides a way to follow, and its path ultimately leads to worshipping Allāh Most High in every possible form.

What most women know about the rulings related to menstruation is that there are actions which they are prohibited from doing. Perhaps they are aware that it is not permitted to pray, fast, or engage in sexual intercourse during menstruation. However, the reality is that the science of menstruation is more than a discussion around prohibitions. In truth, the rulings of menstruation are built upon definitions and conditions.

> The Prophet ﷺ said, "The least menstruation can be is three days, and the most it can be is ten days."
>
> (al-Ṭabarānī, *Al-Muʿjam al-Kabīr*, 7586)

There are several *aḥādīth* that convey a similar time range for menstruation. Through them, it is understood that a woman cannot consider every spot of blood she sees to be menstruation. Rather, her vaginal bleeding must first abide by a specific definition and its related conditions.

Sometimes people hate to read definitions, but this section cannot be overlooked if one is hoping to understand what menstruation really is from an Islamic perspective.

Menstruation Basics

DEFINITION

Menstruation (*ḥayḍ*) is:

- Blood that originates from the uterus and exits out of the vagina of a female who is at least 9 lunar years old.
- It is not blood due to an illness or injury.
- It is not blood that is seen during pregnancy or after childbirth.

CONDITIONS

Its conditions are:

- Its minimum duration is 3 complete days (72 hours).
- Its maximum duration is 10 complete days (240 hours).
- It must be followed by a purity span (*ṭuhr*) of at least 15 complete days (360 hours) free from any colored vaginal discharge.

RULING

If the blood abides by the definition and conditions of menstruation, the bleeding is ruled as sound, and it becomes the menses habit.

4.1 DEFINITION OF MENSTRUATION

Menstruation (*ḥayḍ*) is blood that originates from the uterus and exits out of the vagina of a female who is at least 9 lunar years old. It is not blood due to an illness or injury. It is also not blood that is seen during pregnancy or after childbirth.

Each word in this definition is significant:

◆ '*Blood*' refers to any colored vaginal discharge.

As previously mentioned, blood can be black, red, brown, yellow, turbid, or green. There is no consideration for how heavy the flow is or if the physical symptoms of menstruation are experienced. Rather, whenever any of these colors are seen during the expected time of menstruation, it will be deemed menses.

◆ '*Originates from the uterus*' means that the bleeding must come from the womb.

For example, bleeding from an anal fissure or urinary tract infection is not menstruation because the blood is not coming from the uterus.

Moreover, for a woman who has had a total hysterectomy, any vaginal bleeding that she sees will never be considered menstruation because she no longer has a uterus.

> ⚠ There is no need to check with a doctor about whether the blood seen at the time of menses is truly coming from the uterus. Unless a woman suspects otherwise, she can assume it does.

◆ '*Exits out of the vagina*' means that the colored discharge must exit the vagina for the ruling of menstruation to come into effect.

According to the Sacred Law, exiting refers to when blood is seen at the edge of the vaginal opening.

Practically speaking, most women know that the blood exited when they see it on their panty liner or after wiping. If a woman extracts the blood herself with a tissue or a tampon, and the blood does not naturally flow out, this falls under the ruling of exiting the vagina.

☑ If a woman feels cramps, but no bleeding exits, then what she feels is of no consequence. Blood must first exit the vagina for menses to start.

◆ '*Of a female who is at least 9 lunar years old*' means that if a girl who is under the age of 9 lunar years old (approximately 8 solar years and 9 months) saw colored vaginal discharge, the bleeding is not considered menstruation. Rather, it is abnormal bleeding.

☑ Medically speaking, most girls start to menstruate around 12 to 14 years of age.

◆ '*Is not blood due to an illness or injury*' excludes colored discharge caused by a confirmed vaginal infection or injury.

This confirmation must come from a doctor, a past experience the woman had, or clear signs that strongly indicate it is not menstrual blood.

For example, if a woman's doctor told her that the vaginal discharge she is experiencing is specifically from an infection, it would not be considered menstruation.

Similarly, if a woman had an injury to her vagina – perhaps due to falling off a bike – then the bleeding seen thereafter will not be considered menstruation, unless she believes otherwise.

◆ '*Is not blood that is seen during pregnancy*' refers to any colored vaginal discharge that a pregnant woman sees.

According to the *Ḥanafī madhhab*, a pregnant woman cannot menstruate.

From a medical perspective, the endometrium lining does not shed when a woman is pregnant. In fact, doctors say that it is not normal for a pregnant woman to see blood, and it could be an early sign of a miscarriage. Refer to Chapters 10 and 14 for details.

◆ '*Or after childbirth*' refers to the blood seen after childbirth. It is called lochia (*nifās*) and it is not termed menstruation.

4.2 CONDITIONS OF MENSTRUATION

There are three conditions associated with the definition of menstruation:

1. Meeting the menstrual minimum.
2. Abiding by the menstrual maximum.
3. A purity span occurring between two menstruations.

☑ All three conditions must be met without exception.

4.3 FIRST CONDITION: THE MENSTRUAL MINIMUM

The menstrual minimum is 3 complete days (72 hours). If the menstrual minimum is not met, then the bleeding cannot be ruled as menstruation. Rather, it is abnormal blood (*istiḥāḍa*).

◆ Counting Three Complete Days

What is intended by a 'day' is a full day and its night, which is 24 hours. Three days of 24 hours equals 72 hours. The minimum days of menstruation will not be counted correctly if the 24-hour stipulation is overlooked.

> Observe how the days are counted in Diagram 4a.

Diagram 4a: The Menstrual Minimum

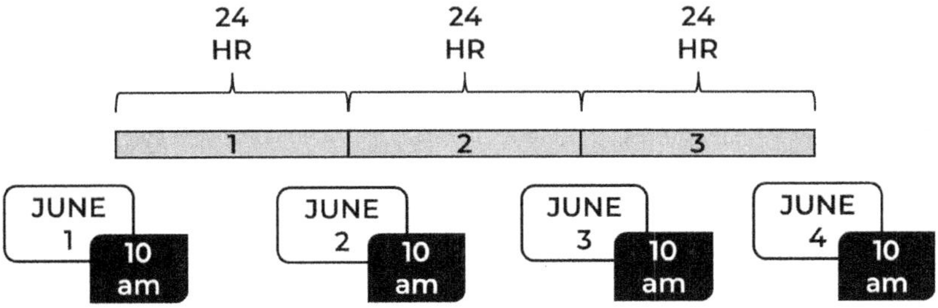

> A woman's menstruation starts on June 1st at 10 am.
>
> ► The menstrual minimum is met after 72 hours on June 4th at 10 am.
>
> ► If a woman is unaware of the 24-hour stipulation, she may mistakenly assume that the menstrual minimum is met on June 3rd.

◆ Color Of Discharge

Any color of vaginal discharge seen within this time takes the ruling of menses, regardless of whether it is red, brown, fresh yellow, or the like. What marks the beginning of menstruation is the first show of colored discharge within the possible days of menses, and it is not necessarily when a red color is seen or when the full flow starts.

> ➔ The colors of blood are discussed in Chapter 3.

◆ Spotting Versus Continuous Flow

Bleeding does not need to be continuous for it to be ruled as menstruation. The real consideration returns to the beginning and ending times of the shows of blood.

If the total duration from the first show of blood to the last show of blood reaches 72 hours, the entire time span is considered menstruation in hindsight, regardless of whether a woman saw blood for the total duration.

This is significant for women who experience spotting when their menstruation starts. If the spotting of blood is seen during the time of expected menstruation and the duration reaches 72 hours, the spotting will count as menstruation.

It also may be different from what doctors say because some do not consider spotting to be menstrual blood. Instead, for many doctors, vaginal bleeding is only menstruation when it becomes a full flow.

> Compare the two examples in Diagram 4b and 4c.

Diagram 4b: The Menstrual Minimum

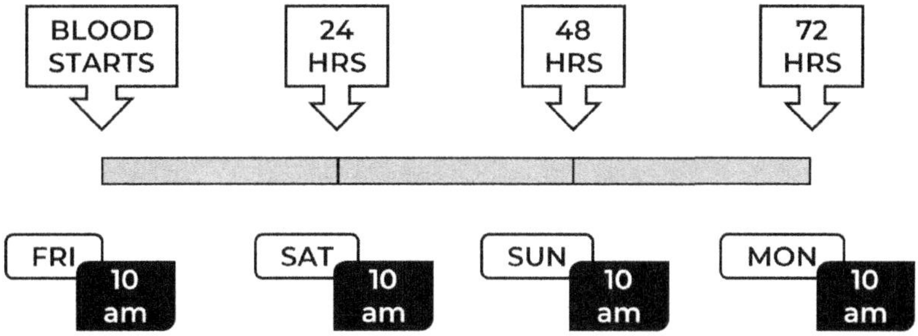

A woman begins to bleed on Friday at 10 am during her expected time of menses. The bleeding finishes on Monday at 10 am.

▶ From the time the blood begins to the time it ceases, there is a duration of 72 hours.

▶ The entire time span of constant blood flow is considered menstruation.

Diagram 4c: The Menstrual Minimum

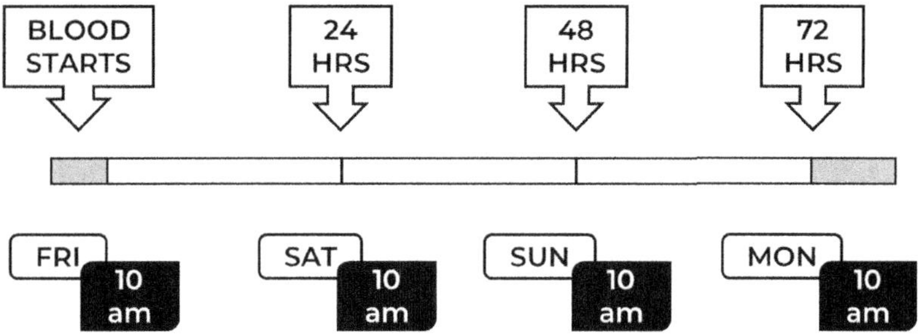

A woman sees a spot of blood on Friday at 10 am during her expected time of menses and then the blood stops. The bleeding returns on Monday at 10 am and stops at 11 am.

> ► From the time the blood begins to the time it ceases, there is a period of 72 hours; in fact, it is 73 hours.
>
> ► The entire time span is considered menstruation in hindsight.
>
> ► Whether she saw blood for the rest of Friday, Saturday, or Sunday is of no consideration according to the rulings.

In retrospect, both situations in Diagram 4b and 4c are ruled as menstruation. Between the first show of blood to the last show of blood, a period of at least 72 hours can be counted.

This fulfills the legal requirement for meeting the menstrual minimum. There is no consideration for whether the blood is a constant flow or spotting.

Scholars explain that the reason it is not a condition for the bleeding to be continuous is because this is the nature of menstrual blood. It is normal and common for it to be an on-and-off flow.

☑ What happens in-between the shows of blood is of no consequence because menstrual bleeding does not need to be continuous.

4.4 SECOND CONDITION: THE MENSTRUAL MAXIMUM

The menstrual maximum is 10 complete days (240 hours). Any bleeding that exceeds the maximum limit of 10 complete days (240 hours) is not menstruation. Rather, it is abnormal blood (*istiḥāḍa*).

◆ Counting Ten Complete Days

What is intended by a 'day' is a full day and its night, which is 24 hours. Ten days of 24 hours equals 240 hours. The maximum days of menstruation will not be counted correctly if the 24-hour stipulation is overlooked.

> 🔍 Observe how the days are counted in Diagram 4d.

Diagram 4d: The Menstrual Maximum

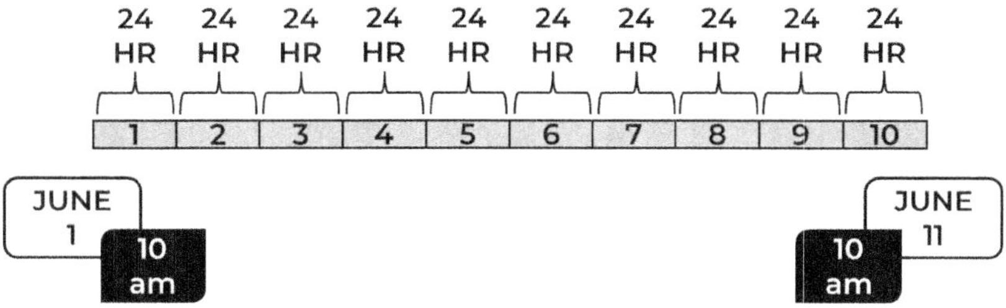

A woman's menstruation starts on June 1st at 10 am.

► The menstrual maximum is met after 240 hours on June 11th at 10 am.

► If a woman is unaware of the 24-hour stipulation, she may mistakenly assume the menstrual maximum is met on June 10th.

◆ Color Of Discharge

Any colored vaginal discharge seen within the 240 hours takes the ruling of menses. The vaginal discharge can be any color, such as red, brown, fresh yellow, or the like.

◆ Spotting Versus Continuous Flow

The bleeding does not need to be continuous during the 10 days for it to be considered menstruation. The consideration is the beginning and ending times of the blood.

Therefore, as previously mentioned, spotting or a constant flow of blood will take the ruling of menstruation. This is upon the condition that the time span between the shows of blood reaches the menstrual minimum as stated in Section 4.3.

Observe which days are considered menses in Diagram 4e.

Diagram 4e: The Menstrual Maximum

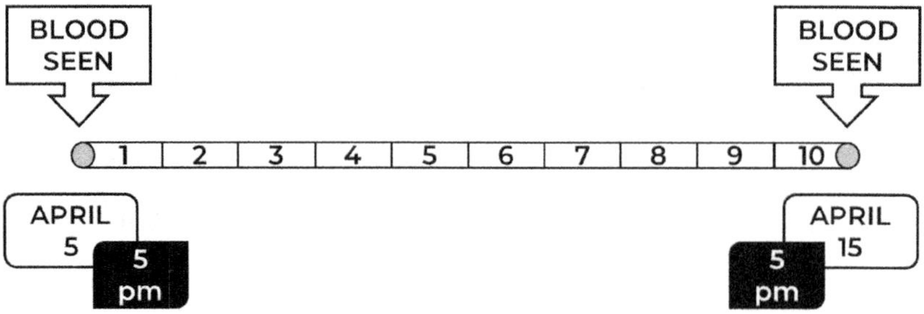

> A woman sees a spot of blood on April 5th at 5 pm during her expected time of menses. Ten days later, she sees another spot on April 15th at 5 pm.
>
> ▶ The entire time span is ruled as menstruation in hindsight.
>
> ▶ Whether she saw blood for the total duration of 10 days is of no consideration according to the rulings.

◆ Not Exceeding The Maximum Limit

If the bleeding does not exceed 10 days (240 hours) and the third condition of a minimal purity is met, then the entire duration will be ruled as menstruation.

If the blood exceeds the menstrual maximum of 240 hours, the woman must revise her situation.

> ➔ The details of what to do when bleeding exceeds the maximum are covered in Chapter 7.

4.5 THIRD CONDITION: PURITY SPAN BETWEEN TWO MENSES

A purity span (*ṭuhr*) of at least 15 complete days (360 hours) must separate between two menstrual bloods. Thus, after menstrual bleeding finishes, a purity span must immediately follow it. Two menstruations cannot succeed each other. There needs to be a separator between them.

- ✧ The purity span must be a minimum duration of 15 complete days (360 hours).
- ✧ The purity span needs to be free from all colored discharge, which includes spotting.

Compare the two examples in Diagram 4f and 4g.

Diagram 4f: Minimum Purity Span

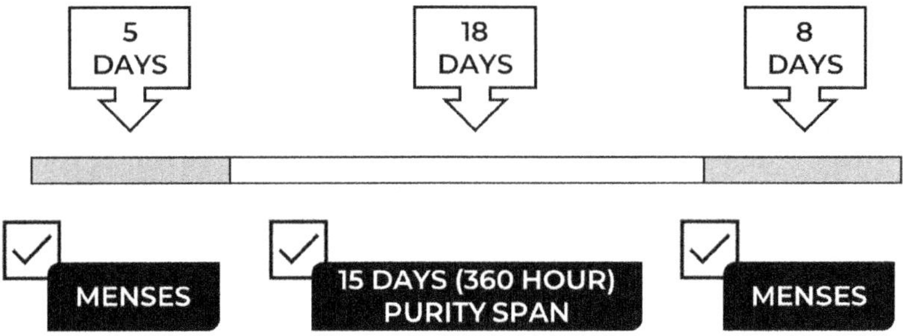

A woman sees 5 days of blood in her expected time of menstruation, 18 days free of blood follow it, and then 8 days of blood occur.

► The 18-day span free of colored discharge is long enough to separate between the two bloods.

► Consequently, each blood can be ruled as menstruation.

Thus, from the end of the first menstrual blood to the beginning of the second menstrual blood, a minimal purity span of 15 complete days (360 hours) must occur for the second show of blood to be ruled as menses. If the second bleeding occurs before 15 complete days, then it will not be ruled as menstruation.

View an example of what happens when the purity span is less than 15 days in Diagram 4g.

Diagram 4g: Minimum Purity Span

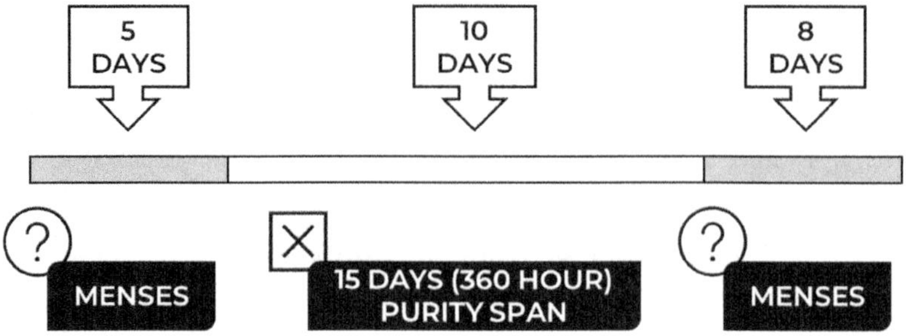

A woman sees 5 days of blood in her expected time of menstruation, 10 days free of blood follow it, and then 8 days of blood occur.

► The 10 days without bleeding are not long enough to separate between the two bloods. Consequently, the second blood will not be ruled as menstruation.

► The first blood will also need to be reevaluated based on the woman's menses and purity habits.

► The habits will determine which days are menses and which days are not menses.

► The habits will also guide her in knowing when she should stop praying.

4.6 ESTABLISHING A MENSES HABIT

If the blood abides by the definition and conditions of menstruation, the bleeding is ruled as sound, and it becomes a woman's menses habit. A sound menses only needs to be seen once for it to become a habit.

ESTABLISHING A MENSES HABIT

- Most recent menses a woman saw.
- Blood is not less than 3 days (72 hours).
- Blood is not more than 10 days (240 hours).
- A purity span of at least 15 days (360 hours) free of blood immediately follows it.
- Only need to see it once to become a habit.
- Obliged to record it.

4.7 RECORDING THE MENSES HABIT

It is obligatory upon every woman to record her menses habit.

4.8 TYPES OF HABITS

The habit (*ʿāda*) refers to the last sound blood or sound purity that a woman saw.

A woman can potentially have three habits:

- A menses habit
- A lochia habit
- A purity habit

Every menstruating woman will have a menses habit and a purity habit. However, not every woman will have a lochia habit. In fact, if a woman never gives birth or miscarries a developed fetus, she will not have a lochia habit.

◆ Can any blood or purity span be taken as a habit?

No. Only a sound blood or a sound purity can be taken as a habit – meaning that the blood and purity must abide by the definitions and conditions set by the Sacred Law.

☑ A woman cannot take abnormal uterine bleeding (*istiḥāḍa*) or an unsound purity as a habit.

◆ Which blood or purity is used for a habit?

The habit refers to the last – meaning the most recent – sound blood or sound purity that a woman experienced.

🔍 Examine the possibilities in Diagram 4h.

Diagram 4h: Types of Habits

MAY		JUNE		JULY
8 DAYS	20 DAYS	6 DAYS	25 DAYS	7 DAYS
✓ MENSES		✓ MENSES		✓ MENSES

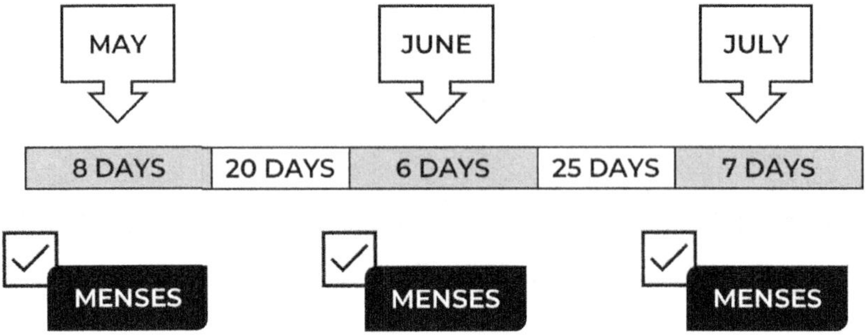

A woman sees 8 days of menstrual blood in May, 6 days of menstrual blood in June, and 7 days of menstrual blood in July.

▶ The July bleeding is the most recent sound blood she saw.

▶ Consequently, her menses habit will be established as 7 days. This is upon the condition that a purity span of at least 15 complete days free of blood follows it.

◆ How many times establish a habit?

A sound blood or sound purity only needs to be seen once for it to become a woman's habit.

She does not need to experience the same cycle next month to prove that this is her new habit. Instead, the habit is established through seeing a sound blood and/or sound purity once.

It is not unusual for women to have slight variations in the days of their cycle from month to month. As long as the days of blood and purity fluctuate within the sound ranges, they will be used to establish a habit.

Taking Diagram 4h as an example, one month she sees 8 days of menstrual blood and 20 days of purity, and then the next month she sees 6 days of menstrual blood and 25 days of purity. This variation in numbers is normal and healthy.

◆ When is the habit used?

The habit is needed in various circumstances as mentioned in Section 3.6. One example is when a woman experiences abnormal uterine bleeding (*istiḥāḍa*). The habit will be used to distinguish between what is ruled as menstrual bleeding, lochia bleeding, and abnormal bleeding.

◆ Can a woman make up a habit?

No. It is a common mistake that women who have abnormal bleeding give themselves a menses habit of 10 days or a purity habit of 15 complete days.

This is incorrect. A woman cannot make up a habit for herself. Rather, she must physically see it occur within her life. The only exception is for a menstrual beginner and a lochia beginner (*mubtadaʾa*).

- ✧ The menstrual beginner is a girl who is experiencing menstruation for the first time in her life. If her bleeding exceeds the menstrual maximum, she is given a habit of 10 days of menses and 20 days of purity. Because she has no prior experience of menstruation, she uses these habits until her bleeding normalizes.

- ✧ The lochia beginner is a woman who is experiencing lochia for the first time in her life. If her bleeding exceeds the lochia maximum, she is given a lochia habit of 40 days. The details related to the lochia beginner can be found in Chapters 11, 12, and 13.

4.9 HABIT IN PLACE & HABIT IN NUMBER

At a technical level, the menstrual habit can refer to two things: habit in place (*makān/zamān*) or habit in number (*ʿadad*).

- **Habit In Place / Menstrual Place:** The expected time that menstruation is supposed to occur according to a woman's purity habit. It could also refer to the place in the month that her menstruation is expected to occur, like in the beginning, middle, or end of the month.

- **Habit In Number:** The expected number of days that a woman will menstruate according to her menses habit.

As a general principle, any time blood is seen within the menstrual place, it will always be ruled as menstruation, providing that the bleeding reaches the menstrual minimum of 72 hours.

> Observe the habit in place and number in Diagram 4i.

Diagram 4i: Habit Terminology

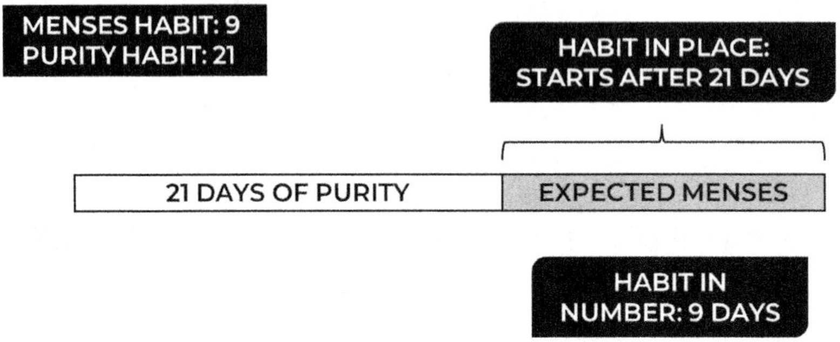

> A woman has a menses habit of 9 days and a purity habit of 21 days.
>
> ► After 21 days of purity elapses, her expected time of menstruation will start. This is known as the habit in place or the menstrual place.
>
> ► The expected number of days that she will menstruate is 9 days.

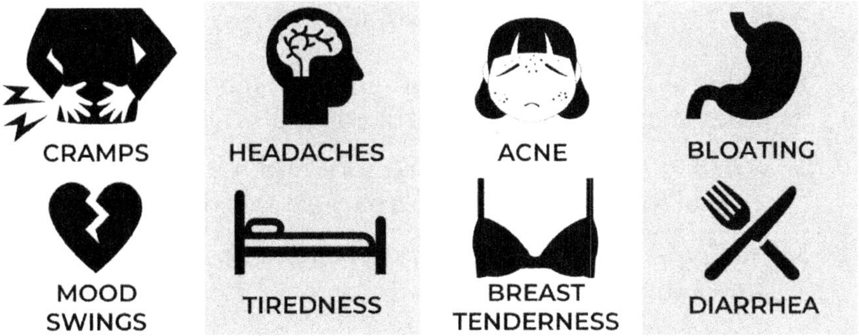

PMS SYMPTOMS

PMS (premenstrual syndrome) is the name for the physical and emotional symptoms that women can experience in the weeks before their period. Symptoms usually stop during or at the beginning of the menstrual period.

It is not fully understood why women get PMS, but it may be because of changes in their hormone levels during the menstrual cycle.

There is no cure for PMS, but symptoms may be managed successfully with lifestyle changes, dietary modifications, supplements, and other therapies.

Recommendations include:

- **Lifestyle:** Exercising regularly, cutting back on caffeine, and sleeping more.
- **Dietary:** Reducing salt intake and eating foods that provide calcium, such as yogurt, almonds, kale, and beans.
- **Supplements:** Taking calcium, magnesium, evening primrose oil, chasteberry, and essential fatty acids can help reduce symptoms according to studies.
- **Therapies:** Practicing mindfulness or breathing exercises may assist in reducing stress levels.

It is useful to keep a PMS diary and record any improvement in symptoms when trying out these suggestions.

REVIEW QUESTIONS

1. What is the Sacred Law definition of menstruation? What does each phrase mean within the definition?
2. What is the menstrual minimum and maximum? What is the ruling for blood that fails to meet this time range?
3. How many days of purity must separate between a menses and a menses?
4. What is the definition for the term habit? How many times must a sound blood or sound purity be seen for it to become a habit?

Chapter 5

Rulings in Practice

IN THIS CHAPTER

- ✧ Ruling in the moment vs retrospect
- ✧ Possible days of menses
- ✧ Blood stopping before 72 hours
- ✧ Blood stopping at or after 72 hours

Allāh Most High says:

﴿ لَا يُكَلِّفُ ٱللَّهُ نَفْسًا إِلَّا وُسْعَهَا ﴾

> Allāh does not obligate any soul beyond its capacity.
>
> (*al-Baqara*, 2:286)

Allāh Most High is all-Merciful and He knows the limits of His creation. He revealed the Sacred Law as a comprehensive form of guidance to mankind. Menstruation rulings are part of that divine guidance, and they are a mercy to women.

The practical rulings of the Sacred Law direct a woman with how to act when her bleeding starts or stops so that she is not left questioning what to do. They fall under two main categories:

- ✧ Rulings in the Moment
- ✧ Rulings in Retrospect

The rulings in the moment are the daily guidelines that instruct a woman as she moves along in her life. They tell her what she should be doing day by day, night by night, hour by hour, minute by minute. Does she pray now? Does she fast now? Can she have sexual intercourse? Is this blood menses? Is it abnormal bleeding?

Because the future is unknown and she cannot be certain with what to expect, there is a very limited picture of her situation. A woman can only assess her circumstance based on what is known in the moment.

It is almost like a puzzle. One piece is given like "Today I am seeing blood," so the ruling is 'x' and the puzzle piece is placed here. Now tomorrow "I am not seeing blood," so the ruling is 'y', and the puzzle piece is placed there.

This process continues until all the pieces of the puzzle fit together, and the image that the puzzle makes becomes clear. Depending on the picture that forms, a woman may go back on the ruling she originally followed.

Thus, the ruling in the moment may change in hindsight once all the events unravel and a woman's situation can be judged more accurately. This is known as the ruling in retrospect.

For example, the onset of bleeding during the expected time of menstruation will be considered menses. However, if it does not reach 72 hours, it will be ruled as abnormal bleeding in retrospect.

It is important to keep in mind that even if the ruling changes in retrospect, the woman is not sinful for the change in the ruling. She was merely following what the Sacred Law instructed her to do.

The Sacred Law is guiding her. It is like she is on a path and if she veers one way, it is only because the Sacred Law told her to go that way. She is not lost or trying to find directions. She knows the direction, but she does not always know the final destination. In truth, no one does. Only Allāh Most High knows what the future holds.

5.1 RULING IN THE MOMENT VS. RULING IN RETROSPECT

The rulings in the moment are the daily guidelines that tell a woman how to act when her bleeding starts or stops.

The rulings in retrospect are the retroactive rulings that come about when the details of a woman's circumstance change. They can overturn a ruling in the moment.

It is important to recognize this distinction when learning the rulings related to the possible days of menses.

5.2 POSSIBLE DAYS OF MENSES (PDM)

The possible days of menses are the potential days that a woman could experience menstruation during the month.

◆ When do the possible days start?

As a general principle, a woman's menstruation can potentially begin when she sees blood after a purity span of at least 15 complete days (360 hours) free of blood.

More precisely, the expected timing is known by a woman's purity habit. When the days of her purity habit elapse, the possible days of menses officially begin – providing that her bleeding starts.

> ☑ When the expected time of menstruation is based on the purity habit, it is known as the habit in place or the menstrual place (*makān*).

> Examine the possibilities in Diagram 5a.

Diagram 5a: Possible Days of Menses

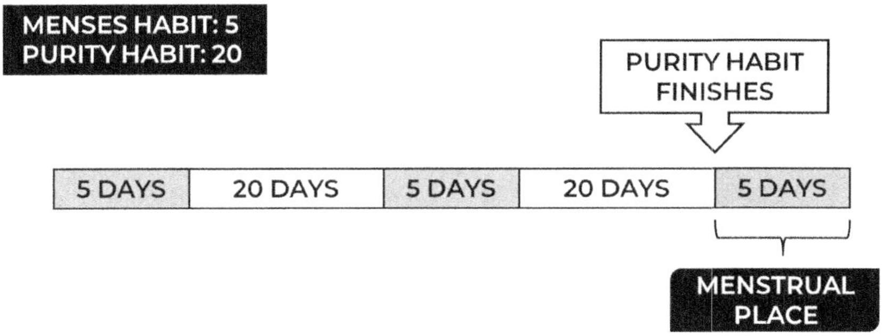

> A woman has a menses habit of 5 days and a purity habit of 20 days.
>
> ▶ Once her 20-day purity habit elapses, the expected time of menstruation begins, which is commonly termed the menstrual place.

> The habit and the menstrual place are discussed in Sections 4.8 and 4.9.

◆ What if no blood is seen?

If bleeding does not begin after her purity habit is finished, she is obliged to continue praying and fasting *Ramaḍān* until the bleeding starts. If she stops her obligatory worship before blood appears, she is sinful.

◆ What if blood comes earlier?

If the bleeding starts before her purity habit is finished, she applies the early blood formula, which is taught in Chapter 18.

> Read a summary of the rulings in Chart 5b.

Chart 5b: When the Possible Days of Menses Start

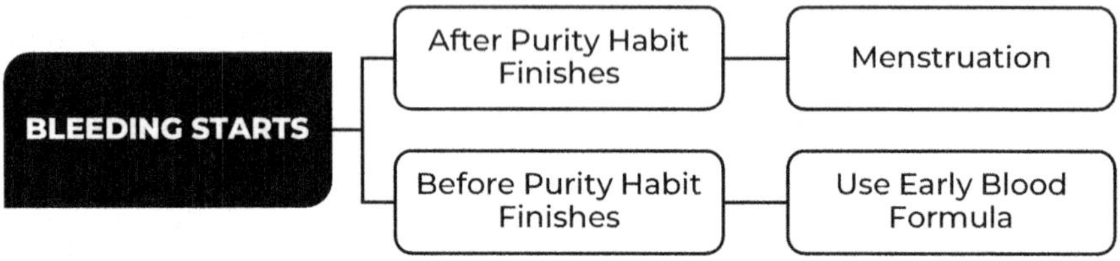

◆ When do the possible days finish?

The possible days of menses last up to 10 complete days (240 hours) counting from the onset of blood.

> Observe how the days are counted in Diagram 5c.

Diagram 5c: Ten Possible Days of Menses

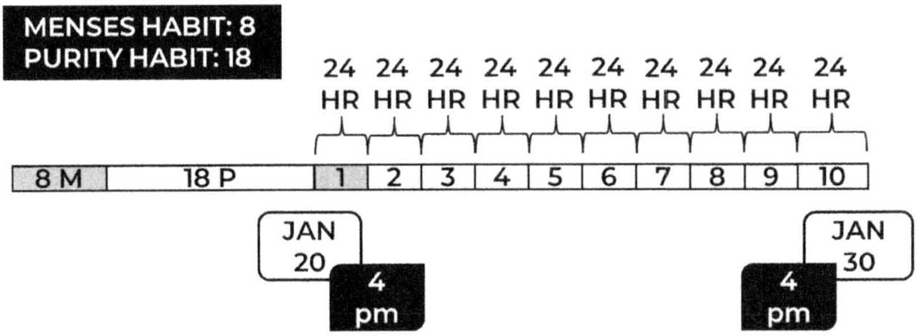

A woman has a menses habit of 8 days and a purity habit of 18 days. After her menstruation ends, she sees 18 days of purity like her habit, and then bleeding starts on January 20th at 4 pm during her expected time of menses.

► Her possible days of menses start when she sees blood on January 20th at 4 pm.

► The possible days of menses end after 10 complete days (240 hours) on January 30th at 4 pm.

5.3 RULINGS FOR THE POSSIBLE DAYS OF MENSES (PDM)

There are three main rulings for the possible days of menses. Sections 5.4 to 5.12 discuss these rulings in detail along with pointing out some of their consequences.

For women who do not experience problems with abnormal bleeding, this section will hopefully be a sufficient guide of how to act within the possible days of menses. It will provide principles for various circumstances that women often find themselves in, as well as answers to common questions.

As for women who experience abnormal uterine bleeding (*istiḥāḍa*), the guidelines given will not provide an overall solution for their problem. Rather, they should read this section to understand how the principles work, and then contact a teacher who may further help them based on their menstrual and purity habits.

Rulings for Possible Days of Menses (PDM)

1. Whenever blood is seen within the possible days of menses, it is always considered menses.
2. Whenever blood stops before 3 complete days (72 hours) within the possible days of menses, it is ruled as abnormal bleeding (*istiḥāḍa*), and a woman is obliged to make *wuḍū*ʾ and pray.
3. Whenever blood stops at 3 complete days (72 hours) or more within the possible days of menses, the blood is ruled as menstruation (*ḥayḍ*), and a woman is obliged to take a *ghusl* and pray.

5.4 FIRST PDM RULING: WHENEVER BLOOD IS SEEN

Whenever blood is seen within the possible days of menses, it is always considered menses.

'*Whenever blood is seen*' means all colored vaginal discharge other than completely white or clear. There is no consideration for the shade of color, the thickness of the blood, or what symptoms accompany it.

The consequences of this ruling are:

❶ All prohibitions apply. She cannot pray. She cannot fast. She cannot have sexual intercourse with her husband. She must adhere to the prohibitions and act like a menstruating woman.

❷ She must always consider any bleeding that she sees within these days to be menstruation, regardless of whether it is spotting, a full flow, or it stops and suddenly returns.

> The prohibitions were briefly mentioned in Section 1.4. They are discussed in detail in Chapter 9.

Observe how the days are counted in Diagram 5d.

Diagram 5d: First PDM Ruling

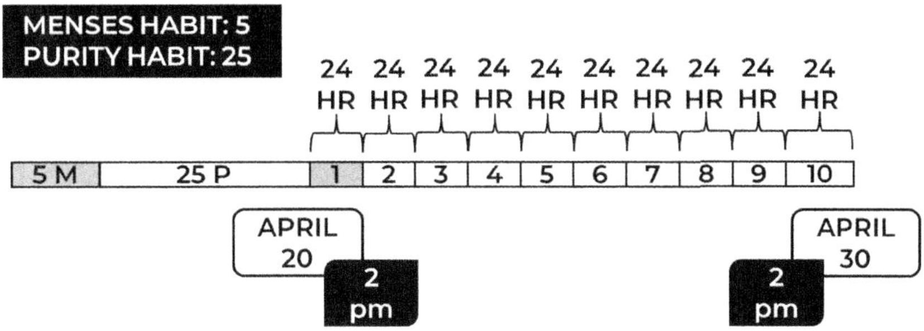

A woman has a menses habit of 5 days and a purity habit of 25 days. After her menstruation ends, she sees 25 days of purity like her habit, and then bleeding starts on April 20th at 2 pm.

► On April 20th at 2 pm, she considers this bleeding to be menses because it is seen after her purity habit finishes.

► Her possible days of menses start when she sees blood on April 20th at 2 pm, and they end after 10 complete days (240 hours) on April 30th at 2 pm.

► Any time she sees bleeding from April 20th 2 pm to April 30th 2 pm, this blood takes the ruling of menstruation.

► She is obliged to adhere to the prohibitions until the blood stops within the possible 10 days or the menstrual maximum of 240 hours is reached.

Keep in mind that this is a ruling in the moment, and depending on what happens, there is a chance that this ruling may change in hindsight. The future is unknown, and there is usually no way of determining whether the blood will exceed 10 complete days or stop beforehand until it happens.

5.5 SECOND PDM RULING: WHEN BLOOD STOPS BEFORE 72 HOURS

Whenever blood stops before 3 complete days (72 hours) within the possible days of menses, it is ruled as abnormal bleeding (*istiḥāḍa*), and a woman is obliged to make *wuḍūʾ* and pray.

◆ '*Stops*' means that there is no sighting of colored vaginal discharge. When a woman checks her *kursuf*, she sees white discharge, clear discharge, or no discharge. She is also reasonably certain that the bleeding will not return.

◆ '*Before 3 complete days*' means that from the onset of blood to the time it stops, the duration is less than 72 hours. The blood did not meet the stipulated menstrual minimum. Consequently, this blood is now considered unsound blood (*istiḥāḍa*) in retrospect.

◆ *Istiḥāḍa* does not require a *ghusl* when it stops, but rather it requires *wuḍūʾ* before praying.

Be aware that not every woman will practice this PDM ruling. For some, when their menses starts, they experience a steady menstrual flow from beginning to end. For others, they see random spotting, and this PDM ruling may be applicable for their situation.

> Observe what happens when blood stops before 72 hours in Diagram 5e.

Diagram 5e: Second PDM Ruling

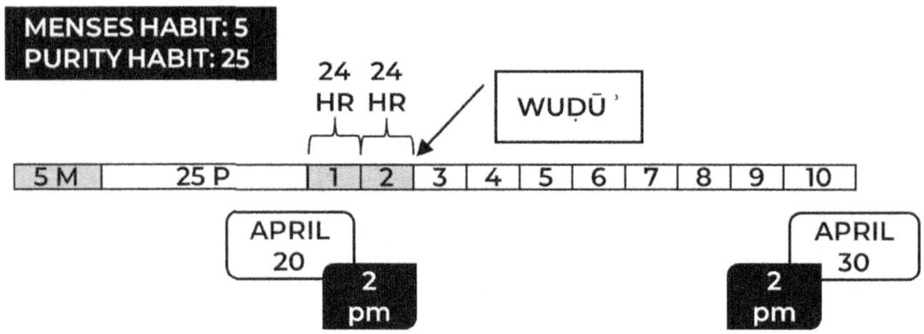

Building on the situation given in Diagram 5d, on April 22nd at 2 pm, the blood stops.

► When the amount of time from April 20th 2 pm to April 22nd 2 pm is calculated, it is apparent that the menstrual bleeding only lasted 48 hours.

► The bleeding is less than 3 complete days (72 hours), and it is now ruled as abnormal bleeding (*istiḥāḍa*) in retrospect.

► She must make *wuḍūʾ* and resume praying.

► She also makes up the prayers missed on April 20th to April 22nd.

5.6 PROCESS FOR BLOOD STOPPING BEFORE 72 HOURS

If a woman thinks that her bleeding will stop before the menstrual minimum of 72 hours, she must:

❶ Delay praying until closer to the end of the prayer time.

She delays praying just in case the bleeding returns. She delays it to the extent that she has enough time to make *wuḍūʾ* and pray before the prayer time exits. She should not miss the prayer of that time if it is confirmed that her bleeding has stopped.

☑ For the *ʿAṣr* prayer time, she delays praying until closer to the end of the preferred prayer time. Refer to Section 6.10.

❷ Make up all the prayers missed for the days that were assumed to be menses.

In retrospect, because the bleeding stopped before the menstrual minimum of 72 hours, what she saw is ruled as abnormal uterine bleeding (*istiḥāḍa*). *Istiḥāḍa* does not prohibit the actions that sound blood prohibits. Consequently, she owes the performance of the missed prayers in hindsight.

☑ She is not sinful for missing these prayers because she had a valid excuse.

❸ Note if the bleeding is followed by a purity span of at least 15 complete days (360 hours).

If the blood does not return within the possible days of menses and a purity span of at least 15 complete days (360 hours) free of blood follows it, this blood is ruled as abnormal uterine bleeding (*istiḥāḍa*) with certainty.

☑ She continues to pray her prayers and fast if it is *Ramaḍān* because she is not seeing any blood.

❹ Consider any blood that returns within the possible days of menses to be menses.

If the blood returns within the 10 possible days of menses, based on PDM Ruling #1, the reappearance of blood will take the ruling of menstruation.

☑ Any time blood is seen within the possible days of menses, it is ruled as menses.

5.7 THIRD PDM RULING: WHEN BLOOD STOPS AT OR AFTER 72 HOURS

Whenever blood stops at 3 complete days (72 hours) or more within the possible days of menses, it is ruled as menstruation (*ḥayḍ*), and a woman is obliged to take a *ghusl* and pray.

◆ '*Stops*' means that there is no sighting of colored vaginal discharge. When a woman checks her *kursuf*, she sees white discharge, clear discharge, or no discharge. She is also reasonably certain that the bleeding will not return.

◆ '*At 3 complete days*' means that from the onset of blood to the time it stops, the duration is at least 72 hours. The blood met the menstrual minimum. So, menstruation is confirmed with certainty.

◆ '*Ghusl*' refers to the purificatory shower that removes a person from major ritual impurity. It is obligatory to take a *ghusl* when menstrual bleeding either stops within the 10 possible days or the menstrual maximum of 10 complete days (240 hours) is reached.

The *ghusl* is described in Sections 6.2 to 6.3.

Observe the difference in the rulings for when bleeding stops before and after the menstrual minimum in Diagram 5f.

Diagram 5f: Blood Stopping Before or After 72 Hours

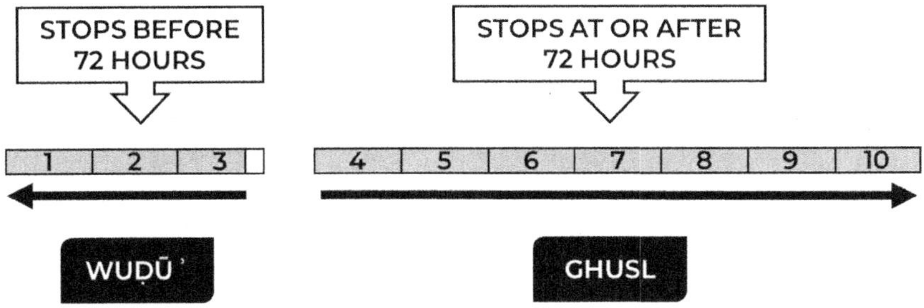

The consequences for meeting the menstrual minimum are:

1. The blood she is seeing is definitely ruled as menstruation. Even if the blood surpasses 10 complete days, part of the overall bleeding will be ruled as menstruation.

2. She is not required to make up any missed prayers due to menstruation, but she must make up her missed fasts if the menses occurred during *Ramaḍān*.

3. Whenever this bleeding stops, she is required to take a *ghusl* before she begins praying.

View a practical example of the third PDM Ruling in Diagram 5g.

Diagram 5g: Third PDM Ruling

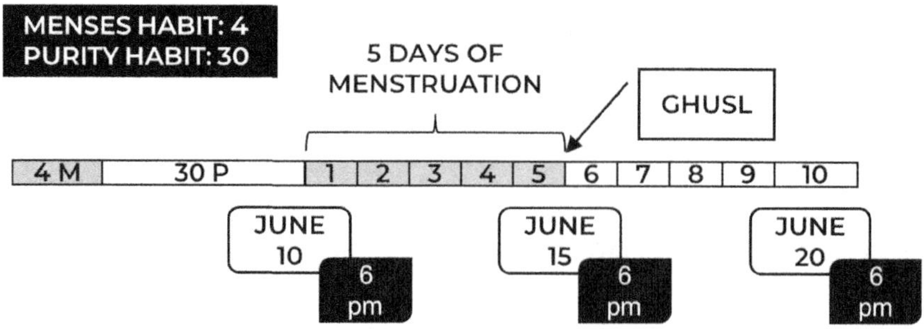

A woman has a menses habit of 4 days and a purity habit of 30 days. After her menstruation ends, she sees 30 days of purity like her habit, and then bleeding starts on June 10th at 6 pm.

► On June 10th at 6 pm, she considers this bleeding to be menses because it is seen after her purity habit finishes. She stops praying and acts like a menstruating woman.

► Her possible days of menses start when she sees blood on June 10th at 6 pm, and they end after 10 complete days (240 hours) on June 20th at 6 pm.

► Any time she sees bleeding from June 10th 6 pm to June 20th 6 pm, this blood takes the ruling of menstruation.

► She is obliged to adhere to the prohibitions for menstruation until the blood stops within the possible 10 days or the menstrual maximum of 240 hours is reached.

► When her blood reaches 3 complete days (72 hours) on June 13th at 6 pm, menstruation is confirmed with certainty.

► Any time the blood stops thereafter, she must take a *ghusl* before starting to pray again.

► On June 15th at 6 pm, her blood stops after 5 complete days.

► She takes a *ghusl* and begins praying.

► If the bleeding does not return and a purity span of at least 15 complete days (360 hours) free of blood follows it, her menses habit changes to 5 complete days.

5.8 BLEEDING EXCEEDING THE MENSES HABIT IN PDM

If a woman reaches her menses habit during the possible days of menses and she is still bleeding, she continues to act like a menstruating woman.

✅ If she is bleeding within the 10 possible days, this is proof that she is still menstruating.

> 🔍 Observe what was done in Diagram 5g when the blood exceeds the woman's menses habit of 4 days. She continued to act like a menstruating woman on Day 5 (June 15th), despite the bleeding surpassing her 4-day habit.

5.9 BLEEDING RETURNING AFTER IT PREVIOUSLY STOPPED IN PDM

If the bleeding stops and later returns within the possible days of menses, it is obligatory to take another *ghusl* – providing that the menstrual minimum of 72 hours is met.

> 🔍 Observe when she takes a second *ghusl* in Diagram 5h.

Diagram 5h: Bleeding Returns After Stopping

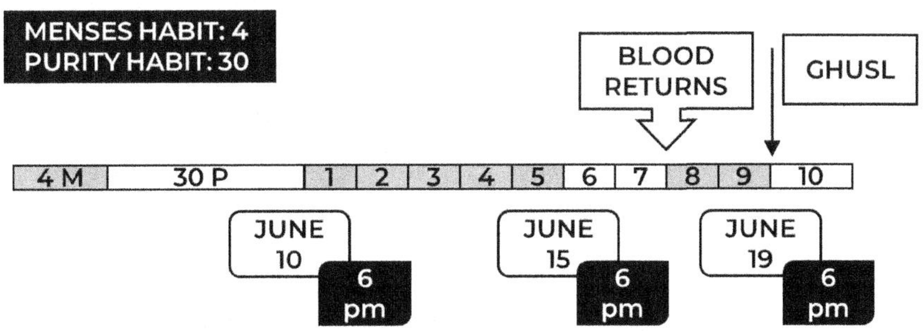

The bleeding in Diagram 5g returns on Day 8 (June 17th) at 6 pm and stops at the completion of Day 9 (June 19th) at 6 pm.

▶ She must take another *ghusl* when the blood stops at the completion of Day 9 (June 19th).

5.10 WORSHIP PERFORMED DURING GAPS OF PURITY IN PDM

If menstrual bleeding returns within the possible days of menses, it is considered menses in addition to the time span in which no blood was seen. Bleeding does not need to be continuous for it to be classified as menses. Thus, all the prayers and fasts that she performed during the days without blood are invalid in retrospect.

☑ Allāh Most High will reward her for following His commandments, even if the prayers and fasts she performed are invalid in hindsight.

🔍 Observe what happens when bleeding returns in Diagram 5i.

Diagram 5i: Worship Performed After Bleeding Returns

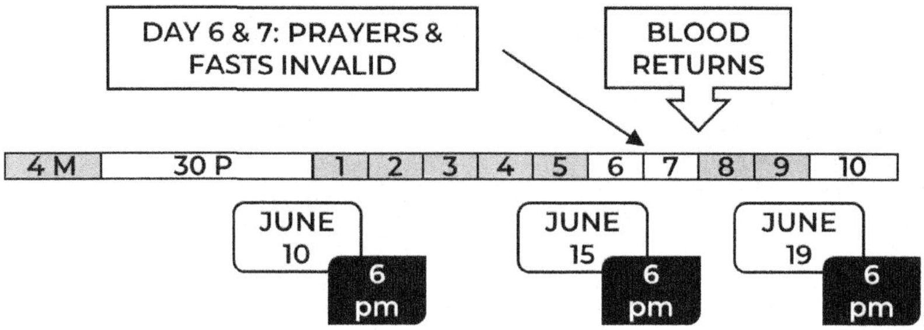

When bleeding returns on Day 8, the prayers and fasts offered on Days 6 and 7 are ruled as invalid in retrospect.

▶ She is not required to make up any of the prayers she performed on Days 6 and 7. The only exception is the performance of makeup prayers owed from previous years or vowed prayers since the debt to Allāh Most High was not lifted.

▶ She is required to make up any obligatory fasts performed on Days 6 and 7 as the fasts do not count in hindsight.

POSSIBLE DAYS OF MENSES PROTOCOL

- From the onset of bleeding in a woman's expected time of menses, she has 10 possible days (240 hours) to menstruate.
- Whenever she sees blood during the possible days of menses, she acts like a menstruating woman.
- Even if the bleeding exceeds her menses habit, she continues to act like a menstruating woman.
- If the blood returns within the 10 days after having stopped, it takes the ruling of menses.
- The gaps of purity during the 10 possible days of menses are considered menstruation in retrospect.
- A *ghusl* is obligatory when menstrual bleeding either stops within the 10 possible days or the menstrual maximum of 10 complete days (240 hours) is reached.
- If the entire span of bleeding does not exceed the menstrual maximum of 240 hours, then what she sees becomes her new habit, as long as a purity span of at least 15 complete days free of blood follows it.
- She cannot consider any bleeding beyond 10 complete days (240 hours) to be menstruation. Once the menstrual maximum of 10 complete days (240 hours) is reached, menstruation can be no more.

5.11 CHANGE IN THE HABIT

If the total bleeding does not exceed the menstrual maximum of 240 hours, then what she sees becomes her new habit. This is upon the condition that a purity span of at least 15 complete days free of blood follows it.

- ✧ A sound menses only needs to be seen once for it to become a habit.
- ✧ The most recent sound menses will be used as her habit.

> ⚠ A woman cannot make up a habit for herself. Rather, she must physically see it occur within her life.
>
> ➔ The details related to the types of habits were discussed in Section 4.8.
>
> 🔍 Observe what her menses habit becomes in Diagram 5j.

Diagram 5j: Change in Habit

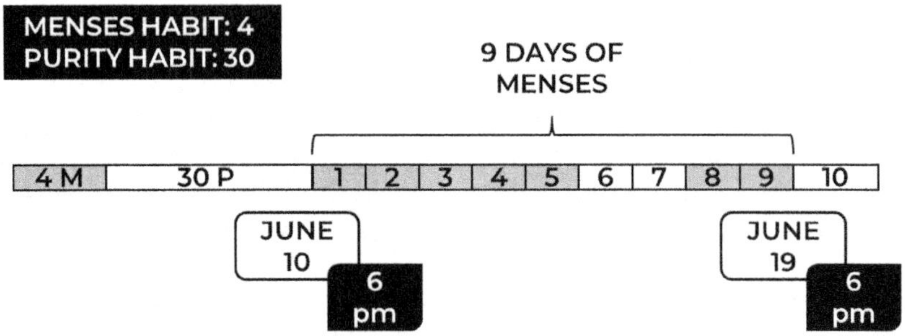

> With the situation in Diagram 5j, she sees 15 days free of blood after the bleeding stops at the completion of Day 9.
>
> ► Her menses habit changes from 4 days to 9 complete days.

5.12 BLEEDING EXCEEDING THE MENSTRUAL MAXIMUM

When the menstrual maximum of 240 hours is reached, it is obligatory to take a *ghusl* and begin praying, even if the bleeding continues. There can be no increase in the maximum time.

If the blood exceeds the menstrual maximum of 240 hours, the woman must revise her situation.

> The details of what to do when bleeding exceeds the maximum are covered in Chapter 7.

			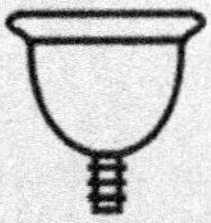
SANITARY PAD	**CLOTH PAD**	**TAMPON**	**MENSTRUAL CUP**
Sticks to the underwear.	Secured with buttons.	Inserted inside the vagina.	Inserted inside the vagina.
Disposable.	Reusable.	Disposable.	Reusable.

PERIOD PRODUCTS

There are several products that a woman can use during her period. Disposable sanitary pads are the most popular option. They are widely available, convenient, and easy to wear. Instead of disposable pads, some women choose to use reusable cloth pads because they are cheaper, better for the environment, and involve less exposure to plastic.

Non-virgins can also use internal products, like the tampon and the menstrual cup. The tampon is inserted inside the vagina and sits just below the cervix. It absorbs the blood and is removed by pulling its string, which hangs outside the vagina. The menstrual cup is completely inserted inside the vagina, but it sits at the lower portion of the vaginal canal. It catches the blood and must be emptied every few hours.

5.13 ABNORMAL BLEEDING SCENARIOS

The scenarios given in this chapter are basic and straightforward. For a woman with abnormal uterine bleeding (*istiḥāḍa*), the rulings she follows may be different depending on her circumstance.

The important thing to note is that a woman's situation needs to be reevaluated if one of three things occur:

- ✧ Her bleeding does not meet the menstrual minimum of three complete days (72 hours).
- ✧ Her bleeding exceeds the menstrual maximum of 10 complete days (240 hours).
- ✧ Her bleeding is not followed by a purity span of 15 complete days (360 hours) free of blood.

It is advisable that women in these circumstances ask a teacher about their situation so that they do not miss performing any obligatory prayers or fasts.

REVIEW QUESTIONS

1. What is a ruling in the moment? What is a ruling in retrospect?
2. What are the possible days of menses? When do they start?
3. What are the three main rulings related to the possible days of menses? Explain each.
4. What is the ruling for menstrual blood that exceeds the habit within the possible days of menses?
5. What is the ruling for menstrual blood that stops and returns within the possible days of menses?
6. What are the conditions for the bleeding to become her new menses habit?

Chapter 6

The Ghusl & Related Questions

IN THIS CHAPTER

- ✧ Obligatory actions of *ghusl*
- ✧ Complete *ghusl* with *sunna* actions
- ✧ *Ghusl* time and the habit
- ✧ Blood ending before or at the maximum

Allāh Most High says:

﴿وَيَسْـَٔلُونَكَ عَنِ ٱلْمَحِيضِ قُلْ هُوَ أَذًى فَٱعْتَزِلُوا۟ ٱلنِّسَآءَ فِى ٱلْمَحِيضِ وَلَا تَقْرَبُوهُنَّ حَتَّىٰ يَطْهُرْنَ
فَإِذَا تَطَهَّرْنَ فَأْتُوهُنَّ مِنْ حَيْثُ أَمَرَكُمُ ٱللَّهُ إِنَّ ٱللَّهَ يُحِبُّ ٱلتَّوَّٰبِينَ وَيُحِبُّ ٱلْمُتَطَهِّرِينَ﴾

> They ask you about menstruation. Say: "It is an impurity. So, keep away from women during menstruation, and do not have intercourse with them until they are purified. When they purify themselves, then you may approach them in the manner specified by Allāh. Verily Allāh loves those who always turn to Him in repentance and those who purify themselves.
>
> (*al-Baqara*, 2:222)

This verse was revealed after the Prophet ﷺ was asked how to interact with wives who are menstruating. Allāh Most High first instructs believing men to avoid sexual intercourse during menses. Once a woman's menstrual blood ceases and she purifies herself, then sexual intercourse becomes permissible.

Consequently, some scholars interpret the phrases to mean that 'those who always turn to Allāh in repentance' (*at-tawwābīn*) are those who avoid sexual intercourse with their wives while they are menstruating.

Whereas 'those who purify themselves' (*al-mutaṭahhirīn*) are those who use water to cleanse themselves from the ritual states of impurity, like performing the *ghusl* after menstrual bleeding stops.

6.1 RULING FOR THE PURIFICATORY SHOWER (GHUSL)

A *ghusl* is obligatory to perform once menstrual bleeding ends during the possible days of menses or the menstrual maximum of 240 hours is reached.

6.2 OBLIGATORY ACTIONS OF THE GHUSL

The obligatory actions of the *ghusl* are the actions that must be performed for the *ghusl* to be ruled as valid.

They are to rinse the nose, the mouth, and the entire body with water at least once. Water must reach every part of the outer body that is possible to rinse without undue hardship.

The *ghusl* is achieved with the use of water, and there is no requirement to use soap, shampoo, or conditioner.

During the *ghusl* a woman must:

- Rinse the inside of the nose, the inside of the mouth, and the entire outer body with water at least once.
- Ensure that water reaches all of her hair, underneath the skin of the clitoral hood, the external orifice of the genitals, and the skin underneath the eyebrows.
- Wet the inside of the belly button and the inside of any hole that is not sealed, like earring holes.

☑ In the *Ḥanafī madhhab*, making the intention to perform the *ghusl* is not obligatory, but rather it is a *sunna* action.

6.3 COMPLETE GHUSL WITH SUNNA ACTIONS

The complete *ghusl* is a *ghusl* that includes the obligatory actions and the *sunna* actions. In various *aḥādīth*, the wives ﷺ of the Prophet ﷺ describe how the Prophet ﷺ performed the *ghusl*.

Step-by-step process for the *ghusl*:

❶ Make an intention in the heart to perform the *ghusl* for the sake of Allāh Most High, while saying '*bismi Llahir Raḥmānir Raḥīm*' with the tongue before revealing one's nakedness (*ʿawra*). This should be done while also washing the hands up to the wrists.

❷ Wash away any filth (*najāsa*) that may be on any part of the body.

❸ Wash both the front and the back private parts, even if they are free from filth (*najāsa*).

❹ Perform a complete *wuḍūʾ* with the *sunna* actions like what is done for the prayer.

❺ Pour water over the body three times, making sure that the entire body is rinsed each time. This is easily achieved under a shower head.

It is related that one first begins with the head, then continues with the right shoulder, then the left shoulder, and then rinses the remainder of the body. Repeat three times.

☑ It is *sunna* to use the hand to help the water flow along the limbs (*dalk*) during the first washing, and thereafter it is recommended. The body parts should be washed successively.

☑ The proper manners (*adab*) of the *ghusl* are the same proper manners as in *wuḍūʾ* except that one does not face the *qibla*, talk, or say *dhikr* aloud while naked. The actions that are disliked in *wuḍūʾ* are also disliked during the *ghusl*.

6.4 DEFINITION OF THE GHUSL TIME

The *ghusl* time is a broader term that refers to the time it takes for a woman to prepare for the *ghusl* and perform the obligatory actions of the *ghusl*. Some scholars say the time it takes to get dressed is also considered.

Scholars do not mention a specific time for how long this would take, but with the modern-day convenience of accessible running water, many estimate it to be 10 to 15 minutes.

> Observe the difference between the *ghusl* and the *ghusl* time in Chart 6a.

Chart 6a: Ghusl Time vs. the Ghusl

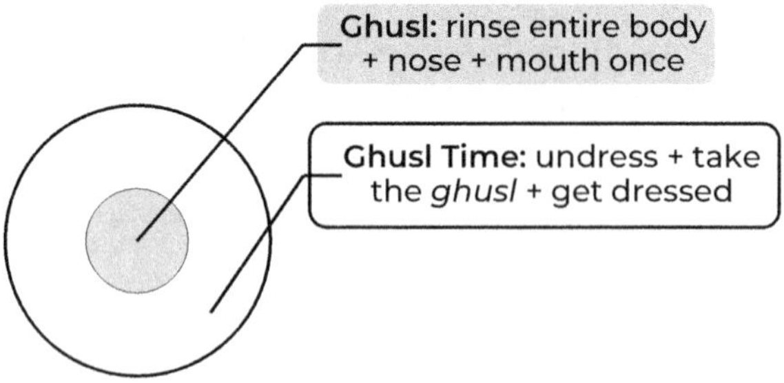
Ghusl: rinse entire body + nose + mouth once
Ghusl Time: undress + take the ghusl + get dressed

6.5 GHUSL TIME & THE HABIT

With respect to the *ghusl* time and the habit:

- When menstrual bleeding ends before the menstrual maximum of 240 hours, the *ghusl* time is **added** to the menses habit.

- When menstrual bleeding ends at the menstrual maximum of 240 hours, the *ghusl* time is **not** added to the menses habit.

> Read a summary of this ruling in Chart 6b.

Chart 6b: Ghusl Time Added to the Habit

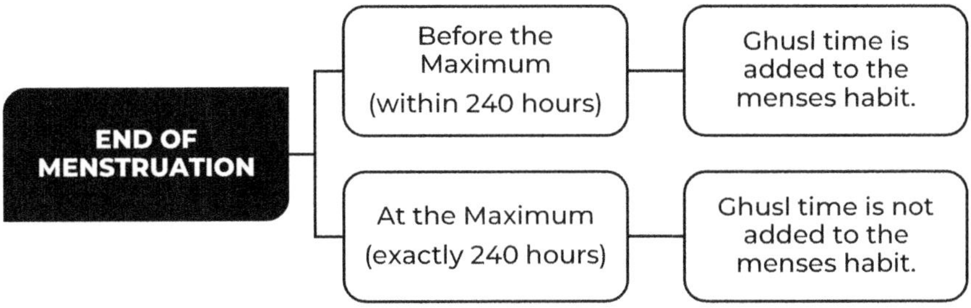
END OF MENSTRUATION
Before the Maximum (within 240 hours)
Ghusl time is added to the menses habit.
At the Maximum (exactly 240 hours)
Ghusl time is not added to the menses habit.

The *ghusl* time is added to the menses habit when blood stops before 10 days because of the opinion held by key Companions رضي الله عنهم that a woman is still in a state of menses until she takes a *ghusl*.

> Compare the difference in the ruling in Diagrams 6c and 6d.

Diagram 6c: Blood Stops Before the Maximum

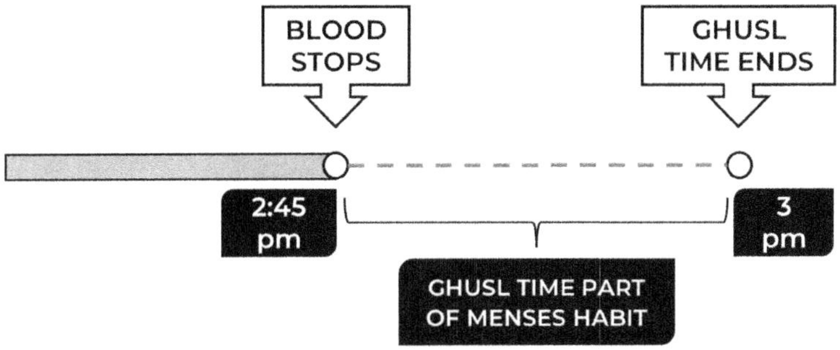
BLOOD STOPS
GHUSL TIME ENDS
2:45 pm
3 pm
GHUSL TIME PART OF MENSES HABIT

> A woman's menstruation stops on Day 8 at 2:45 pm.
>
> ▶ The bleeding stops before the menstrual maximum. She will add 15 minutes to her end time.
>
> ▶ She does not exit the state of menstruation until 3 pm. Thus, she will record her menses habit as ending at 3 pm.

On the other hand, if her menstruation stopped exactly at 240 hours, the *ghusl* time is not added to the menses habit because the menstrual maximum has been reached.

Diagram 6d: Blood Stops at the Maximum

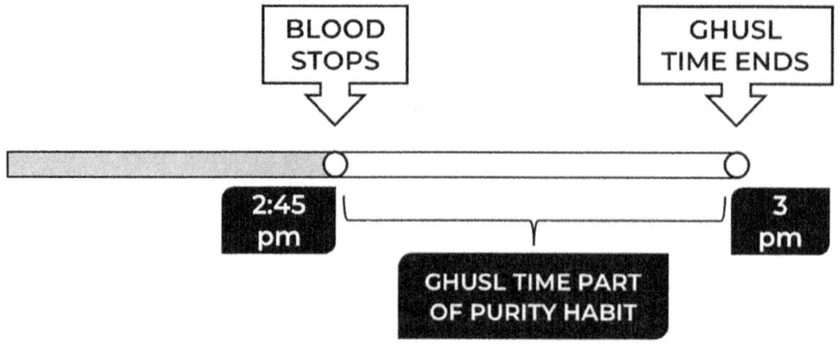

A woman's menstruation stops at 240 hours at 2:45 pm.

► The bleeding stops at the menstrual maximum. She will not add 15 minutes to her end time.

► She exited the state of menstruation at 2:45 pm. Thus, she will record her menses habit as ending at 240 hours.

When the *ghusl* time is added to the menses habit, it affects many related rulings like:

- Delaying the *ghusl* until closer to the end of the prayer time.
- Recording when menstruation ends.
- Determining if the obligatory prayer of that time is owed.
- Establishing if the next day's fast is valid.
- Knowing when sexual intercourse is permissible.

Sections 6.6 to 6.10 detail these rulings.

6.6 BLOOD ENDING BEFORE THE MAXIMUM

When bleeding ends before the maximum, it means that the menstrual minimum of 3 complete days (72 hours) has been met, but the blood stops before reaching the menstrual maximum of 10 complete days (240 hours).

The stopping can occur in three ways:

- Before the habit
- At the habit
- After the habit

> 🔍 Observe what it means for blood to stop before the maximum in Chart 6e.

Chart 6e: Blood Ending Before the Maximum

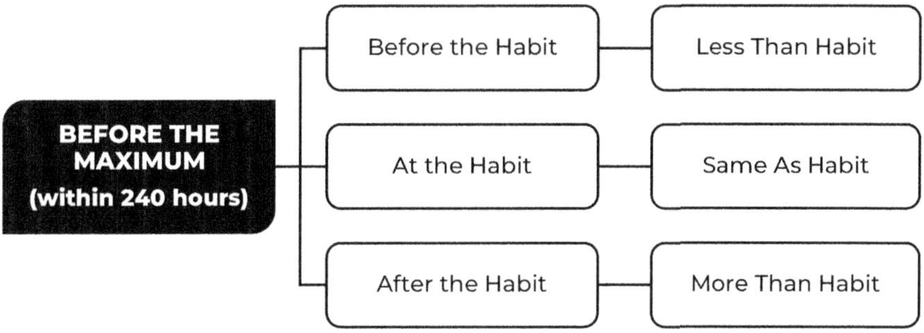

✅ **Example of Before the Habit:** A woman has a menses habit of 8 days and the next month her bleeding stops on day 5.

✅ **Example of At the Habit:** A woman has a menses habit of 7 days and the next month her bleeding stops on day 7 at the same time.

✅ **Example of After the Habit:** A woman has a menses habit of 6 days and the next month her bleeding stops on day 8.

6.7 BEFORE THE HABIT RULINGS

When bleeding stops before the habit, the assumption is that there is a strong chance the bleeding will return. Consequently, the rulings in this category are different from the other categories.

◆ Is delaying the *ghusl* necessary?

Yes. When a woman's bleeding ends before the habit, she is required to delay taking her *ghusl* until closer to the end of the prayer time. She does this to check if the bleeding will return.

The scholars do not give an exact time of when she must check. Each woman knows her circumstance and must do what is best for the timing of her situation. If it is confirmed that the bleeding has stopped, she should not miss performing the prayer of that time.

> ⚠ If she fears missing the prayer, then she takes a *ghusl* and prays.
>
> ➔ For the ʿ*Aṣr* prayer time, she delays taking the *ghusl* until closer to the end of the preferred prayer time. See Section 6.10.

◆ Is the *ghusl* time added to the habit?

Yes. As shown in Diagram 6c, whenever blood stops before the maximum, the *ghusl* time is added to the habit. She is free from a state of menses once the actions of the *ghusl* time are complete.

For example, a woman last saw blood on Day 4 at 5 pm. She records her menses as ending at 5:15 pm. See Table 3a for a sample record.

◆ Does she owe the prayer of that time?

Depends. From the time the blood ceases, if she has enough time to complete the *ghusl* and say 'Allāh' from 'Allāhu Akbar' before the prayer time exits, she owes the obligatory prayer. Otherwise, no.

> 🔍 Observe what happens when her bleeding ends in Diagram 6f.

Diagram 6f: Before the Habit Rulings

A woman's bleeding stops at 2 pm during the *Ẓuhr* prayer time. The *ʿAṣr* prayer time enters at 4 pm.

► Between 2 pm and 4 pm, there is enough time to complete the *ghusl* and say 'Allāh' from 'Allāhu Akbar.'

► She owes the *Ẓuhr* prayer.

◆ Is her fast valid if the bleeding stops before *Fajr*?

Depends. A condition for the validity of the fast is that a woman is free from the state of menstruation for the entire duration of the fasting day, which is from the entrance of the *Fajr* prayer time to the entrance of the *Maghrib* prayer time.

Thus, if a woman's bleeding stops before *Fajr* and there is enough time to complete the *ghusl* and say 'Allāh' from 'Allāhu Akbar' before *Fajr* enters, her fast is valid. This is because she is free from the state of menstruation when *Fajr* enters. Otherwise, the fast is not valid.

☑ Even if she delays taking her *ghusl* until after *Fajr* enters, the same ruling applies. However, she is responsible for making up her *ʿIshāʾ* and *witr* prayers.

🔍 Observe what happens when her bleeding ends in Diagram 6g.

Diagram 6g: Before the Habit Rulings

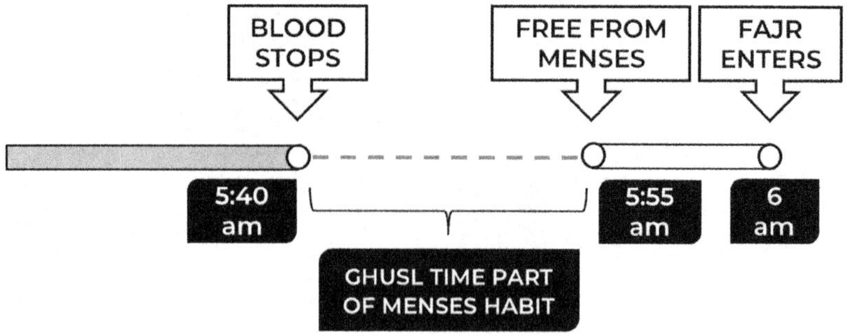

> A woman's bleeding stops on Day 7 at 5:40 am in *Ramaḍān*. *Fajr* enters at 6 am.
>
> ► She has enough time to complete the *ghusl* and say 'Allāh' from 'Allāh Akbar' before *Fajr* enters.
>
> ► Her fast is valid.

◆ Is sexual intercourse permissible after the *ghusl*?

No. When the blood stops early, a woman is not permitted to engage in sexual intercourse until the completion of her habit.

- ✧ This is the ruling even if she is now praying after her *ghusl*.
- ✧ Sexual intercourse is unlawful out of precaution because there is a strong chance that the blood will return in her habitual time.
- ✧ Sexual intercourse only becomes permissible once she reaches the completion of her habit.
- ✧ She is not obliged to take another *ghusl* at her habit before engaging in sexual intercourse.

> Observe what happens when her bleeding ends in Diagram 6h.

◆ Is another *ghusl* needed at her habit?

It is recommended to take a precautionary *ghusl* at the completion of the habit. This is a safeguard for her prayers in case a purity span of less than 15 days (360 hours) follows the end of her bleeding.

☑ It is not a condition for her to perform the precautionary *ghusl* before engaging in sexual intercourse.

🔍 Observe what happens when her bleeding ends in Diagram 6h.

Diagram 6h: Before the Habit Rulings

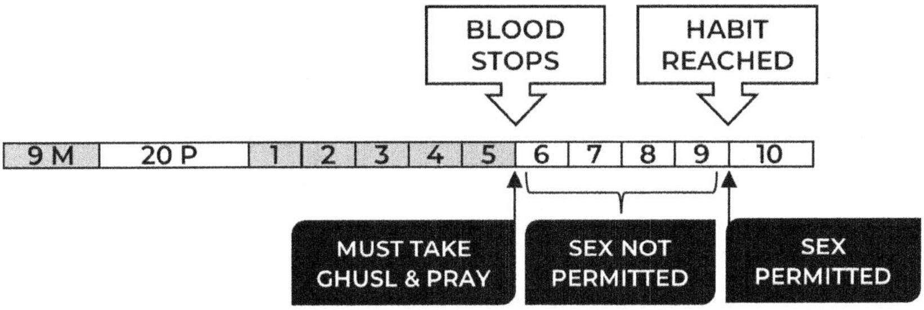

A woman has a habit of 9 days and this month her menstrual blood stops on Day 5.

► **Day 5:** When the blood stops before the habit, she is obliged to wait towards the end of the prayer time to check if the bleeding really ceased. If no colored discharge is seen, she takes a *ghusl* and begins praying.

► **Day 6 to 9:** Even though she is praying, sexual intercourse is not permitted until the completion of her habit on Day 9.

► **Day 10:** At the completion of her 9-day habit, sexual intercourse is permissible. It is also recommended to take a precautionary *ghusl* to safeguard her prayers in case bleeding returns before a purity span of 15 complete days (360 hours).

6.8 AT OR AFTER THE HABIT RULINGS

When blood stops at or after the habit, both situations take the same rulings. Unlike bleeding that stops before the habit, the chance of blood returning after it has stopped is less likely.

◆ Is delaying the *ghusl* necessary?

No. When a woman's bleeding ends at/after the habit, it is recommended to delay taking her *ghusl* until closer to the end of the prayer time just in case the bleeding returns. However, if she does not delay it, there is no issue.

◆ Is the *ghusl* time added to the habit?

Yes. As shown in Diagram 6c, whenever blood stops before the maximum, the *ghusl* time is added to the habit. She is free from a state of menses once the actions of the *ghusl* time are complete.

For example, a woman last saw blood on Day 9 at 8 pm. She records her menses as ending at 8:15 pm. See Table 3a for a sample record.

◆ Does she owe the prayer of that time?

Depends. From the time the blood ceases, if she has enough time to complete the *ghusl* and say 'Allāh' from 'Allāhu Akbar' before the entire prayer time exits, she owes the obligatory prayer. Otherwise, no.

> 🔍 Observe what happens when her bleeding ends in Diagram 6f. The same applies to blood stopping at/after the habit.

◆ Is her fast valid if the bleeding stops before *Fajr*?

Depends. If a woman's bleeding stops before the entrance of *Fajr* and there is enough time to complete the *ghusl* and say 'Allāh' from 'Allāhu Akbar' before *Fajr* enters, her fast is valid. This is because she is free from the state of menstruation when *Fajr* enters. Otherwise, the fast is not valid.

> Observe what happens when her bleeding ends in Diagram 6g. The same applies to blood stopping at/after the habit.

◆ Is sexual intercourse permissible after the *ghusl*?

Yes. Once the *ghusl* is finished, she is free to have sexual intercourse with her spouse.

> ⚠ It is not permissible to engage in sexual intercourse before the *ghusl*.
>
> Observe what happens when her bleeding ends in Diagram 6i.

Diagram 6i: At / After the Habit Rulings

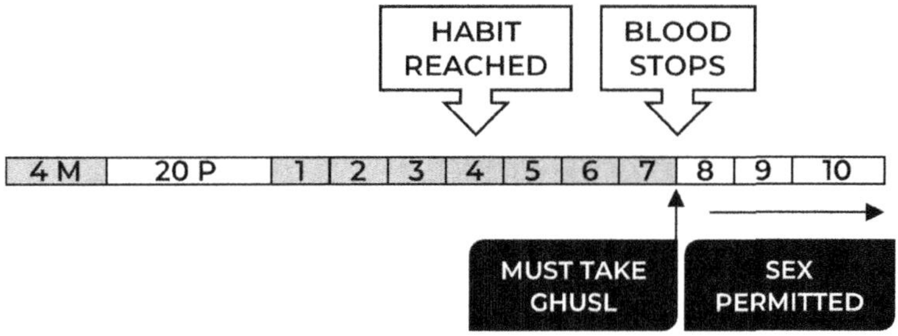

> A woman has a menses habit of 4 days. During her next cycle, her bleeding continues after her habit and stops on Day 7.
>
> ► Sexual intercourse is permitted after the *ghusl* on Day 7.

◆ Is another *ghusl* needed at her habit?

No. This ruling does not apply because the precautionary *ghusl* is only recommended when bleeding stops before the habit.

6.9 BLOOD ENDING AT THE MAXIMUM

When blood ends at the menstrual maximum, it means that it stopped exactly at 10 complete days (240 hours). Thus, the *ghusl* time is not added to the habit because menstruation can never be more than 10 complete days (240 hours).

☑ There can be no increase in the maximum time. When the maximum is reached, the state of menstruation ends.

◆ **Is delaying the *ghusl* necessary?**

No. The possible days of menses are over and there is no chance of menstrual blood returning after it has stopped.

◆ **Is the *ghusl* time added to her habit?**

No. As shown in Diagram 6d, whenever blood stops at the maximum, the *ghusl* time is not added to the habit. Menstruation ends at 240 hours. The *ghusl* time is part of the purity time (*ṭuhr*).

For example, a woman last saw blood at the completion of 10 days (240 hours) at 4 pm. She does not add the *ghusl* time to her end time. Thus, she is free from the state of menses at 4 pm.

◆ **Does she owe the prayer of that time?**

Depends. From the time the blood stops, if a woman has enough time to say 'Allāh' from '*Allāhu Akbar*' before the prayer time exits, she owes the prayer of that time, even if she has not yet taken the *ghusl*. Practically speaking, this is the length of a second.

The consideration for owing prayers returns to the woman's state within the last moment of the prayer time. When the maximum is reached, she is no longer in a state of menses. As such, she is legally in a time of purity (*ṭuhr*), and the ritual prayer is due upon her.

> 🔍 Observe what happens when her bleeding ends in Diagram 6j.

Diagram 6j: Blood Ending at the Maximum

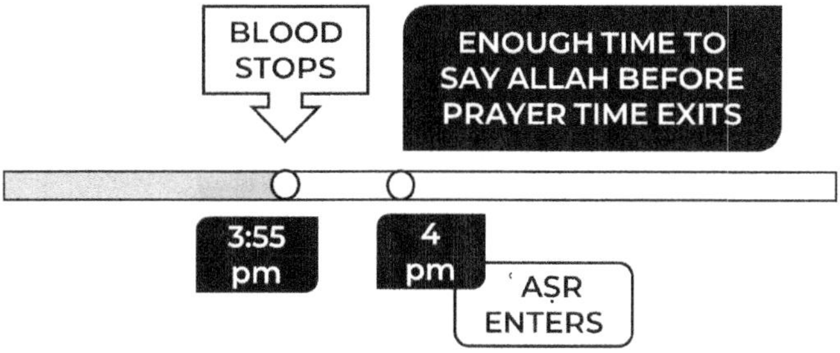

A woman's bleeding stops at 10 complete days (240 hours) at 3:55 pm. *ʿAṣr* enters at 4 pm.

► Legally, she is free from menstruation at 3:55 pm. There is enough time to say 'Allāh' from *'Allāhu Akbar'* before the prayer time exits. Technically, she must perform the *Ẓuhr* prayer.

► However, she is still within a state of major ritual impurity until she takes a *ghusl*. She cannot pray in this state.

► As a result, after her *ghusl* is finished, she is required to make up the *Ẓuhr* prayer before she prays the *ʿAṣr* prayer, but she is not sinful for missing the *Ẓuhr* prayer.

◆ Is her fast valid if the bleeding stops before *Fajr*?

Depends. If the maximum is reached before the entrance of *Fajr*, her fast will count, even if *Fajr* enters while she is taking a *ghusl*. This is because she is free from the state of menstruation when *Fajr* enters. Otherwise, the fast is not valid.

✅ If there is enough time to say 'Allāh' from 'Allāhu Akbar,' she must also make up the *ʿIshāʾ* and *witr* prayers before praying her *Fajr* prayer, but she is not sinful for missing them.

🔍 Observe what happens when her bleeding ends in Diagram 6k.

Diagram 6k: Blood Ending at the Maximum

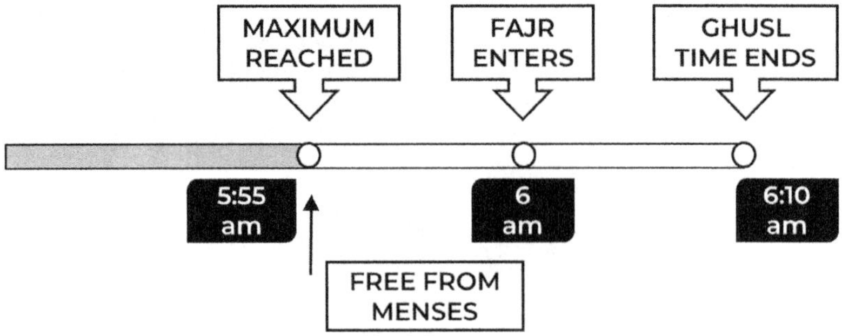

A woman's bleeding stops at 10 complete days (240 hours) at 5:55 am in *Ramaḍān*. *Fajr* enters at 6 am.

► The *ghusl* time is not added to the menses habit. Thus, when *Fajr* enters, she is free from the state of menstruation and her fast counts.

► She makes up the *ʿIshāʾ* and *witr* prayers and then prays *Fajr*. She is not sinful for missing the prayers.

◆ Is sexual intercourse permissible before the *ghusl*?

Yes. She is legally in a time of purity (*ṭuhr*). As such, it is permissible – but not recommended – to have sexual intercourse before taking a *ghusl*.

It is best to take a *ghusl* before having sexual intercourse to avoid the difference of opinion with scholars who say it is obligatory to take the *ghusl* first, like Imām al-Shāfiʿī.

◆ Is another *ghusl* needed at her habit?

No. This ruling does not apply because the precautionary *ghusl* is only recommended when bleeding stops before the habit.

Read a summary of the rulings for this chapter in Table 6l.

Table 6l: Blood Ending Before or At the Maximum (Menses & Lochia)

MENSES / LOCHIA ENDS	BEFORE HABIT	AT OR AFTER HABIT	AT MAXIMUM
Legal Ruling of Ghusl	Obligatory before praying.	Obligatory before praying.	Obligatory before praying.
Delaying The Ghusl	Required to wait until closer to the end of the prayer time.	Recommended to wait closer to the end of the prayer time.	No ruling because the possible days are over.
Ghusl Time & The Habit	*Ghusl* time is included in the habit.	*Ghusl* time is included in the habit.	*Ghusl* time is not included in the habit.
Legal Status for the End of Menses	Ends after the *ghusl* time is added to the habit.	Ends after the *ghusl* time is added to the habit.	Ends at 240 hours (menses) / 960 hours (lochia).
Owing the Obligatory Prayer of That Time	Owes the prayer if she has enough time to complete the *ghusl* and say 'Allāh' before the prayer time exits.	Owes the prayer if she has enough time to complete the *ghusl* and say 'Allāh' before the prayer time exits.	Owes the prayer if she has enough time to say 'Allāh' before the prayer time exits.
Validity of Fast	Fast is valid if she has enough time to complete the *ghusl* and say 'Allāh' before the *Fajr* prayer time enters.	Fast is valid if she has enough time to complete the *ghusl* and say 'Allāh' before the *Fajr* prayer time enters.	Fast is valid if the maximum is reached before the *Fajr* prayer time enters.
Sexual Intercourse	Impermissible until the completion of the habit.	Impermissible until after the *ghusl*.	Permissible before the *ghusl* but not recommended.
Precautionary Ghusl	Recommended at the habit.	No ruling because the habit has been reached.	No ruling because the possible days are over.

6.10 PREFERRED PRAYER TIME

This point is specific to the ʿ*Aṣr* prayer time. The ʿ*Aṣr* prayer time contains a prohibitively disliked (*makrūh taḥrīmān*) time at its end, which is while the sun is setting.

- ✧ The prohibitively disliked time begins when the sun loses its glare such that it is easy to directly look at it. The color of the sun is usually a deep orange. It is sinful to pray within this time.

- ✧ From the moment the ʿ*Aṣr* prayer time enters to until the prohibitively disliked time begins, this duration is termed the preferred prayer time. It is permissible to pray within this time without any dislike.

Some scholars estimate that the prohibitively disliked time begins 15 to 20 minutes before the ʿ*Aṣr* prayer time exits. However, this estimation may differ from place to place because the length of the ʿ*Aṣr* prayer time varies from country to country, especially during the summer when the daytime is longer.

To estimate when the disliked time starts, one can look at the color of the sky or the sun. There are also websites that calculate it too.

> 🔍 Observe the preferred prayer time in Diagram 6m.

Diagram 6m: Preferred Prayer Time

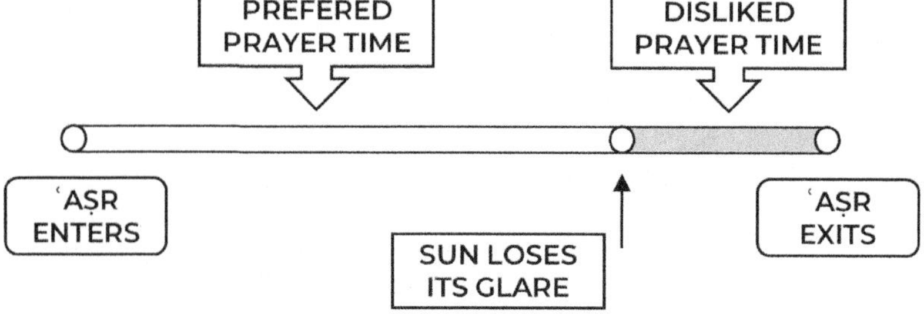

Knowing about the preferred prayer time is needed when a woman's bleeding stops before 72 hours, or it stops before her menstrual habit is complete.

The general ruling for a woman in this circumstance is that she must delay making *wuḍūʾ* or taking her *ghusl* until closer to the end of the prayer time.

However, for the *ʿAṣr* prayer time, she will purify herself and pray before the actual prohibitively disliked time begins so that she avoids praying in that time.

Observe when she takes a *ghusl* in Diagram 6n.

Diagram 6n: Preferred Prayer Time

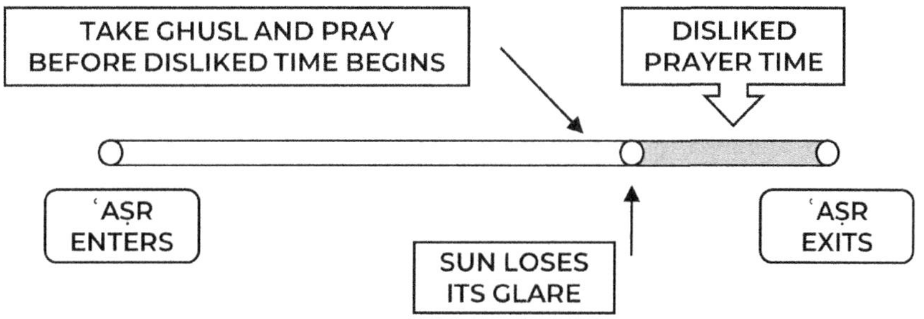

REVIEW QUESTIONS

1. What is the *ghusl*? What is the *ghusl* time?
2. When is the *ghusl* time added to the habit? How does this impact the rulings?
3. When is the *ghusl* time not added to the habit? How does this impact the rulings?
4. When is sexual intercourse permitted for each category?

Chapter 7

Blood Exceeding Ten Days

IN THIS CHAPTER

- ✧ Common misconceptions
- ✧ Possible days of menses
- ✧ Rulings in retrospect
- ✧ Solving problems

Once bleeding exceeds 10 days, a woman cannot consider the excess blood to be menstruation. However, there is a lot of confusion around this ruling. Thus, before explaining the rulings related to bleeding exceeding 10 days (240 hours), a few common misconceptions need to be busted.

Misconception #1: When bleeding exceeds 10 days (240 hours), a woman continues to refrain from praying because she is still bleeding.

> ➔ **Busted:** Once the menstrual maximum is reached, a woman is obliged to take a *ghusl* and start praying – even if she is still bleeding. Menstruation can be no more. This is the ruling regardless of whether the bleeding that exceeds the menstrual maximum of 240 hours is spotting or a full flow.

Misconception #2: When bleeding exceeds 10 days (240 hours), a woman gives herself a habit of 10 days of menstruation and 15 days of purity. She uses this habit until her bleeding normalizes.

> ➔ **Busted:** As discussed in Chapter 4, a woman cannot create a habit for herself. The habit is based upon what she saw in the

past. When the bleeding exceeds 10 days, a woman with a habit must return to her respective menstrual and purity habits. She uses her habits to determine which part of the 240-hour time span is deemed to be menses, and which part of it is deemed to be abnormal uterine bleeding (*istiḥāḍa*). Any bleeding seen outside her menses habit will automatically be ruled as abnormal blood. Refer to Diagram 7c for an example.

Misconception #3: When returning to the habit, a woman counts the first day of her menstruation from the time the bleeding began.

➔ **Busted:** When the bleeding exceeds 10 days, a woman must return to her menstrual and purity habits. The purity habit determines when her expected time of menstruation begins (menstrual place), and the menses habit determines how many days are deemed to be menstruation. Both habits are needed to resolve her issue. Thus, it's not necessarily the case that the first day of blood will coincide with the first day of her menses habit. Refer to Diagram 7d for an example.

7.1 RULINGS FOR POSSIBLE DAYS OF MENSES (PDM)

As for the ruling in the moment, the same principles discussed in Chapter 5 for the possible days of menses apply. She follows the rulings for the possible days of menses (PDM) because she cannot be certain that the bleeding will exceed the maximum until it happens.

Brief recap of the PDM rulings:

- Whenever a woman sees blood during the possible days of menses, she considers it to be menses.
- When the blood exceeds her habit within the possible days of menses, she continues to act like a menstruating woman.
- She must wait for the blood to either stop within the possible days of menses or for the bleeding to reach the menstrual maximum of 240 hours.

⚠ The PDM rulings may differ for a woman who is constantly experiencing abnormal bleeding. Women in these situations should speak to a scholar.

Observe what she does during the possible days of menses in Diagram 7a.

Diagram 7a: Possible Days of Menses Rulings

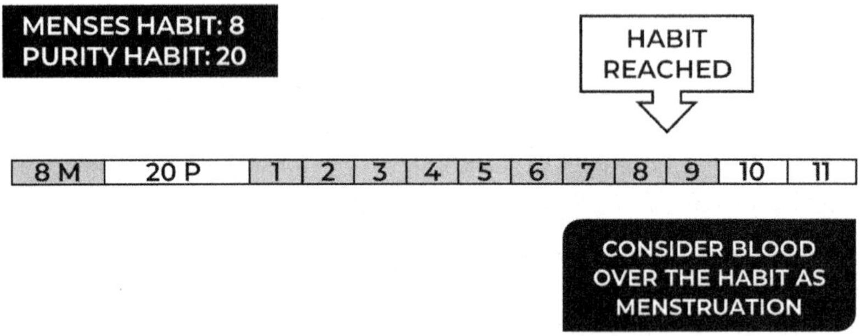

A woman has a menses habit of 8 days and a purity habit of 20 days. After the completion of her 20-day purity habit, she sees blood.

▶ She considers this bleeding to be menstruation because it is seen within her expected time of menses.

▶ When she reaches her menses habit at the completion of Day 8, she is still bleeding.

▶ At this time, she considers the blood to be menstruation because she is still within her possible days of menses.

7.2 BLOOD REACHING THE MAXIMUM

When the menstrual maximum of 240 hours is reached, she is obliged to take a *ghusl* and begin praying. There can be no increase in the maximum time.

7.3 BLOOD EXCEEDING THE MAXIMUM

If the bleeding does not stop when the menstrual maximum is reached, a woman is obliged to:

- Take a *ghusl* at 10 complete days (240 hours).
- Start praying.
- Return to her menstrual and purity habits.
- Consider the blood seen outside the habit and beyond the maximum of 240 hours as unsound blood.
- Make *wuḍūʾ* for her prayers and not *ghusl.*
- Make up the days of missed prayers over the habit.

> Observe when she takes her *ghusl* and begins to pray in Diagram 7b.

Diagram 7b: Blood Exceeding the Maximum

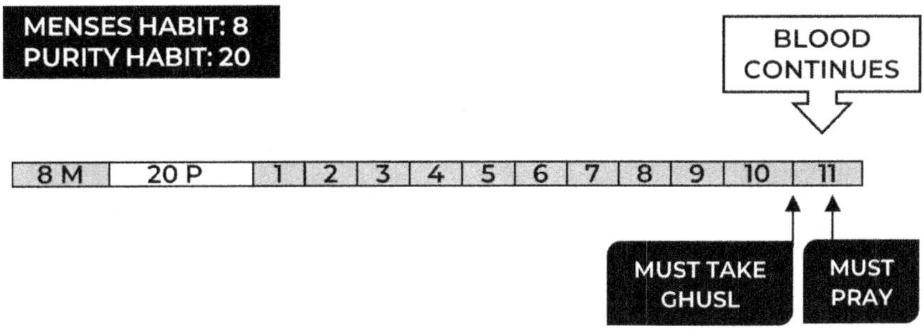

> Building on the situation in Diagram 7a, at the completion of Day 10 (240 hours), the bleeding continues.
>
> ► Even though she is still bleeding, she is obliged to take a *ghusl* at 240 hours and begin praying.
>
> ► She would not miss any prayers on Day 11 onwards because this bleeding is not menstruation.

► She performs her prayers with *wuḍū'* and she does not take a *ghusl* for her prayers.

► If this situation occurred during *Ramaḍān*, she would begin fasting.

7.4 RETURNING TO THE HABIT

When her bleeding exceeds the maximum of 240 hours, her situation must be reevaluated using her menstrual and purity habits. The habits will determine which days are ruled as menstruation or purity.

Observe which days are considered menstruation in retrospect in Diagram 7c.

Diagram 7c: Returning to the Habit

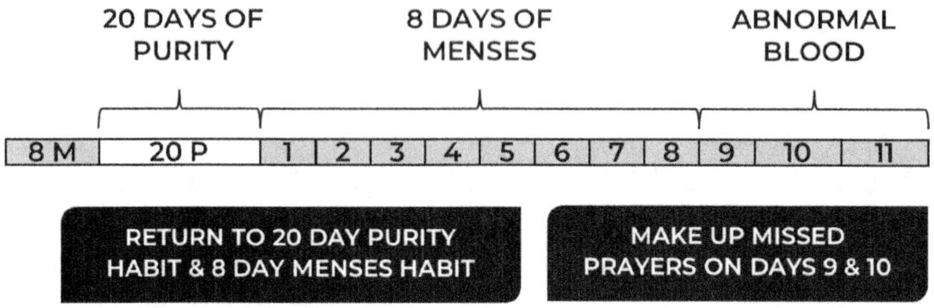

Building on the scenario in Diagram 7b, her situation will be reevaluated using her habits. Her menses habit is 8 days, and her purity habit is 20 days.

► According to her menstrual and purity habits, she will consider the 8 days of bleeding that come after the 20 days of purity to be menstruation. This is the ruling regardless of whether the bleeding was spotting or a full flow.

► Days 9 and 10 of the bleeding are in excess of her 8-day menses habit. In retrospect, they are no longer ruled as menstruation and are deemed to be days of legal purity.

► She must make up the obligatory (*farḍ*) and *witr* prayers missed on days 9 and 10. She is not sinful for missing these prayers, but rather she owes their performance in retrospect.

► The rulings for performing worship during abnormal uterine bleeding (*istiḥāḍa*) apply to her, which are discussed in Chapter 17.

► If she continues to bleed, she cannot stop praying until another 20 days elapses. She counts Day 1 of her legal purity span from the end of her menses habit of 8 complete days (Day 9 in Diagram 7c).

The way the situation in Diagram 7c was resolved would look very different if a purity span of 18 days preceded the bleeding. Her menses and purity habits are still used to resolve her situation, but the days of bleeding that are ruled as menstruation are different.

When a woman returns to her habits, it is not necessarily the case that the first day of bleeding will be the first day of menstruation. Diagram 7d briefly shows what would happen to a woman who has a 20-day purity habit and an 8-day menses habit.

Observe which days are considered menstruation in retrospect in Diagram 7d.

Diagram 7d: Returning to the Habit

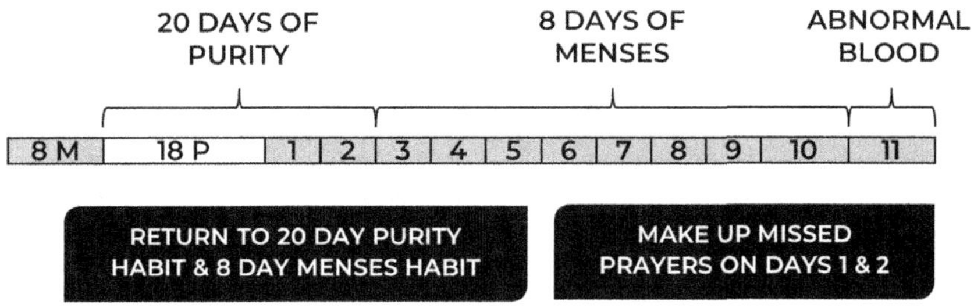

A woman has a menses habit of 8 days and a purity habit of 20 days. After the completion of 18 days of purity, she sees blood. The bleeding exceeds 240 hours.

► When abnormal bleeding occurs, the purity habit is used to determine the menstrual place. In retrospect, the first day of menstruation is counted after the 20-day purity habit elapses.

► The first two days of bleeding – in addition to Day 11 – are ruled as abnormal bleeding.

The scenarios given are basic and they are specifically designed to demonstrate certain points.

In real life, when a woman experiences abnormal bleeding, determining which days are menstruation or purity may not be as simple. In fact, there is an entire science behind solving menstruation problems!

Women should double check their situation with a teacher. In addition, if they are able, they should dedicate the time and effort to study these rulings in detail.

Chart 7e gives a useful summary of the rulings related to women with a menses habit.

Chart 7e: Summary of Rulings for Women With a Habit

BLEEDING STOPS BEFORE OR AT 240 HOURS	BLEEDING EXCEEDS THE MAXIMUM OF 240 HOURS
• The blood becomes her new menses habit if a purity span of 15 days (350 hours) free of blood follows it.	• She returns to her menses and purity habits to know which days are menses and which days are not menses.

HEAVY MENSTRUAL BLEEDING

When period changes happen – such as a heavier flow than usual – it can be hard to decide if calling a doctor is necessary. Sometimes irregularities happen occasionally, and sometimes they happen more frequently. It is advisable to see a doctor if any of the following symptoms are experienced:

- Having a menstrual flow that soaks through one or more pads or tampons every hour for several hours in a row.
- Needing to double up on pads to control the blood flow.
- Needing to change pads or tampons during the night.
- Having menstrual periods lasting more than 7 days.
- Having a menstrual flow with blood clots the size of a coin or larger.
- Having a heavy blood flow that keeps one from doing the things that one would do normally.
- Having constant pain in the lower part of the stomach during one's periods.
- Being tired, lacking energy, or feeling short of breath.

Untreated heavy or prolonged bleeding can stop a woman from living her life. It can also cause lowered iron levels or anemia. Anemia is a common blood problem that can leave a person feeling tired or weak.

Thus, if a woman has a bleeding problem, it could lead to other health problems. Consequently, it is best for women to seek proper medical attention and not ignore these symptoms.

REVIEW QUESTIONS

1. What are common misconceptions about the rulings related to blood that exceeds 10 days?
2. What does a woman do if her bleeding exceeds the menstrual maximum? Give an example.

Chapter 8

The Kursuf

IN THIS CHAPTER

- Definition of the *kursuf*
- How to wear the *kursuf*
- Rulings related to the *kursuf*
- Stopping the onset of menses

In a *ḥadīth* found in the *Muwaṭṭaʾ* of Imām Mālik, the maid servant of the Mother of Believers ʿĀʾisha said:

> "Women used to send small boxes to ʿĀʾisha, the Mother of the Believers, that had a piece of cotton cloth (*kursuf*) contained in them in which there was a yellow discharge upon it from menstrual blood. They would ask her about the prayer. She would say to them, 'Do not be hasty (to take a *ghusl*) until you see a white discharge.'" By that she meant purity from menses.
>
> (*Muwaṭṭaʾ*, 85)

The Mother of Believers ʿĀʾisha taught the female Companions that menstruation does not end until white discharge is seen. Moreover, what is understood from this transmission is that the female Companions used a cotton cloth (*kursuf)* to determine when their colored discharge ended.

8.1 DEFINITION OF THE KURSUF

The *kursuf* is a cotton cloth placed at the vaginal opening, and it is used to determine the actual color of discharge when it exits the vagina. Lighter colored discharges like yellow or turbid – in addition to normal vaginal discharge like white or clear – may change color after they exit the vagina and are exposed to air.

Thus, the only way to ascertain the real color of these discharges is to wear a *kursuf* and to judge the discharge while it is still fresh. If the *kursuf* is worn correctly, meaning that it is placed at the vaginal opening and properly secured between the labia minora (inner lips), there is hardly any chance that air will reach it and alter its color.

> ☑ The legal rulings are based upon the color of fresh discharge, and any change in color thereafter is ignored.

8.2 PADS & PANTYLINERS

Pads and panty liners are different. They are placed far from the vaginal opening, and the color of the discharge seen on them may have changed. Consequently, the color of discharge found on pads and pantyliners is usually disregarded with regards to establishing a ruling.

This is only for the colors yellow, turbid, white, and clear. As for if a woman sees black, red, or brown blood on a pad or panty liner, there is no doubt that what she is seeing is blood.

> ☑ Pads and panty liners can be worn during a woman's menstrual period to absorb blood, but they cannot be used to determine the color of fresh discharge.

8.3 WEARING THE KURSUF

The *kursuf* is worn externally at the vaginal opening, secured between the labia minora. It is not typically placed inside the vagina.

The *kursuf* can be made from tissue paper, toilet paper, paper towels, or a piece of cut up cotton t-shirt that is washed for reuse. The type of material used for a *kursuf* depends on a woman's body. Each woman should use whichever material works best for her. Some women's bodies are more sensitive than others and they cannot wear tissue paper at their labia. Others are less sensitive, and they can use any material.

How to wear a *kursuf*:

The easiest way to wear the *kursuf* is when sitting on the toilet or squatting. It is suggested that a woman follow these steps:

1. Rinse the labia (lips) with water.

2. Dry the area.

3. Fold a tissue into a small rectangle that is approximately 2 inches wide by 3 inches long. A cotton facial pad or cutup cotton t-shirt can also be used.

4. Lay the folded tissue on top of the labia minora (inner lips).

5. Stand up. The lips will fold over the *kursuf*.

✓ By following this method, a woman can ensure that the *kursuf* is placed at the vaginal opening, secured between the labia minora, and it will not shift around or fall out while walking.

> Diagram 8a summarizes these points.

Diagram 8a: How to Wear a Kursuf

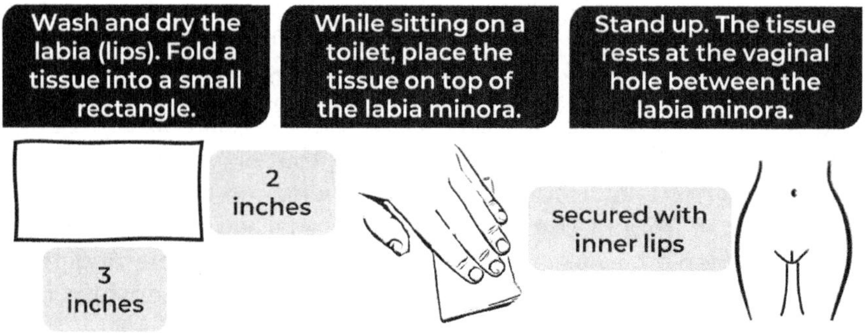

Wash and dry the labia (lips). Fold a tissue into a small rectangle.
While sitting on a toilet, place the tissue on top of the labia minora.
Stand up. The tissue rests at the vaginal hole between the labia minora.
2 inches
3 inches
secured with inner lips

8.4 RULING FOR DISCHARGE FOUND ON THE KURSUF

Once a woman removes the *kursuf*, whatever color is immediately seen will determine the legal ruling. Any change in color afterwards is of no legal consequence.

8.5 DISCHARGE EXITS YELLOW

If the discharge exits yellow on the *kursuf* and dries white, then the discharge is considered yellow. This means that it is blood, and it takes the legal consequences of blood.

- ✧ If seen within the possible days of menstruation, yellow takes the ruling of menstrual blood, and a woman is still deemed to be menstruating.
- ✧ If seen within a time of purity, yellow is ruled as abnormal uterine bleeding (*istiḥāḍa*), and a woman follows its related rulings.

> Refer to Chapter 16 for the rulings related to abnormal bleeding.
>
> Chart 8b summarizes these points.

8.6 DISCHARGE EXITS WHITE

If the discharge exits white or clear on the *kursuf* and dries yellow, then the discharge is considered white or clear. This means that it takes the rulings related to normal vaginal discharge.

- ✧ If seen within the possible days of menstruation, white or clear marks the end of a woman's menstrual blood.
- ✧ If seen within a time of purity, white or clear takes the rulings related to normal vaginal discharge discussed in Chapter 3.

> Chart 8b summarizes these points.

Chart 8b: Summary of Rulings for Lighter Colored Discharges

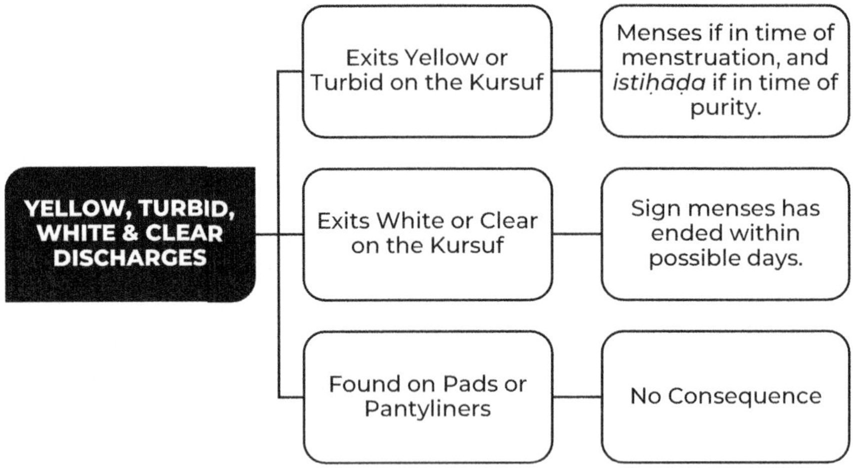
YELLOW, TURBID, WHITE & CLEAR DISCHARGES
Exits Yellow or Turbid on the Kursuf
Menses if in time of menstruation, and istiḥāḍa if in time of purity.
Exits White or Clear on the Kursuf
Sign menses has ended within possible days.
Found on Pads or Pantyliners
No Consequence

8.7 AVOIDING MULTIPLE GHUSLS

The *kursuf* can aid in catching scant discharge that exits towards the end of a woman's menstruation when the flow of blood becomes lighter.

Towards the end of menstruation, it may take a longer time for the bleeding to descend to the vaginal opening. This can pose problems for a woman who sees that her panty liner is clean and takes a *ghusl*, but the bleeding later returns.

A similar issue may occur when women resort to wiping and see nothing on the toilet paper used. Some may find themselves taking a *ghusl* more than once because they assume that their menstruation has finished when in reality it has not.

> ☑ Using a *kursuf* can catch scant discharge and help a woman determine if her bleeding has truly ended.

8.8 USING THE KURSUF TO CHECK THE END OF BLEEDING

When the bleeding begins to lessen to the extent that it may soon finish, a woman starts to wear the *kursuf*. It will help her to determine when her bleeding officially stops. The exact day that she chooses to use a *kursuf* to check will differ from woman to woman. As such, it is important that each woman become familiar with how her body operates. The following are suggestions based on practical experience.

◆ What does a woman take note of?

She should pay attention to:

- ✧ The change in colors normally seen.
- ✧ The heaviness of flow experienced.
- ✧ The number of days menses usually lasts.

Change In Colors: Some women see a spectrum of colors during their days of menstruation. The bleeding could start off with dark colors and then gradually move to lighter colors as the days pass. Perhaps the colors change from red to brown to dark yellow to light yellow and lastly to white. In this situation, it is advisable to begin wearing the *kursuf* when the light yellow is close to finishing because it is the last color seen before menstrual bleeding officially stops.

Change In Flow: If she is someone who sees the same color, but her strength of flow differs from heavy to light, then she will start wearing the *kursuf* when her bleeding begins to spot. For instance, the bleeding progresses from a full flow to a light flow, and it tapers off with dots of blood. The *kursuf* is worn when spotting starts.

Change In Days: If she is someone who usually has 8 days of bleeding, then she starts to wear the *kursuf* around Day 7 when the bleeding is close to finishing.

☑ Some women may use all three factors to determine their end.

> ⚠ Most women have some type of recognized pattern, and each woman must discover her pattern by paying attention to her body.

◆ **How long does a woman wear the *kursuf*?**

The length of time depends on each woman's body. Based on surveying many women, wearing the *kursuf* from anywhere between 30 to 90 minutes before checking is best.

The intention is to use the *kursuf* to determine whether the colored discharge has ceased; consequently, a woman should wear it for as long as she needs to achieve this goal.

☑ It may also help to walk around to help the discharge move down towards the vaginal opening.

☑ Married woman can insert the *kursuf* inside the vagina to check. This can help catch discharge that is descending at a slower pace.

◆ **How many times is the *kursuf* used for checking?**

The *kursuf* only needs to be checked once in the prayer time and not multiple times.

8.9 WHO WEARS THE KURSUF

The scholars state that for a virgin it is only *sunna* to wear the *kursuf* during the time of menses. Outside of the time of menses, she does not need to wear it.

As for the non-virgin, the *kursuf* is recommended at all times. This may be because non-virgins tend to excrete more vaginal discharge. However, if doing so causes irritation or harm, a non-virgin can choose to not wear it during her time of purity.

8.10 STOPPING THE ONSET OF MENSES

The *kursuf* can be used to delay the onset of menses. The rulings differ depending on where and when the *kursuf* is worn.

◆ If menstrual bleeding has not yet started and the *kursuf* is worn externally at the vaginal opening, then once blood wets the *kursuf*, menstruation begins.

- ✧ The external *kursuf* is placed at the opening of the vagina and not inside of it, as described in Section 8.3. Therefore, it does not prevent the exiting of discharge from the vagina. As such, once blood exits the vagina, menses begins.

◆ If menstrual bleeding has not yet started and the *kursuf* is inserted inside the vagina, menses will only begin when the internal *kursuf* is removed or blood leaks out of the vagina.

- ✧ The internal *kursuf* prevents the exiting of discharge from the vagina. Therefore, even if the *kursuf* becomes wet with blood inside the vaginal canal, menses does not begin.

☑ This ruling could be useful to know for a woman who is performing ʿ*umra* and she thinks that her menstruation may start soon. She can wear an internal *kursuf* like a tampon before her menstruation starts and perform the ʿ*umra* rites.

🔍 Diagram 8c demonstrates the rulings for the internal *kursuf*.

Diagram 8c: Stopping the Onset of Menses

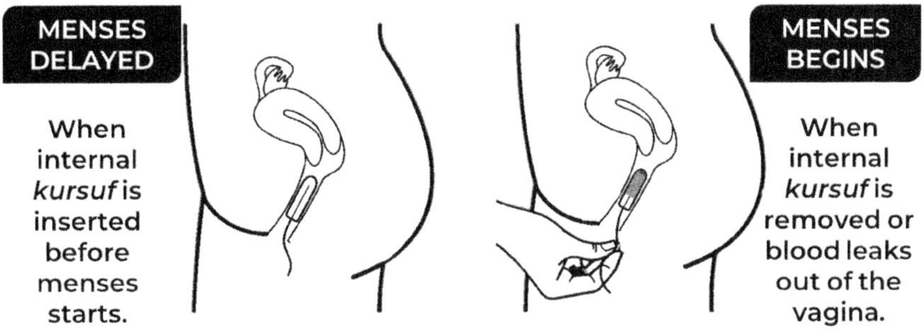
MENSES DELAYED
When internal kursuf is inserted before menses starts.
MENSES BEGINS
When internal kursuf is removed or blood leaks out of the vagina.

◆ If the blood is blocked after menstrual bleeding began, then the blocking does not cancel the legal status of menstruation.

- ✧ Blocking the blood after menstruation starts does not cause the state of menstruation to end.
- ✧ Menstruation only ends when colored discharge naturally stops within the possible days of menses or the menstrual maximum is reached.

> ⚠ Menstrual bleeding that starts off as spotting is included in this ruling. Blocking the vagina after spotting starts will not cancel the state of menstruation.
>
> 🔍 Chart 8d summarizes these points.

Chart 8d: Summary of Rulings for Stopping the Onset of Menses

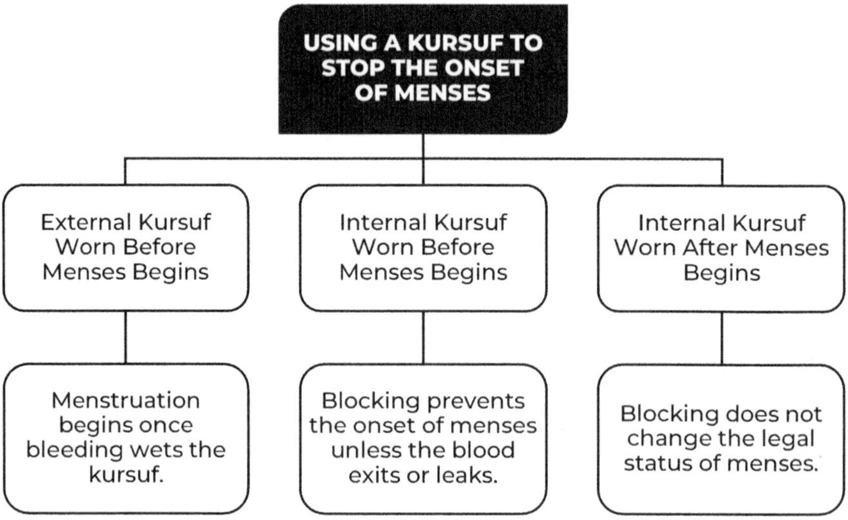

8.11 USING THE KURSUF FOR ABNORMAL BLEEDING

If it is placed inside the vagina, the *kursuf* can block abnormal bleeding (*istiḥāḍa*) from exiting. Therefore, a non-virgin can insert the *kursuf* internally to perform worship that requires *wuḍūʾ*.

- ✧ The *wuḍūʾ* will remain until the internal *kursuf* is removed or blood leaks out of the vagina.
- ✧ A tampon or mooncup can also be used if the bleeding is heavy.

If the *kursuf* is placed externally at the vaginal opening as described in Section 8.3, it does not block discharge from exiting the vagina. Therefore, the exiting of colored discharge on the *kursuf* during the days of purity breaks *wuḍūʾ*.

> ➔ Refer to Chapter 17 for the rulings related to praying while bleeding.

REVIEW QUESTIONS

1. What is the *kursuf*? Why is it used? How is it different from a pad or panty liner?
2. Why is fresh discharge so important?
3. How does a woman wear a *kursuf*?
4. What are the various usages for a *kursuf* during menses?
5. What are the various usages of the *kursuf* during purity?

Chapter 9

Prohibited & Permitted Acts

IN THIS CHAPTER

- ✧ Why Allāh prohibits things
- ✧ Detailed rulings related to each prohibition
- ✧ Detailed rulings related to permissible acts

Allāh Most High says:

﴿ قُلْ إِن كُنتُمْ تُحِبُّونَ ٱللَّهَ فَٱتَّبِعُونِى يُحْبِبْكُمُ ٱللَّهُ وَيَغْفِرْ لَكُمْ ذُنُوبَكُمْ وَٱللَّهُ غَفُورٌ رَّحِيمٌ ﴾

> Say (O Prophet): "If you really love Allāh, then follow me, and Allāh shall love you and forgive your sins. Allāh is Most-Forgiving, Most-Merciful.
>
> (*Āli ʿImrān*, 3:31)

Allāh Most High commanded the Prophet ﷺ to say these words to mankind to convey a clear message: If mankind really loves their Creator, then they will follow the Prophet's ﷺ noble way and teachings.

In return, through following his ﷺ way, Allāh Most High will show the believers His love by increasing them in their blessings, making them firm on their faith, and forgiving their misdeeds.

The Prophet ﷺ instructed the female Companions ؓ with what they can and cannot do in a state of menstruation and lochia. The believing women of his time followed him ﷺ out of their love for Allāh, and it is upon the believing women of today's time to do the same.

The concept of an act being prohibited can be off-putting for some. However, the believer must have a firm conviction that Allāh Most High is Wise, and He prescribes things in accordance with His divine wisdom. Most certainly, He does not enjoin an act except that it is in the best interest of His creation. Likewise, He does not forbid an act except that it protects His creation from its harm.

Despite the obligations and prohibitions being in a person's best interests, sometimes there may not be an explanation given for them or the wisdom behind them is obscure. The prohibitions related to menstruation often fall under this category. Thus, a believing woman must focus her attention on earning Allāh Most High's eternal pleasure and abiding by the prohibitions purely for His sake.

Nevertheless, some scholars discuss the wisdoms behind a few of the prohibitions related to menstruation. For example, some state that the reason why Allāh Most High has forbidden menstruating women to fast is out of mercy for them. The blood loss can cause weakness and other symptoms which may make fasting difficult or possibly harmful for her.

There are differences of opinion in the schools of law (*madhāhib*) regarding what is permissible or impermissible during the time of menstruation. According to the *Ḥanafī madhhab,* while a woman is in a state of menstruation (*hayḍ*) or a state of lochia (*nifās*), it is impermissible (*ḥarām*) to:

1. Perform the ritual prayer or prostrate.
2. Fast.
3. Touch the Qurʾān.
4. Recite the Qurʾān.
5. Enter any mosque.
6. Make *ṭawāf.*
7. Engage in sexual intercourse.
8. Be directly touched between the navel to the knee.
9. Be divorced.

❶ Praying

9.1 PERFORMING THE RITUAL PRAYER DURING MENSES

It is not permitted for a menstruating woman to pray any type of prayer. This includes the obligatory (*farḍ*) prayer, the *witr* prayer, the *sunna* prayer, and the voluntary (*nafl*) prayer.

Additionally, because Allāh Most High lifted the obligation for her to pray, she is not required to make up (*qaḍā*ʾ) any of the prayers missed due to her menses.

> The Mother of the Believers ʿĀʾisha ﷺ said, "...We used to get our periods at the time of the Prophet ﷺ, and he ﷺ never commanded us to offer the prayers missed during menses."
>
> (*Bukhārī*, 321)

9.2 RECOMMENDED FORMS OF WORSHIP

In the *Ḥanafī madhhab*, it is an overall recommendation for a menstruating woman to make *wuḍū*ʾ for each prayer time, sit in her usual place of worship, and make *dhikr* for the time that it normally takes her to pray so that she does not lose her habit of worship while in this state.

☑ For a comprehensive list of other types of recommended worship, refer to Section 1. 5.

9.3 BLEEDING STARTS DURING THE PRAYER

If a woman's menstruation starts while she is praying, the prayer becomes invalid from a legal perspective. For example, a woman is praying the *Maghrib* prayer, and while she is engaged in the prayer, menstrual blood exits. Her prayer is legally invalid, but Allāh Most High will reward her for her good intentions.

The question now arises of whether she needs to make up this prayer after her menstruation ends. The ruling for this situation revolves around the type of prayer that she was praying when the bleeding started.

◆ If the menstrual bleeding started while she was performing an obligatory prayer (*farḍ*), she does not need to make up this prayer.

- ✧ The consideration for owing prayers returns to the woman's state within the last moment of the prayer time.
- ✧ In this case, when the *Maghrib* prayer time exits, she is classified as a menstruating woman, and menstruating women are not obliged to perform the obligatory prayers.

◆ If the bleeding started while she was performing a *sunna* or a voluntary (*nafl*) prayer, she is required to make up this prayer after her menstruation ends.

- ✧ Allāh Most High commands the believers to not invalidate their works (*Muḥammad*, 47:33). Thus, acts of good must be completed once they are initiated.
- ✧ Therefore, because she initiated the *sunna* or *nafl* prayer, she must complete its performance when her menses ends.

> Read a summary of these rulings in Table 9a.

9.4 BLEEDING STARTS AFTER THE PRAYER TIME ENTERED

If a woman's menstruation starts after the prayer time entered, but she has not performed the obligatory prayer (*farḍ*) yet, she does not need to make up the prayer after her menses finishes.

☑ The consideration for owing prayers returns to the woman's state within the last moment of the prayer time. In this situation, she is in a state of menses at the end of the time.

> ⚠ The etiquette of a believer is to pray at the earliest part of the prayer time, even if she knows that her menses may start soon.

Table 9a: Summary of the Rulings for Making Up Prayers

ACTION	OBLIGATORY PRAYER	SUNNA / NAFL PRAYER
Missed Prayers During Menses	No Makeup	No Makeup
Menses Starts While Praying	No Makeup	Makeup
Menses Starts Before Praying	No Makeup	No Makeup

9.5 CALL TO PRAYER

A menstruating woman is not obliged to answer the call to prayer. It is permissible for her to repeat the words of the *adhān* and make supplication (*duʿāʾ*) afterwards.

9.6 PROSTRATION OF RECITATION OR GRATITUDE

The prostration is a sacred act associated with the prayer, and its performance requires ritual purity. Therefore, a menstruating woman cannot perform the prostration of recitation (*sajdat ʾl-tilāwa*) or the prostration of gratitude (*sajdat ash-shukr*).

Furthermore, if a menstruating woman hears a verse of prostration, she is not obliged to prostrate. She is also not required to perform the prostration after her menstruation finishes.

? What is the prostration of recitation (*sajdat ʾl-tilāwa*)?

There are fourteen verses of prostration in the *Qurʾān*. The general principle is that whenever a believer recites or hears one of these verses, they are obliged to prostrate. To perform the prostration outside of prayer, one covers for prayer, stands facing the *qibla*, and says *'Allāhu Akbar'* without raising the hands. Then one prostrates and says the *dhikr*: *Subḥān rabbīl-ʿalā* three times. Thereafter, one says *'Allāhu Akbar'* again and stands up.

❷ Fasting

9.7 FASTING DURING MENSES

It is not permitted for a menstruating woman to fast any type of fast. This includes the obligatory (*farḍ*) fast, the mandatory (*wājib*) fast, the *sunna* fast, and the voluntary (*nafl*) fast.

Unlike the prayer, she is required to make up any obligatory fasts that she misses from the month of *Ramaḍān*. She makes them up after *Ramaḍān* is over during a time when she is not menstruating.

☑ Scholars state that the wisdom in making up her missed fasts and not her missed prayers is based upon *Ramaḍān* only occurring once a year. Making up approximately ten fasts (or less) a year is not difficult – as opposed to making up her missed prayers every month for an entire year.

> The Mother of the Believers ʿĀʾisha ﵂ said, "We would menstruate at the time of the Messenger of Allāh ﷺ. Then, when we would become pure, he ﷺ would command us to make up our fasts, but he ﷺ would not command us to make up our prayers."
>
> (*Muslim*, 335, *Tirmidhī*, 787; *Abū Dāwūd*, 262)

9.8 MENSTRUAL BLEEDING STARTS DURING THE FAST

If a woman's menstruation begins during the fasting time, the fast does not count.

One of the conditions for a valid fast is that a woman must be free from the state of menstruation from the time the *Fajr* prayer enters to the time the *Maghrib* prayer enters. If her menstruation occurs during any part of the fasting time, the fast is not valid.

- ✧ Even if her menstruation begins only a few minutes before *Maghrib* enters, her fast becomes legally invalid, but Allāh Most High will reward her for her good intentions.

- ✧ She is obliged to make up this fast after her menstruation ends.
- ✧ The ruling of making up the vitiated fast applies to all types of fasts, whether it be an obligatory (*farḍ*) fast, a mandatory (*wājib*) fast, a *sunna* fast, or a voluntary (*nafl*) fast.

9.9 MISSING RAMAḌĀN FASTS

Women are required to make up any missed *Ramaḍān* fasts due to menstruation or lochia after *Ramaḍān* is finished at a time when they are able. Women should record the number of fasting days missed so that they do not forget how many fasts are owed.

9.10 EATING DURING THE DAY IN RAMAḌĀN

A menstruating woman is permitted to eat and drink during the day in *Ramaḍān*, but she should do so discretely and not in public.

If she believes that it is unlawful for her to eat or drink, then it is necessary (*wājib*) for her to do so because refraining from food or drink with the intention of fasting is sinful.

MENSTRUATION STARTS DURING THE DAY IN RAMADAN

- She stops fasting.
- This day of fasting does not count.
- She must make up this fast after *Ramaḍān* ends.
- She continues to not fast until her menstruation finishes or the menstrual maximum of 10 complete days is reached.
- She must make up her missed fasts after *Ramaḍān* ends at a time when she is able.

9.11 MENSES STOPS DURING THE DAY IN RAMAḌĀN

If a woman's menstruation stops during the day in *Ramaḍān* – meaning any time from the entrance of *Fajr* to the entrance of *Maghrib* – then she takes a *ghusl*, starts praying, and acts like a fasting person until the *Maghrib* time enters due to the sacredness of the month of *Ramaḍān*.

- ✧ It is mandatory (*wājib*) for her to abstain from eating and drinking for the remainder of this day in *Ramaḍān*.
- ✧ She must make up this day after *Ramaḍān* ends in a time when she is able.
- ✧ She is required to fast the following day and the remainder of *Ramaḍān*.

? Why does she have to refrain from eating if the fast does not count?

This ruling only applies to the month of *Ramaḍān* and not during other times of the year. *Ramaḍān* is a sacred time in which believers are heavily encouraged to engage in acts of good with fasting being the main act of virtue. Thus, out of respect for this holy ritual, she acts like a fasting person because she is now free from menses during the fasting time. However, it does not count as a real fast because she was menstruating for part of that day.

9.12 MENSES STOPS DURING THE NIGHT IN RAMAḌĀN

If a woman's menstruation stops in *Ramaḍān* during the night – meaning any time from the entrance of *Maghrib* to the entrance of *Fajr* – then she takes a *ghusl*, begins praying, and she is required to fast the following day and the remainder of *Ramaḍān*.

> Compare what a woman does when bleeding starts and stops during the day in *Ramaḍān* in Chart 9b.

Chart 9b: Summary of Rulings During *Ramaḍān*

BLEEDING STARTS DURING THE DAY IN RAMAḌĀN	BLEEDING STOPS DURING THE DAY IN RAMAḌĀN
• Fasting is unlawful. • Eating is done discretely. • Make up the fast later.	• Take a *ghusl* and pray. • Refrain from food and drink. • Make up the fast later.

9.13 ʿITIKĀF

If a woman's menstrual bleeding starts during the *sunna* *ʿitikāf* in the last ten nights of *Ramaḍān*, then her *ʿitikāf* ends. After her period finishes, she must make up the *ʿitikāf* when she is able.

- ✧ She only owes one day of *ʿitikāf* and not all ten.
- ✧ The makeup *ʿitikāf* is for a full day with its night from the entrance of *Maghrib* to *Maghrib* the following day.
- ✧ She must fast during the day, either a *nafl* or makeup fast.

9.14 KAFFĀRAT AL-FIṬR

Menstruation does not break the consecutiveness of the 60-day expiation due for purposely breaking a fast in *Ramaḍān* (*kaffārat al-fiṭr*). However, bleeding that was considered menstruation but is ruled as abnormal uterine bleeding (*istiḥāḍa*) in retrospect breaks the consecutiveness of the 60-day fast. Likewise, lochia breaks the consecutiveness of the expiation.

? What is *kaffārat al-fiṭr*?

If one purposely breaks a *Ramaḍān* fast without a lawful excuse, an expiation is due, which is known as *kaffārat al-fiṭr*. The expiation is to fast sixty consecutive days without interruption. If one does not fast the days consecutively, then the 60-day period is restarted each time the continuity of the fasts is broken.

❸ Touching The Qurʾān

9.15 TOUCHING THE QURʾĀN DURING MENSES

It is not permitted for a menstruating woman to directly touch a verse of the Qurʾān or the *muṣḥaf* (Arabic Qurʾān), including its insides, its page margins, and its cover.

The same ruling applies to touching the Bible, Torah, and Psalms.

> The Prophet ﷺ said, "Only a person in a state of ritual purity should touch the Qurʾān."
>
> (*Muwaṭṭaʾ* of Imām Mālik, 296)

9.16 TOUCHING THE QURʾĀN WITH A BARRIER

It is permissible for a menstruating woman to touch a verse of the Qurʾān or the *muṣḥaf* with a non-attached barrier.

- The non-attached barrier must be completely removable from the *muṣḥaf* – meaning that it is not permanently attached to it.
- Examples of a non-attached barrier are a cloth, box, or bag.

For example, if the *muṣḥaf* is stored in a bag, it is permissible for a menstruating woman to hold or touch the bag. Likewise, if she holds the *muṣḥaf* with a separate cloth, it is permissible.

As for touching it with the clothing that she is wearing, it is not permitted because the clothing is connected to her body. For example, a menstruating woman cannot hold the *muṣḥaf* with the sleeves of her shirt.

9.17 TRANSLATIONS OF THE QURʾĀN

It is not permitted to touch a translation of the Qurʾān without ritual purity, even if the book does not contain the Arabic script within it.

9.18 TAFSĪR BOOKS

As for a commentary (*tafsīr*) of the Qurʾān, the ruling returns to how much of the text is Qurʾān as opposed to *tafsīr*.

- ✧ If the Qurʾān is more, then it is not permitted to touch the book or its pages without ritual purity.
- ✧ If the *tafsīr* is more, then it is permitted to touch the book and its pages. However, it is not permitted to touch the verses of the Qurʾān without ritual purity.

9.19 BOOKS OF SACRED KNOWLEDGE

It is permissible to touch books of law (*fiqh*), Arabic grammar (*naḥw*), and other subjects of sacred knowledge without ritual purity. It is also permissible to touch *duʿāʾ* and *dhikr* books.

However, when a woman is not in a state of menstruation, it is recommended and better to touch them with *wuḍūʾ*.

As for the verses of the Qurʾān contained within any of these books, it is not permitted to touch them without ritual purity.

9.20 OBJECTS WITH QURʾĀN INSCRIBED ON THEM

If a complete verse of the Qurʾān is inscribed on an object – such as a wall or an ornament – the more precautionary position is that it is not permissible to touch the object or verse without ritual purity.

If a verse of the Qurʾān is written on a piece of paper alone, it is not permitted to touch the paper or verse without ritual purity.

☑ Amulets with a verse of the Qurʾān written upon them should be wrapped in a cloth before being worn.

9.21 PHONES & ELECTRONIC DEVICES

As for phones or tablets with Qurʾān programs, there is a difference of opinion amongst contemporary scholars.

- ✧ The more precautionary opinion is that when the app is open and verses appear on the screen, it is not permissible to hold the device or touch its screen without ritual purity – unless it is done with a pen or barrier.

- ✧ Another opinion is that when the app is open and verses are on the screen, it is permissible to hold the device, but it is not permissible to touch the screen without ritual purity.

☑ According to both views, when the app is closed, the device takes the ruling of a phone or tablet, and it can be touched without ritual purity.

9.22 READING WITH EYES ONLY

If no touching or holding is involved, it is permissible to read the Qur᾽ān with one's eyes. For example, a menstruating woman can read the Qur᾽ān while sitting in front of a computer screen.

Read a summary of the rulings in Table 9c.

Table 9c: Summary of Rulings for Touching the Qur᾽ān

TOUCHING DIRECTLY	RULING
***Muṣḥaf* or Verse**	Impermissible
Bible, Torah, & Psalms	Impermissible
Translation of the Qur᾽ān	Impermissible
***Tafsīr* Book - Qur᾽ān Is More**	Impermissible
***Tafsīr* Book - *Tafsīr* Is More**	Permitted
Books Of Sacred Knowledge	Permitted
***Du῾ā᾽* and *Dhikr* Books**	Permitted
Reading With Eyes - No Touching	Permitted

4 Reciting The Qurʾān

9.23 RECITING THE QURʾĀN DURING MENSES

It is not permitted for a menstruating woman to recite the Qurʾān, even if it is less than a complete verse.

The definition for reciting is to move the lips while producing sound, even if it be whispering to oneself.

As for a Qurʾān teacher, she is permitted to say the verses word by word while teaching, pausing briefly after each word.

> ✅ If a woman is concerned about keeping up with her Qurʾān memorization or classes, she can seek the advice of scholars concerning the *Mālikī madhhab*'s position in this matter.

9.24 RECITING FOR REWARD

Despite the reward mentioned for it, it is not permissible to recite *Sūrat al-Kahf* on Fridays or *Sūrat al-Mulk* in the evening during menses, even if a woman has a habit of doing so when she is not menstruating.

It is also not permissible to recite a portion (*juz*) of the Qurʾān or *Sūrat Yā Sīn* for the deceased.

> The Prophet ﷺ said, "A menstruating women or a person in a state of sexual impurity should not recite any part of the Qurʾān."
>
> (*Tirmidhī*, 131)

9.25 QURʾĀNIC SUPPLICATIONS

It is permissible for a menstruating woman to make *duʿāʾ* with Qurʾānic verses, providing that the verses contain the meaning of supplication, praise, remembrance, or protection, and it is read with this intention.

The following are examples:

- It is permissible to read *Sūrat ʾl-Ikhlāṣ*, *Sūrat ʾl-Falaq*, *Sūrat ʾl-Nās*, and *Ayyat ʾl-Kursī* with the intention of seeking protection.
- It is permissible to read the *rabbanā* supplications from the Qurʾān and *Sūrat ʾl-Fātiḥa* with the intention of making supplication.
- It is permissible to say '*bismiLlāh*' before eating or starting an act.
- It is permissible to say '*alḥamduliLlāh*' when finishing eating.

CONDITIONS FOR SAYING QURʾĀNIC SUPPLICATIONS

- The menstruating woman's intention is to make *dhikr* or *duʿāʾ*, and it is not for reciting the Qurʾān.
- The verses contain the meanings of *dhikr* or *duʿāʾ*, unlike verses that relate stories or legal rulings.

9.26 OTHER FORMS OF DHIKR

It is permissible for a menstruating woman to make supplications narrated from the *sunna*, recite *ṣalāwāt*, and engage in *dhikr*.

9.27 READING THE QURʾĀN WITH THE HEART

It is permissible for a menstruating woman to read the Qurʾān with her heart, which means that no sound exits her lips.

9.28 LISTENING TO THE QURʾĀN

It is permissible for a menstruating woman to listen to the Qurʾān.

Read a summary of the rulings in Table 9d.

Table 9d: Summary of Rulings for Reciting the Qurʾān

RECITING	RULING
Qurʾān With Lips & Sound	Impermissible
Qurʾān for Reward	Impermissible
Qurʾān for Deceased	Impermissible
Qurʾānic Supplications & Dhikr	Permitted
Prophetic Supplications, *Dhikr*, & *Ṣalāwāt*	Permitted
Reading Qurʾān With Heart Only	Permitted
Listening to Qurʾān	Permitted

❺ Entering A Mosque

9.29 ENTERING A MOSQUE DURING MENSES

It is not permitted for a menstruating woman to enter a mosque (*masjid*), regardless of whether she is passing through it to reach another location or remaining within it.

The only exception is in the case of a necessity, such as fear of a wild beast, a criminal, or extreme cold. In this circumstance, scholars state that the proper etiquette is to make *tayammum* before entering if it is possible.

> The Prophet ﷺ said, "I do not make the *masjid* lawful for a menstruating woman or for a person in a state of sexual impurity."
>
> (*Abū Dāwūd*, 232)

9.30 MENSTRUATION STARTS IN THE MOSQUE

If her menstruation starts while she is in the mosque, she must leave immediately.

9.31 ENTERING ISLAMIC CENTERS

A mosque is an area that is permanently designated to be a *masjid* for the worship of Allāh until the Day of Judgement, whereas a *muṣalla* is a temporary place of worship.

If the Islamic center is not a mosque, it is permitted for a menstruating woman to enter it.

However, she must avoid entering the main prayer area (*muṣalla*) of the center because it could take the ruling of a mosque.

She is permitted to attend lectures and programs if they are held in other rooms in the center.

> ☑ Women should check with their local *imām* to find out whether they are entering a mosque or an Islamic center.

9.32 COURTYARDS IN MAKKAH & MADĪNA

It is permitted to walk within the courtyards outside *al-Masjid al-Ḥarām* in Makkah and *al-Masjid al-Nabawī* in Madīna. However, it is not permitted to enter the mosques.

9.33 ʿ*ĪD* PRAYER AREA

If the ʿ*Īd* prayer is conducted outside the mosque, such as at a convention center or an open field, it is permitted to enter the prayer area during menstruation.

9.34 GRAVEYARDS

As for graveyards, it is permissible for a menstruating woman to enter them, providing that she does not wail or follow the funeral prayer procession.

Read a summary of the rulings in Table 9e.

Table 9e: Summary of Rulings for Entering a Mosque

ENTERING & REMAINING	RULING
Mosque	Impermissible
Islamic Center	Permitted
Mosque Courtyard	Permitted
ʿĪd Prayer Area	Permitted
Graveyard	Permitted

6 Making Ṭawāf

9.35 MAKING ṬAWĀF DURING MENSES

It is not permitted for a menstruating woman to circumambulate (make *ṭawāf*) around the *Kaʿba*, regardless of whether the *ṭawāf* is obligatory (*farḍ*), mandatory (*wājib*), *sunna*, or voluntary (*nafl*).

This prohibition is separate from the prohibition of entering a mosque. The actual act of making *ṭawāf* is not permitted, such that even if the *Kaʿba* was hypothetically not inside the mosque, making *ṭawāf* remains impermissible.

9.36 MENSTRUATION STARTS BEFORE OR DURING ṬAWĀF

If a woman's menstruation starts before she begins to make *ṭawāf*, then she must wait until her menstruation finishes and she takes a *ghusl*. Thereafter, she can enter the mosque and make *ṭawāf*.

If a woman's menstruation starts while she is making a *ṭawāf*, then she must stop making *ṭawāf* and leave the mosque immediately. She must wait until her menstruation finishes and she takes a *ghusl* before completing her *ṭawāf*.

No penalty is owed for a woman who delayed performing the obligatory *ṭawāf* for *ḥajj* because she was menstruating from the 10th to 12th of *Dhū'l Ḥijjah*.

What if my menses starts before I do the *ṭawāf* and will only finish after my group leaves?

If a woman's menstruation starts before she can make the obligatory *ṭawāf*, she must wait until her menstruation finishes before performing the *ṭawāf*, even if it entails extending her trip.

If this is not possible, she should take medication to stop the flow immediately. She should inquire from the local pharmacists what is the safest maximum dosage that she can take to stop her blood flow.

However, if all avenues have been explored and it is not possible to do any of them, as an absolute final resort, she can make *ṭawāf* to remove herself from a state of *iḥrām* and offer the penalty for doing *ṭawāf* in a state of menses. She must also repent for performing *ṭawāf* in a state of ritual impurity.

Women should plan ahead as best as they can so that they do not find themselves in this situation. Likewise, travel agencies should leave ample time for women to stay in Makkah to perform their *ṭawāf* in case they menstruate unexpectedly.

9.37 ṬAWĀF PENALTIES

If a woman makes *ṭawāf* while she is menstruating, a penalty is owed. The penalty due differs according to the type of *ṭawāf* she performed.

◆ The obligatory *ṭawāf* for *ḥajj* is called *ṭawāf al-ifāḍa* or *ṭawāf az-ziyāra*. If a woman performs the obligatory *ṭawāf* for *ḥajj* while she is menstruating, the *ṭawāf* counts, but it is sinful and she owes a camel as a penalty.

◆ If she performs a mandatory (*wājib*) *ṭawāf*, a *sunna ṭawāf*, or a voluntary (*nafl*) *ṭawāf* while she is menstruating, the *ṭawāf* counts, but it is sinful and she owes a sheep as a penalty.

- ✧ The farewell *ṭawāf* (*al-wadāʿ*) for *ḥajj* is a mandatory (*wājib*) *ṭawāf*.

- ✧ The welcoming *ṭawāf* (*al-qudūm*) for *ḥajj* is a *sunna ṭawāf*.
- ✧ A *nafl ṭawāf* is any voluntary *ṭawāf* that is not a specific *ḥajj* or *ʿumra* rite, or a *ṭawāf* conditioned for a particular time.

◆ The *ṭawāf al-ʿumra* is obligatory to perform for a valid *ʿumra*. If a woman performs it while menstruating, the *ṭawāf* counts, but it is sinful and she owes a sheep as a penalty.

☑ All slaughtering must be completed in the Sacred Precinct (*Al-Ḥaram*).

☑ A woman is not required to perform the slaughtering herself. She can appoint an agent to carry out the slaughtering on her behalf. She should ask her group leaders how to pay for a slaughtering penalty if necessary.

9.38 DROPPING ṬAWĀF PENALTIES

If the woman repeats her *ṭawāf* in a state of ritual purity before she leaves Makkah, the penalty is dropped, and she no longer owes the penalty of slaughtering an animal.

Read a summary of the rulings in Table 9f.

Table 9f: Summary of *Ṭawāf* Penalties

TYPE OF ṬAWĀF	PENALTY OWED
Obligatory *Ḥajj Ṭawāf*	Camel
ʿUmra Ṭawāf	Sheep
Mandatory *Ṭawāf*	Sheep
Sunna *Ṭawāf*	Sheep
Nafl *Ṭawāf*	Sheep

9.39 PERMISSIBLE ACTS DURING ḤAJJ & ʿUMRA

It is permissible for a menstruating woman to enter into a state of *iḥrām* for *ḥajj* and *ʿumra*. It is also permissible to take the *sunna ghusl* for *iḥrām* beforehand.

As for the *ḥajj* rites, it is permissible for a menstruating woman to perform the standing at ʿArafat (*wuqūf*), spend the night at Muzdalifa, camp at Minā, stone the *jamarāt*, and perform the slaughtering.

MEDICATION DURING ḤAJJ OR ʿUMRA

It is permitted to take medication to delay the menstrual period for *ḥajj* or *ʿumra*. Two medications are commonly used by women: birth control pills or Primolut N.

Even if a woman takes medication, if she begins to bleed and the blood falls within her time of menses, it will be ruled as menses – including spotting or a light flow. Thus, she should give ample time for her body to become used to the effects of the medicine so that this does not occur.

If a woman chooses to take birth control pills, she should start taking the pills months before she travels. By doing so, she can manipulate her cycle so that the dates for her expected time of menses are moved forward. The hope is that her expected time of menses will not fall within the actual days of *ḥajj* or *ʿumra*, and any bleeding seen will be ruled as abnormal blood.

If a woman does not want to take birth control that early, then she can take Primolut N (Norethisterone 5g tablets) before leaving her home country. She continues to take the medicine while on *ḥajj* or *ʿumra*. In most cases, when the medication is stopped, withdrawal bleeding will occur approximately two or three days later.

It is best to consult a doctor for when one should start taking any of these medications, as well as what is the recommended dose, because each person's situation will be unique.

9.40 PERFORMING THE SAʿĪ

The *saʿī* can only be done after a *ṭawāf*, and it cannot be done beforehand. Therefore, a menstruating woman cannot perform the *saʿī* until her *ṭawāf* is complete.

- If a woman's menstruation starts after completing the *ṭawāf*, then she can perform the *saʿī* while in a state of menstruation.
- However, she cannot enter the mosque. She should enter the area of the *saʿī* from the back doors and not walk through the mosque to reach it.

> The Mother of the Believers ʿĀʾisha ﷺ said, "Ṣafīya bint Ḥuyayy ﷺ started her menses after performing the *ṭawāf al-ifāḍa*. I mentioned her menstruation to the Prophet ﷺ to which he ﷺ remarked, 'Then perhaps she will detain us!' I said, 'O Messenger of Allāh, indeed she performed the *ṭawāf al-ifāḍa* and finished the *ṭawāf* around the Kaʿba. It was after this that her menses started.' Thereupon the Messenger of Allāh ﷺ said, 'Then let her depart.'"
>
> (*Muslim*, 1211)

9.41 FAREWELL ṬAWĀF & MENSES

The farewell *ṭawāf* (*al-wadāʿ*) is mandatory to perform for those who are not residents of Makkah.

If a woman's menstruation begins after the obligatory *ṭawāf* for *ḥajj*, but before she can perform the farewell *ṭawāf* (*al-wadāʿ*), its performance is dropped, and she does not owe a makeup *ṭawāf* or an expiation.

Thus, she will not be required to delay her departure to complete the farewell *ṭawāf*.

❼ Engaging In Sexual Intercourse

9.42 SEXUAL INTERCOURSE DURING MENSES

It is not permitted for a menstruating woman to engage in sexual intercourse.

If both spouses willingly engage in this act, they must each repent and ask for Allāh Most High for forgiveness.

Additionally, it is recommended for the husband to give in charity.

- ✧ If the blood was red, or if it was done at the beginning of her menstruation, he gives the equivalent of 4.25 grams of gold.
- ✧ If the blood was yellow, or if it was done in the middle or end of her menstruation, he gives the equivalent of 2.125 grams of gold.
- ✧ The money should be given to poor and needy individuals who are eligible *zakāt* recipients.

☑ The monetary equivalent is calculated based on the price of gold per gram, which can be found online. Multiply 4.25 or 2.125 by the price of gold per gram to calculate how much is paid.

> ﴾ And they ask you about menstruation. Say, "It is an impurity. So, keep away from women during menstruation; and do not have intercourse with them until they are purified..." ﴿
>
> (*al-Baqara*, 2:222)

9.43 KNOWING THE TIME OF MENSES

The impermissibility of engaging in sexual intercourse is established by the wife informing her husband that she is menstruating.

❽ Touching Between Navel To Knee

9.44 TOUCHING BETWEEN THE NAVEL TO KNEE DURING MENSES

It is not permitted for a husband to directly touch the skin between his wife's navel to knees during menstruation. This is the ruling regardless of whether sexual desire is present or not.

- ✧ The prohibited area begins just below her navel and ends just below her knees.
- ✧ The knees, backside, hips, and thighs are included in this prohibition.

☑ The prohibition only applies to her and not to him. A menstruating woman can touch this respective area on her spouse's body. She can also stimulate and sexually please her husband with her hands.

> The Mother of the Believers Maymūna ﷺ said, "Whenever the Messenger of Allāh ﷺ wanted to touch any of his wives (for sexual intimacy) during her menstruation, he ﷺ would order her to wear an *izār* (lower garment)."
>
> (*Bukhārī*, 303)

9.45 PERMISSIBLE TOUCHING

It is permitted for her husband to touch the prohibited area over a barrier. For example, the wife places a sheet over this part of her body, or she wears leggings.

As for skin-to-skin contact with other areas of her body, such as the chest, back, arms, and calves, it is permissible.

☑ Sexually pleasing a woman while she is menstruating is permissible.

Read a summary of the rulings in Table 9g.

Table 9g: Summary of Rulings for Sexual Touching

AREA OF WOMAN'S BODY	RULING
Vaginal or Anal Intercourse	Impermissible
Skin-to-Skin Contact Between Navel & Knees (Includes Knees, Backside, Hips, and Thighs)	Impermissible
Between Navel & Knees With a Barrier	Permitted
Skin-to-Skin Contact With Chest, Back, Arms, and Calves	Permitted
Seeking Sexual Pleasure	Permitted

9 Being Divorced

9.46 BEING DIVORCED DURING MENSES

It is not permitted for a man to divorce a woman in a state of menstruation or lochia. However, even though it is unlawful, if he does it, the divorce counts.

Divorcing a woman in a state of menstruation will extend her post-marital waiting period (*ʿidda*) beyond three menstrual cycles. The menstruation in which the divorce is given does not count towards the *ʿidda*. Instead, the counting of three menstrual cycles for her *ʿidda* will begin from the next menstrual period, despite her being confined to her home after the divorce is given.

This will result in unnecessary hardship for her. Thus, scholars say that the husband is required to take her back, allow this current menstruation, as well as another purity, and a second menstruation to pass. Thereafter, if he wishes, he can divorce her within a purity span that he has not engaged in sexual intercourse with her.

Why does the divorce count if it is unlawful to divorce her during menstruation?

Many people are surprised by this ruling, but each act is viewed separately and thus possesses its own unique ruling. The *sunna* way to issue a divorce is to divorce a woman once in a purity span (*ṭuhr*) in which sexual intercourse has not taken place.

The Prophet ﷺ disapproved of men divorcing their wives during menstruation, and scholars say that doing it is an innovation (*al-ṭalāq al-bidʿī*). Thus, the timing that the divorce is given makes it unlawful, and as a result, the husband is sinful.

Then why does it count? It counts because the condition for a valid divorce was fulfilled, which is to declare divorce. Thus, issuing a divorce while she is menstruating is not permissible, and he is sinful for what he did, but this does not change the ruling that they are now divorced.

9.47 KHULʿ DURING MENSES

The *khulʿ* is an agreement between the husband and wife to dissolve the marriage contract in lieu of a compensation paid by the wife. It is permissible to issue a *khulʿ* during menstruation because the wife willingly agrees to extend her post-marital waiting period (*ʿidda*).

9.48 RELATED RULINGS DURING IMPURE STATES

The acts which are permitted or prohibited to engage in while in a state of ritual impurity differ for:

- Major ritual impurity, which is a state that requires *ghusl* due to sexual impurity or the cessation of menses / lochia.
- Minor ritual purity, which is a state that requires *wuḍūʾ* due to experiencing a *wuḍūʾ* nullifier.

Read a summary of these differences in Table 9h.

Table 9h: Summary of Rulings Related to Major & Minor Ritual Impurity

ACTION	MAJOR RITUAL IMPURITY		MINOR RITUAL IMPURITY
	Menses or Lochia	**Sexual Impurity (*Janāba*)**	**After Breaking *Wuḍūʾ***
Praying	Unlawful	Unlawful	Unlawful
Fasting	Unlawful	Permissible	Permissible
Touching the Qurʾān	Unlawful	Unlawful	Unlawful
Reciting the Qurʾān	Unlawful	Unlawful	Permissible
Sexual Intercourse	Unlawful	Permissible	Permissible
Touching Between the Navel to Knee	Unlawful	Permissible	Permissible
Entering the Mosque	Unlawful	Unlawful	Permissible
Performing *Ṭawāf*	Unlawful	Unlawful	Prohibitively Disliked
Cutting Nails & Removing Body Hair	Permissible	Slightly Disliked	Permissible

REVIEW QUESTIONS

1. Which acts are prohibited during menstruation and lochia?
2. What are the rulings related to menstruation starting during a prayer or a fast?
3. Which acts are prohibited in a state of minor ritual impurity?

PART THREE:
Lochia Rulings

Chapter 10:

PREGNANCY & BIRTH

Chapter 11:

LOCHIA 101

Chapter 12:

RULINGS IN PRACTICE

Chapter 13

BLOOD EXCEEDING FORTY DAYS

Chapter 14:

MISCARRIAGES

My Lord!
Bless me with
righteous
offspring

Qurʾān
37:100

Chapter 10

Pregnancy & Birth

IN THIS CHAPTER

- ✧ Bleeding during pregnancy
- ✧ Obligation to pray and fast
- ✧ Colored discharge during labor
- ✧ Praying during labor

One of the greatest Muslim women to ever live was Asmāʾ bint Abī Bakr رضي الله عنها, the daughter of the Rightly Guided Caliph Abū Bakr رضي الله عنه and the half-sister of the Mother of the Believers ʿĀʾisha رضي الله عنها. She was also the mother of the well-known Companions ʿAbdullah ibn Zubayr and ʿUrwa ibn Zubayr رضي الله عنهما.

Asmāʾ رضي الله عنها was of the early Muslims, and she played a pivotal role in the migration (*hijra*) of the Prophet ﷺ to Madīna. Although Asmāʾ was heavily pregnant at the time, she was entrusted with delivering provisions to her father رضي الله عنه and the Prophet ﷺ while they were hiding in Ghār Thawr. For three days, she risked her life to secretly bring them food and water.

On the last day of preparing their food sacks, she could not find a rope to tie the containers. She tore her waist belt into two pieces and tied their openings. When the Prophet ﷺ discovered what she had done, he ﷺ was pleased with her sacrifice and guaranteed her two belts in Paradise. Thereafter, she became known as the 'Lady of Two Waistbelts' (*dhat an-niṭāqayn*).

It is narrated that after the Prophet ﷺ and Abū Bakr رضي الله عنه fled, Abū Jahl came searching for them. He interrogated Asmāʾ رضي الله عنها about their whereabouts. She refused to disclose any information, and in a fit of rage, Abū Jahl slapped her across her face. Despite being pregnant, she stood up against Islam's biggest enemy.

When the Prophet ﷺ arrived near Madīna, he summoned for his family to join him. Asmāʾ رضي الله عنها accompanied them, tracking through the hot, barren desert while she was nine months pregnant. As they approached Qubāʾ, she gave birth to ʿAbdullah ibn Zubayr ﷺ. He was the first baby born to the emigrants (*muhājirīn*). She later had seven more children.

What courage and strength she showed in the face of tremendous life trials! She endured the hardship of persecution and the struggle of migrating to a new homeland while in her third trimester. Asmāʾ is a shining example for every pregnant woman. The sacrifices she made for the sake of her religion are remarkable, and the spirit of her perseverance must be modeled.

Pregnant women need to bear in mind that the act of carrying a child in their womb, as well as overcoming the challenges that come with pregnancy, is an act of worship. The nausea, hormonal imbalances, mood swings, and tiredness throughout a woman's pregnancy are a means for reward in disguise.

Consequently, a pregnant woman must not miss out on this golden opportunity to draw nearer to her Lord. She should be dutiful in her prayers, increase in her recitation of the Qurʾān, and make abundant *dhikr* of Allāh Most High. She should fuel her body with lawful food and avoid anything that is unlawful or dubious. She must also frequently pray to Allāh Most High to aid her in her struggles and ask Him for help with raising her child.

10.1 MENSTRUATION DURING PREGNANCY

According to the *Ḥanafī madhhab*, pregnant women are not able to menstruate because the cervix is plugged and nothing can exit the uterus. Thus, any blood or colored vaginal discharge seen during pregnancy is considered abnormal vaginal bleeding (*istiḥāḍa*).

10.2 BLEEDING DURING PREGNANCY

Seeing blood during pregnancy is not normal. A pregnant woman should notify her doctor of the bleeding out of safety for herself and her child. She should also keep a record of any blood that she experiences due to the possibility of miscarrying.

> ➔ The rulings related to miscarriages are discussed in Chapter 14.

What does medical research say about a pregnant woman menstruating?

According to doctors, menstruation only happens when a woman is not pregnant. Each month, the uterus grows a thick blood-rich lining in preparation for an egg to embed there. If a woman does not get pregnant, she will shed this tissue and blood as a menstrual period. However, once an egg embeds in the uterine lining, hormones tell the blood-rich tissue to stay intact to support the growing baby. As a result, a woman will not shed the lining or menstruate again until her pregnancy is over.

10.3 OBLIGATION TO PRAY

A pregnant woman is obliged to pray. Even if she is experiencing abnormal bleeding, she must continue to pray. Menstruation (*hayḍ*) and lochia (*nifās*) are the only vaginal bloods that lift the obligation of performing the ritual prayer.

> ⚠ An increase of white or milky discharge during pregnancy is normal. It takes the same rulings as normal vaginal discharge.

10.4 OBLIGATION TO FAST

As a general ruling, pregnant and nursing women are required to fast during *Ramaḍān*. However, an exception is made for a woman who fears that the act of fasting will harm her or her baby. Her fear must be reasonable, meaning that it must have a genuine basis.

Reasonable fear is known by one of the following:

- Manifest signs.
- A relevant past experience.
- The notification of an upright, Muslim doctor/expert who is familiar with the limits of the Sacred Law.

If a woman does not have access to an upright, Muslim doctor, then she listens to her doctor's medical opinion, asks a Muslim scholar for guidance, and makes her own decision based on what she understands about her situation and the limits of the Sacred Law.

Every woman's circumstance will be different. When in doubt, it is best to try to fast first and see how easy or difficult it may be. One is encouraged to take all the necessary steps available to make fasting easier, like eating a nutrient dense pre-dawn meal (*suḥūr*), sleeping during the day, using baby formula, drinking lots of fluid during the night, consuming healthy fats, and taking it easy overall.

Despite taking these steps, if fasting will be harmful, then a pregnant or nursing woman is not required to fast *Ramaḍān*. If any *Ramaḍān* fasts are missed due to pregnancy or nursing, a woman is required to make them up once *Ramaḍān* has ended at a time when she is able.

Some women may find it easier to fast every other day or every few days, instead of stopping to fast all together. This also ensures that a lesser number of days will be required for makeup in the future.

There is no expiation for a woman who delays making up her missed fasts – even if she delays it past the next *Ramaḍān*. However, it is superior to make them up immediately if she is able, especially if the accumulation of missed fasts will overwhelm her in the future.

10.5 VAGINAL EXAMS

Vaginal exams do not require *ghusl*, but they require *wuḍū*ʾ.

As for breaking the fast, the position of many scholars is that inserting anything wet inside the vagina to the distance of a suppository breaks the fast. Accordingly, because vaginal exams usually involve the insertion of a lubricated vaginal speculum, the fast would be nullified.

However, some contemporary scholars refute this position based on the current medical understanding of a woman's anatomy. Nevertheless, it is superior to avoid the difference of opinion and delay the exam. If this is not possible, then out of precaution, a woman can fast that day and make it up after *Ramaḍān* is over.

THE MUCUS PLUG, BLOODY SHOW, & AMNIOTIC FLUID

When a woman nears the time for labor, her mucus plug dislodges from the cervix, her water breaks, and she may even experience a bloody show.

The mucus plug is a "cork" barrier that seals a pregnant woman's cervix during pregnancy. Along with the amniotic sac, it helps protect the baby from the outside world while a woman is pregnant until she is ready to deliver.

The bloody show is a discharge of mucus that is tinged pink or brown with blood. It means the blood vessels in the cervix are rupturing as it begins to dilate.

Typically, at the beginning of or during labor the amniotic sac that surrounds the baby will rupture. The fluid that leaks from this sac will slowly trickle out of the vagina or quickly gush out, which is commonly known as a woman's water breaking.

Every woman will differ in when they experience these events, and there is no way to tell which incident will take place first.

10.6 COLORED DISCHARGE EXITING BEFORE CHILDBIRTH

Any blood or fluid that exits before childbirth is considered filthy (*najis*), and it does not lift the obligation to pray.

- When the mucus plug falls out or the bloody show occurs, the discharge is filthy, and it breaks *wuḍūʾ*.
- When a woman's water breaks, the amniotic fluid that exits is filthy, and it breaks *wuḍūʾ*.

> ➔ If a woman experiences constant bleeding or fluid exiting her vagina, then she will resort to the Excused Person's Rulings for her *wuḍū'*, which are mentioned in Chapter 17.

10.7 REMOVING FILTH BEFORE PRAYING

Before praying a pregnant woman must wash away any filth (*najāsa*) on her body or clothes that exceeds the excused amount.

Determining the excused amount of filth:

The amount of filth that is permitted to remain on a person's clothes and body during the prayer is filth that is the size of a *dirham* or less. Scholars estimate the size of a *dirham* to be:

- Five grams in weight for solid filth (e.g., feces).
- Five centimeters in diameter for liquid filth (e.g., urine or blood).

If a person prays with the excused amount of filth on their clothes or body, it is slightly disliked (*makrūh tanzīhān*). Thus, it is recommended to remove the filth before praying – although the prayer is valid if it is not removed.

If a person prays with more than this amount on their clothes or body, while having the means to remove it, then the prayer is not valid.

10.8 PRAYING DURING LABOR

A pregnant woman is obliged to perform her obligatory (*farḍ*) and *witr* prayers during labor until most of the baby exits. Any blood seen before childbirth is considered abnormal uterine bleeding (*istiḥāḍa*), and it does not lift the obligation to pray.

Even if a woman is experiencing contractions, she must pray until actual childbirth. The advice from many mothers is to pray as soon as the prayer time comes in, if this is possible. The sooner a woman prays, the less worry it is for her.

When contractions become more intense, it may not be easy or possible to bow as usual or prostrate on the floor. In this circumstance, a woman may need to resort to the sick person's rulings for her prayer. These rulings permit a person to pray sitting up or lying down with head movements.

How to pray during labor:

- If a woman cannot make *wuḍū*ʾ herself, or with the help of someone, she can make *tayammum* with a rock or dirt. When preparing to give birth, she should carry a small rock in her bag or pack a Ziplock bag filled with dirt to use for *tayammum*.

- If a woman is constantly bleeding or fluid is continuously exiting, she will resort to the Excused Person's Rulings for her *wuḍū*ʾ, which are discussed in Chapter 17.

- If a woman cannot cover her body for the prayer by wearing clothing, she can cover herself by throwing a sheet over her body. If delivering in a public hospital, it is advisable to wear a two-piece hijab or sport hijab so that one's hair remains covered.

- If a woman cannot pray standing, then she prays sitting or with head movements.

- Praying with head movements can be done while sitting, lying down on her back, or lying on her side. She moves her head slightly forward for the bowing position (*rukū*ʿ) and somewhat lower than that for the prostration (*sujūd*), such that both are two distinct movements. The prostration movement must be lower than the bowing movement. Otherwise, the prayer is invalid.

- If a woman cannot perform the prayer due to drastic circumstances, someone else should record the number of prayers she missed, and she must make them up later in a time when she is legally able to pray. It helps to assign someone with this duty before going into labor. With child delivery, it is best to expect the unexpected.

10.9 MAKING DUʿĀʾ DURING CHILDBIRTH

It is permissible to make supplication (*duʿāʾ*) and recite *dhikr* during childbirth.

RECOMMENDED DUʿĀʾ & DHIKR

A pregnant woman should make *duʿāʾ* for an easy birth and the righteousness of her children. Allāh Most High tells us that the supplication (*duʿāʾ*) of the distressed person is answered. (*an-Naml*, 27:62)

Even in tough moments like when giving birth, it is important to have trust in Allāh Most High, call upon Him, and seek His protection from any complications.

Recommended supplications are:

اللهُمَّ لا سَهْلَ إلا مَا جَعَلتَهُ سَهْلا وَ أنتَ تَجْعَلُ الحَزْنَ إذا شِئْتَ سَهْلا

Allāhumma lā sahla illā mā jaʿalatahu sahlā,
wa anta tajʿalu l-ḥazana idhā shiʾta sahlā

"O Allāh, there is no ease except in that which You have made easy, and You make the difficult, if You wish, easy."

رَبَّنَا هَبْ لَنَا مِنْ أَزْوَاجِنَا وَذُرِّيَّاتِنَا قُرَّةَ أَعْيُنٍ وَاجْعَلْنَا لِلْمُتَّقِينَ إِمَامًا

Rabbanā hab lanā min azwājinā wa dhurriyyātinā
qurrata ʾaʿyun wajʿalnā lil muttaqīna imāmā

"Our Lord! Bless us with pious spouses and offspring who will be the joy of our hearts and make us models for the righteous." (*al-Furqān*, 25:74)

She can also recite easy forms of *dhikr*, like *subḥānAllāh wa alḥamduliLlah wa lā ilaha illā Allāh wa Allāhu akbar.*

These actions can create a spiritual atmosphere during the labor, increase the family's blessings, and bring mental relief during childbirth.

10.10 OWING THE PRAYER

If the baby exits before the prayer time is over, that prayer is not owed.

The consideration for owing prayers returns to the woman's state within the last moment of the prayer time. Thus, if a woman is in a state of lochia (*nifās*) when the prayer time exits, she does not owe the prayer of this time and she is not required to make up the missed prayer after her lochia finishes.

10.11 POST-MARITAL WAITING PERIOD

If a woman is divorced while she is pregnant, her post-marital waiting period (*ʿidda*) ends once she gives birth.

If she is pregnant with twins or triplets, her post-marital waiting period (*ʿidda*) ends with the birth of the last child.

> ﴾ As for those who are pregnant, their waiting period ends when they give birth to their child. ﴿
>
> (*aṭ-Ṭalāq*, 65:4)

REVIEW QUESTIONS

1. Can a pregnant woman menstruate?
2. What is the ruling for blood seen during pregnancy and during labor?
3. How does a woman pray during labor?

Chapter 11

Lochia 101

IN THIS CHAPTER

- ✧ Definition of lochia
- ✧ Conditions of lochia
- ✧ How to establish a lochia habit
- ✧ Lochia beginner vs. woman with a habit

Asmā' bint 'Umays رضي الله عنها was an exceptional female Companion. She is known for having married three of the Prophet's ﷺ most noble Companions: Ja'far ibn Abī Ṭālib, Abū Bakr aṣ-Ṣiddīq, and 'Alī ibn Abī Ṭālib رضي الله عنهم.

In the early days of Islam, she emigrated to Abyssinia with her first husband, Ja'far ibn Abī Ṭālib رضي الله عنه. It was in Abyssinia that she gave birth to their three sons. The family spent approximately fifteen years in a faraway land until they later returned to Madīna after the conquest of Khaybar.

Shortly after, Ja'far رضي الله عنه was killed in the Battle of Mu'ta. It was an intensely heartbreaking experience for Asmā' رضي الله عنها. By the grace of Allāh Most High, Asmā' رضي الله عنها then married Abū Bakr aṣ-Ṣiddīq رضي الله عنه and remained his beloved wife until he died – only for her to witness another death of her husband.

Despite being pregnant, Asmā' رضي الله عنها accompanied Abū Bakr رضي الله عنه during the Prophet's ﷺ farewell *ḥajj*. As they were traveling on the way to Makkah, Asmā' رضي الله عنها gave birth to Abū Bakr's رضي الله عنه son, Muḥammad رضي الله عنهما, at Dhu'l Ḥulayfa.

Unaware of what to do, Abū Bakr رضي الله عنه asked the Prophet ﷺ about the matter. The Prophet ﷺ told him to instruct Asmā' رضي الله عنها to take a *ghusl* and enter into pilgrim sanctity (*iḥrām*). (*Muslim*, 1209; *Abū Dāwūd*, 1743) Even though she was in a state of lochia (*nifās*), Asmā' رضي الله عنها persisted with performing *ḥajj* and endured the journey ahead.

Giving birth is difficult but caring for a newborn baby while traveling for days in the desert and performing *ḥajj* in that state could not have been any easier. Asmāʾ ﷺ was a woman that was tested with many trials, but she patiently withstood them for the sake of Allāh Most High.

Similarly, every mother is tested with her children. The constant sacrifices that a mother makes are only known to Allāh Most High. Yet she will be rewarded for her actions on the Day of Judgement if she practices a beautiful patience for His sake.

The Prophet ﷺ said, "No fatigue, nor disease, nor sorrow, nor sadness, nor hurt, nor distress befalls a Muslim – even if it were the prick from a thorn – but that Allāh expiates some of his sins for it." (*Bukhārī*, 5641)

Lochia Basics

DEFINITION

Lochia (*nifās*) is:

- Blood that originates from the uterus and comes out of the vagina after the exiting of most of the baby.

Most of the baby exiting means:

- If the head comes out first, then when the chest exits.
- If the feet come out first (breech birth), then when the navel exits.

CONDITIONS

Its conditions are:

- It has no minimum.
- Its maximum duration is 40 complete days (960 hours).
- It must be followed by a purity span (*ṭuhr*) of at least 15 complete days (360 hours) free from any colored vaginal discharge that ends outside the 40 days.
- A minimal purity span (*ṭuhr*) of six months must separate between two lochia.

RULING

If the blood abides by the definition and conditions of lochia, the bleeding is ruled as sound, and it becomes the lochia habit.

11.1 DEFINITION OF LOCHIA

Lochia, also known as post-partum bleeding, is blood that originates from the uterus and comes out of the vagina after the exiting of most of the baby.

Each word in this definition is significant:

◆ '*Blood*' refers to any colored vaginal discharge.

As previously mentioned, blood can be black, red, brown, yellow, turbid, or green. If any of these colors are seen during the possible days of lochia, it will be deemed lochia.

◆ '*Originates from the uterus and comes out of the vagina*' means that the bleeding from the womb must exit through the vagina.

Therefore, any blood that exits from the incision of a cesarean birth (c-section) is not lochia. Rather it is blood from a wound, and it does not follow the rulings of lochia. As for vaginal blood seen after a c-section, it will be ruled as lochia.

◆ '*After the exiting of most of the baby*' means that lochia only begins after most of the baby exits.

- ✧ If the head comes first, then most of the baby is when the chest exits.
- ✧ If the feet come first, then most of the baby is when the navel exits.

☑ From a practical perspective, in most cases in real life, when the crowning of the head occurs in a normal vaginal delivery, the rest of the baby quickly follows.

> ⚠ Any blood seen before childbirth is considered abnormal uterine bleeding (*istiḥāḍa*). Therefore, a pregnant woman is required to pray up until the delivery of the baby.

11.2 CONDITIONS OF LOCHIA

There are four conditions associated with the definition of lochia:

1. Meeting the lochia minimum.
2. Abiding by the lochia maximum.
3. A purity span occurring between lochia and menstruation.
4. A six-month span occurring between two lochia.

✓ All four conditions must be met without exception.

11.3 FIRST CONDITION: THE LOCHIA MINIMUM

There is no minimum length for lochia. Lochia can last for just a moment.

If a woman was to hypothetically experience a dry birth – meaning that no colored vaginal discharge was seen following childbirth – she would be obliged to take a *ghusl* and begin praying. Her lochia habit would be a moment.

✓ This situation is very rare, as even women who have cesarean births (c-sections) experience vaginal blood after childbirth.

? What is a caesarean birth (c-section)?

A cesarean section (c-section) is a surgical procedure performed when a vaginal delivery is not possible or safe, like when the baby is in an abnormal position or the baby's size is too big. It may also be done when the health of the mother or the baby is at risk. During this procedure, the baby is delivered through surgical incisions made in the abdomen and the uterus. The entire c-section procedure takes about 45 minutes. After the baby is delivered, the doctor will close the incisions with stitches or something similar.

11.4 SECOND CONDITION: THE LOCHIA MAXIMUM

The lochia maximum is 40 complete days (960 hours). Any bleeding that exceeds the maximum limit of 40 complete days (960 hours) is not lochia. Rather, it is abnormal blood (*istiḥāḍa*).

◆ Counting Forty Complete Days

What is intended by a 'day' is a full day and its night, which is 24 hours. Forty days of 24 hours equals 960 hours.

The maximum days of lochia will not be counted correctly if the 24-hour stipulation is overlooked.

> 🔍 Observe how the days are counted in Diagram 11a.

Diagram 11a: The Lochia Maximum

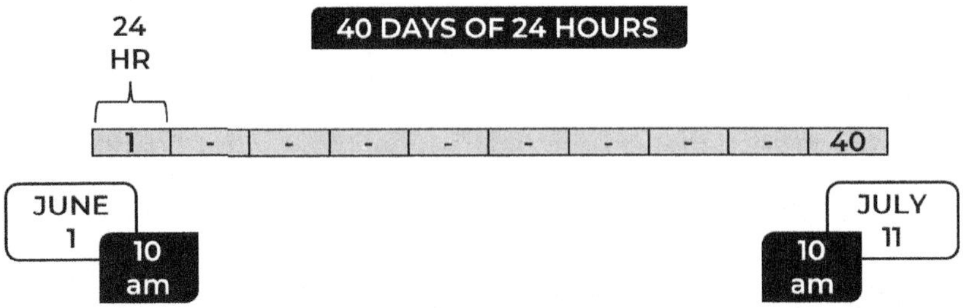

> A woman's gives birth to her first baby on June 1st at 10 am.
>
> ► Her lochia starts after childbirth on June 1st at 10 am
>
> ► The lochia maximum is met at 960 hours on July 11th at 10 am.
>
> ► If a woman is unaware of the 24-hour stipulation, she may mistakenly assume that the lochia maximum is met on July 10th.

◆ Color Of Discharge

Any colored vaginal discharge seen within the 960 hours takes the ruling of lochia. During these 960 hours, the vaginal discharge can be any color, such as red, brown, fresh yellow, or the like.

> ➔ The colors of blood are discussed in Chapter 3.

? What is lochia blood? What is considered normal?

Lochia is the body's way of getting rid of the extra blood and tissue in the uterus that helped the baby grow. It is made up of blood, placental tissue, endometrial lining, and mucus. The blood comes mostly from the area where the placenta detached itself from the uterine wall during birth. The endometrial lining which thickens during pregnancy also sheds. Normal bleeding lasts for 3 to 6 weeks as the uterus heals and returns to its usual shape and size.

Lochia is heaviest the first few days after the baby is born. Blood will be dark or bright red for about three to ten days. It is normal to see clots of blood during this stage. A woman may feel cramping and uterine contractions as the uterus returns to its usual size. As the weeks pass, the blood flow will lighten. The color may change from light red to a watery pink. In its final stage, lochia changes from pink to brown to a yellowish-white color. Women can still see occasional spotting of blood.

◆ Spotting Versus Continuous Flow

The bleeding does not need to be continuous during the 40 days for it to be considered lochia. The consideration is the beginning and ending times of the blood. Therefore, spotting or a constant flow of blood will take the ruling of lochia.

> Observe which days are considered lochia in Diagram 11b.

Diagram 11b: The Lochia Maximum

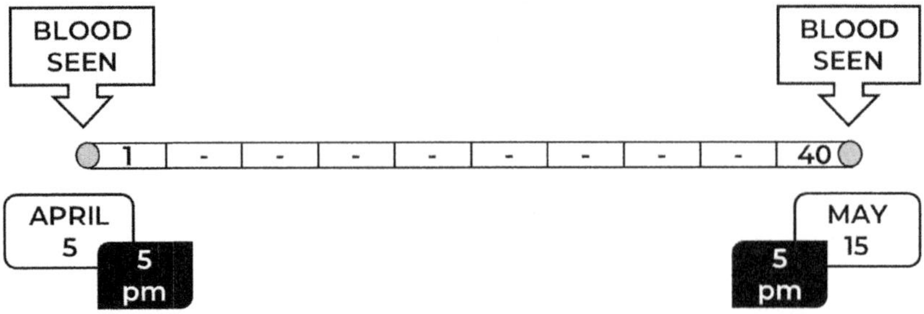

> A woman sees a spot of blood on April 5th at 5 pm after giving birth. Forty days later, she sees another spot on May 15th at 5 pm.
>
> ► The entire time span is considered lochia in hindsight.
>
> ► Whether she saw blood for the total duration of 40 days is of no consideration according to the rulings.

◆ Not Exceeding The Maximum Limit

If the bleeding does not exceed 40 days (960 hours) and the third condition of a minimal purity is met, then the entire duration will be ruled as lochia.

If the blood exceeds the lochia maximum of 960 hours, the woman must revise her situation.

> ➔ The details of what to do when bleeding exceeds the maximum are covered in Chapter 13.

11.5 THIRD CONDITION: PURITY SPAN BETWEEN LOCHIA & MENSES

A purity span (*ṭuhr*) of at least 15 complete days (360 hours) free of blood must separate between a lochia and a menses. Thus, after lochia bleeding finishes, a purity span must immediately follow it.

A woman's lochia and menstruation cannot succeed each other. There needs to be a separator between them.

- ✧ The purity span that follows lochia must be a minimum duration of 15 complete days (360 hours). It also needs to be free from all colored discharge, which includes spotting.

- ✧ The purity span must end outside the 40 possible days of lochia.

☑ Both conditions need to be fulfilled for the next bleeding to be ruled as menses.

➔ For more rulings related to menstruation, refer to Section 12.14.

Observe the purity span that follows the lochia in Diagram 11c.

Diagram 11c: Purity Span Between Lochia & Menses

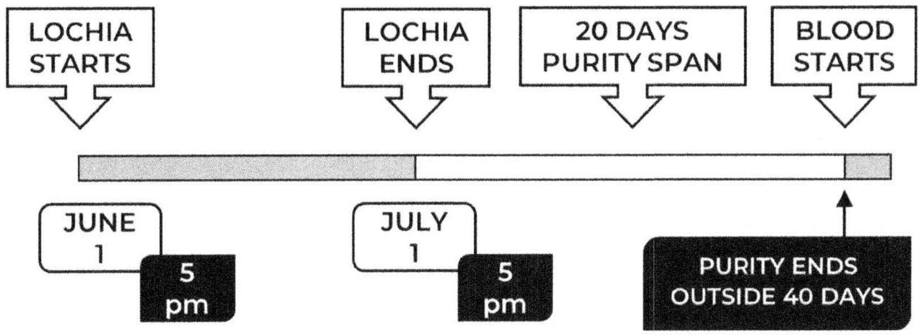

A woman gives birth on June 1st at 5 pm. She bleeds for 30 days. The bleeding is followed by a purity span of 20 days.

► The bleeding did not exceed 40 days.

► It is followed by a purity span of at least 15 complete days that ends outside the 40 days.

► All 30 days are ruled as lochia. The next bleeding can be menses.

11.6 FOURTH CONDITION: SIX-MONTH SPAN BETWEEN TWO LOCHIA

The minimum duration for pregnancy is six months. Thus, a span of at least six months must separate between two lochia.

This condition primarily relates to women who give birth to twins or women who become pregnant very soon after their lochia finishes. These rulings can also apply to certain types of miscarriages.

With twins and triplets, lochia begins with the exiting of most of the first baby according to Imām Abū Ḥanīfa.

- If the babies are born within a time span of less than six months apart from each other, they are deemed to be from the same pregnancy. This means that the blood following the birth of the second or third baby is part of the same lochia from the first baby.

- If a gap of six months or more occurs between the two bloods, then the second bleeding is ruled as a new lochia. This means that the woman had two pregnancies, which will result in her experiencing two separate lochia.

> Compare the two examples in Diagram 11d and 11e.

Diagram 11d: Six-Month Span Between Two Lochia

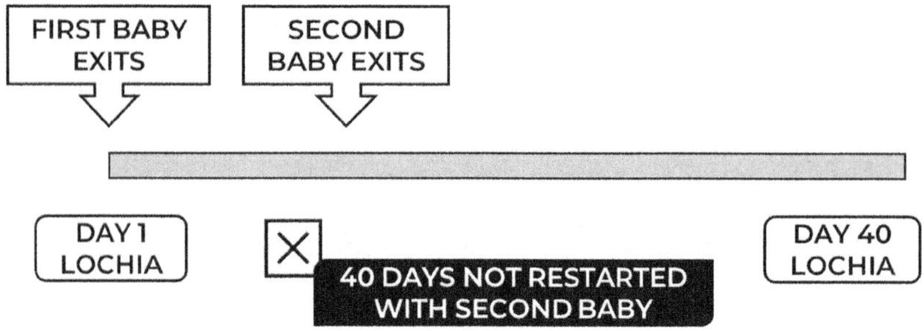

A woman is pregnant with twins. On July 1st, she gives birth to one of the babies. Two days later, she gives birth to the second baby.

► There is a duration of less than six months between the births. The babies are deemed to be from the same pregnancy.

► Thus, the blood that follows the second baby's exiting is part of the same lochia from the first baby. She does not restart a new 40 days with the second birth.

Diagram 11e: Six-Month Span Between Two Lochia

A woman gives birth to her first baby. After her lochia finishes, she becomes pregnant and gives birth to her second child eight months later.

► There is a duration of at least six months that separate between the two bloods.

► She starts a new 40 days of lochia with the second birth.

11.7 ESTABLISHING A LOCHIA HABIT

If the blood abides by the definition and conditions of lochia, the bleeding is ruled as sound, and it becomes a woman's lochia habit.

A sound lochia only needs to be seen once for it to become a habit. Moreover, the most recent sound lochia will be used as her habit.

- ✧ A woman's lochia habit will change with each new birth, providing that the blood meets all the conditions of lochia.

  For example, a woman gives birth to her first baby and bleeds for 20 days. After her second child, she bleeds for 40 days. Her lochia habit will change from 20 days to 40 days – providing that the third condition for lochia is met.

- ✧ A woman cannot make up a habit for herself. Rather, she must physically see it occur within her life.

ESTABLISHING A LOCHIA HABIT

- Most recent lochia a woman saw.
- Blood is not more than 40 days (960 hours).
- A purity span of at least 15 days (360 hours) free of blood immediately follows it and it ends outside the 40 days.
- Only need to see it once to become a habit.
- Obliged to record it.

11.8 RECORDING THE LOCHIA HABIT

It is obligatory upon every woman to record her lochia habit.

11.9 LOCHIA BEGINNER

A lochia beginner (*mubtadaʾa*) is a woman who is experiencing lochia for the first time in her life. This can either occur through the birth of her first baby or the miscarriage of a developed fetus.

A woman can only be a lochia beginner once. After seeing lochia for the first time, her habit is established, and she then becomes a woman with a lochia habit.

> ➔ The rulings related to miscarriages are discussed in Chapter 14.

11.10 WOMAN WITH A LOCHIA HABIT

A woman with a lochia habit (*muʿtāda*) is a woman who has experienced a previous lochia. The lochia habit refers to the last sound lochia that she saw – meaning the most recent.

> ⚠ The rulings related to bleeding exceeding the lochia maximum are different for a lochia beginner and a woman with a lochia habit. Refer to Chapter 13.

REVIEW QUESTIONS

1. What is the legal definition of lochia? What does each phrase within the definition mean?
2. What is the lochia minimum and maximum?
3. How many days of purity must separate between a lochia and menses? Why?
4. How long is the span that must separate between two lochia? Why?
5. Who is a lochia beginner? Who is a woman with a lochia habit?

Chapter 12

Rulings in Practice

IN THIS CHAPTER

- ✧ Possible days of lochia
- ✧ Changes in lochia habit
- ✧ Rulings for lochia beginner
- ✧ Menses after lochia

Out of His compassion, Allāh Most High grants women a lengthy duration to experience lochia. For many mothers, they instinctively recognize the mercy and blessing of this bleeding.

Perhaps Allāh Most High willed for lochia to occur after childbirth so that women are given a chance to adjust to motherhood. They can focus on taking care of their newborn baby without the worry of other matters.

Maybe He created lochia to provide time for their bodies to rest and heal after nine months of pregnancy. Indeed, Allāh is the best of planners.

The Mother of the Believers Umm Salama رضي الله عنها said:

> "During the time of the Prophet ﷺ, the women who experienced bleeding after childbirth would refrain from praying for forty days. The Prophet ﷺ did not command them to make up the prayers missed due to lochia."
>
> (*Abū Dāwūd*, 312)

Scholars deduce from Umm Salama's رضي الله عنها statement that after childbirth a woman will abide by the same prohibitions that apply to a menstruating woman. If she sees blood, she will not pray, fast, or engage in sexual intercourse. Both women are similar in many ways, which is why their rulings are often mentioned together.

12.1 POSSIBLE DAYS OF LOCHIA (PDL)

The possible days of lochia are the potential days that a woman can experience lochia.

◆ When do the possible days start?

The possible days of lochia start when most of the baby exits. Any bleeding that exits beforehand is abnormal uterine bleeding (*istiḥāḍa*), and it is not lochia.

> Observe which blood is considered lochia in Diagram 12a.

Diagram 12a: Possible Days of Lochia

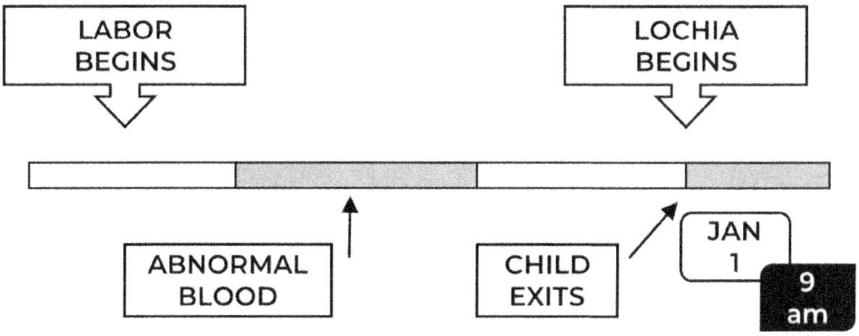

> A woman bleeds during labor and gives birth on January 1st at 9 am.
>
> ► Her lochia begins after childbirth at 9 am.
>
> ► The blood preceding childbirth is abnormal uterine bleeding (*istiḥāḍa*).

◆ When do the possible days finish?

The possible days of lochia last up to 40 complete days (960 hours) counting from the birth of the child.

This does not mean that a woman waits the entire span of 40 days. If her bleeding stops within the 40 days, she must take a *ghusl* and begin praying.

> Observe how the days are counted in Diagram 12b.

Diagram 12b: Forty Possible Days of Lochia

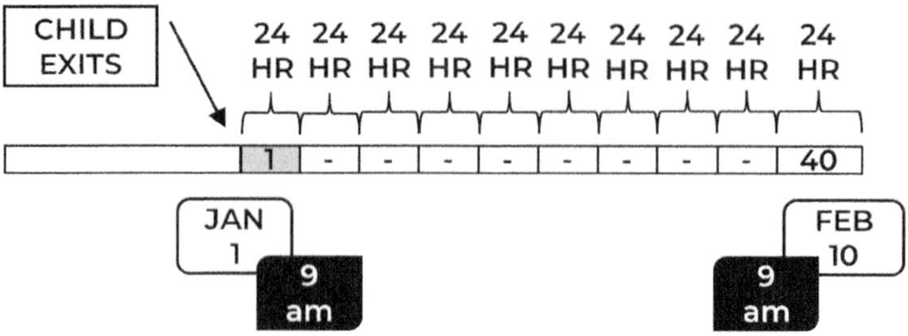

> A woman gives birth on January 1st at 9 am.
>
> ► Her possible days of lochia start on January 1st at 9 am.
>
> ► Her possible days of lochia end on February 10th at 9 am.

12.2 RULINGS FOR THE POSSIBLE DAYS OF LOCHIA (PDL)

There are two main rulings for the possible days of lochia. Sections 12.3 to 12.8 discuss these rulings in detail along with pointing out some of their consequences.

For women who do not experience problems with abnormal bleeding, this section will hopefully be a sufficient guide of how to act within the possible days of lochia.

As for women who experience abnormal uterine bleeding (*istiḥāḍa*), the guidelines given will not provide an overall solution for their problem. Rather, they should read this section to understand how the principles work, and then contact a teacher who may further help them based on their lochia, menses, and purity habits.

Rulings for Possible Days of Lochia (PDL)

1. Whenever blood is seen within the possible days of lochia, it is always considered lochia.
2. Whenever blood stops within the possible days of lochia, it is ruled as lochia (*nifās*), and a woman is obliged to take a *ghusl* and pray.

12.3 FIRST PDL RULING: WHENEVER BLOOD IS SEEN

Whenever blood is seen within the possible days of lochia, it is always considered lochia.

'*Whenever blood is seen*' means all colored vaginal discharge other than completely white or clear. There is no consideration for the shade of color, the thickness of the blood, or what symptoms accompany it.

The consequences of this ruling are:

❶ All prohibitions apply. She cannot pray. She cannot fast. She cannot have sexual intercourse with her husband. She must adhere to the same prohibitions for a menstruating woman.

❷ She must always consider any bleeding that she sees within these days to be lochia, regardless of whether it is spotting, a full flow, or it stops and suddenly returns.

➔ The prohibitions were briefly mentioned in Section 1.5. They are discussed in detail in Chapter 9.

Observe how the days are counted in Diagram 12c.

Diagram 12c: First PDL Ruling

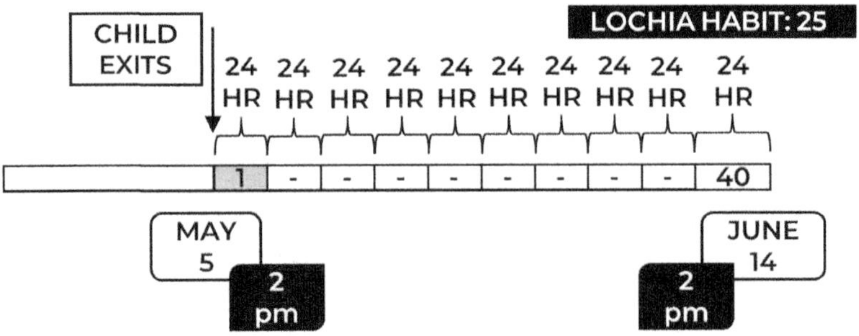

A woman with two children has a lochia habit of 25 days. She gives birth to her third child on May 5th at 2 pm.

► Her possible days of lochia start when she gives birth, and they end after 40 complete days (960 hours) on June 14th at 2 pm.

► Any time she sees bleeding from May 5th 2 pm to June 14th 2 pm, this blood takes the ruling of lochia.

► She is obliged to abide by the prohibitions until the blood stops within the 40 possible days or the lochia maximum of 960 hours is reached.

Keep in mind that this is a ruling in the moment, and depending on what happens, there is a chance that this ruling may change in hindsight. The future is unknown, and there is usually no way of determining whether the blood will exceed 40 complete days or stop beforehand until it happens.

12.4 SECOND PDL RULING: WHEN BLOOD STOPS

Whenever blood stops within the possible days of lochia, it is ruled as lochia (*nifās*), and a woman is obliged to take a *ghusl* and pray.

◆ *'Stops'* means that there is no sighting of colored vaginal discharge. When a woman checks her *kursuf*, she sees white discharge, clear discharge, or no discharge. She is also reasonably certain that the bleeding will not return.

- ✧ The blood does not need to reach 3 complete days like with menstruation. This is because there is no minimum for lochia. The fact that she gave birth is proof that the blood which follows is lochia. The blood does not need to reach 3 days to establish certainty.

- ✧ Therefore, any time the bleeding stops within the possible days of lochia – even if it is before 3 complete days – she is obliged to take a *ghusl*.

◆ '*Ghusl*' refers to the purificatory shower that removes a person from major ritual impurity. It is obligatory to take a *ghusl* when bleeding either stops within the 40 possible days or the lochia maximum of 40 complete days (960 hours) is reached.

> ➔ The *ghusl* is described in Sections 6.2 to 6.3.

The consequences of this ruling are:

❶ Even if the blood surpasses 40 complete days, part of the overall bleeding will be ruled as lochia.

❷ She is not required to make up any missed prayers due to lochia, but she must make up her missed fasts if the lochia occurred during *Ramaḍān*.

❸ Whenever this bleeding stops, she is required to take a *ghusl* before she begins praying.

> Observe when the *ghusl* is taken in Diagram 12d.

Diagram 12d: Second PDL Ruling

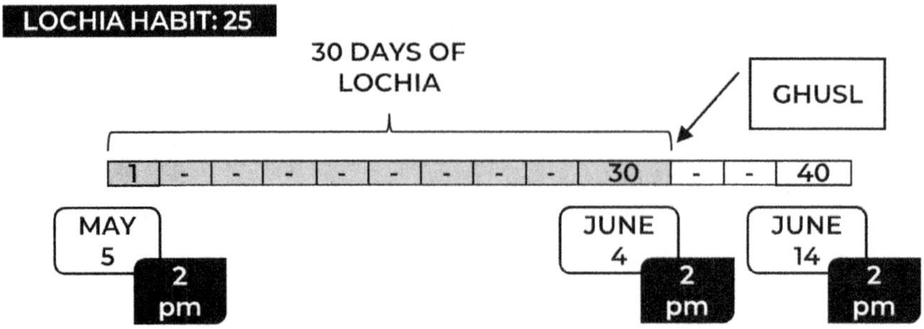

Building on the situation in Diagram 12c, her blood stops after 30 complete days on June 4th at 2 pm.

► She takes a *ghusl* on June 4th and begins praying.

► If the bleeding does not return and a purity span of at least 15 complete days (360 hours) free of blood follows it, her lochia habit changes to 30 complete days.

12.5 BLEEDING EXCEEDING THE LOCHIA HABIT IN PDL

If a woman with a lochia habit reaches her habit during the possible days and she is still bleeding, she continues to abide by the prohibitions.

✅ If she is bleeding within the 40 possible days, this is proof that she is still experiencing lochia.

🔍 Observe what she did when the blood exceeded her lochia habit of 25 days in Diagram 12d. She continued to abide by the prohibitions on Day 26, despite the bleeding surpassing her 25-day lochia habit.

12.6 BLEEDING RETURNING AFTER IT PREVIOUSLY STOPPED IN PDL

If the bleeding stops and later returns within the possible days of lochia, it is obligatory to take another *ghusl*.

> Observe when she takes a second *ghusl* in Diagram 12e.

Diagram 12e: Bleeding Returns After Stopping

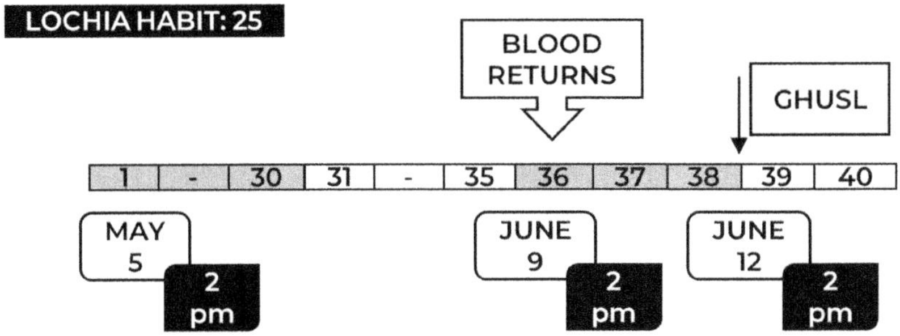

> The bleeding returns on Day 36 (June 9th) at 2 pm and stops at the completion of Day 38 (June 12th) at 2 pm.
>
> ► She must take another *ghusl* when the blood stops at the completion of Day 38 (June 12th).

12.7 WORSHIP PERFORMED DURING GAPS OF PURITY IN PDL

If bleeding returns within the possible days of lochia, it is considered lochia in addition to the time span in which no blood was seen.

Bleeding does not need to be continuous for it to be classified as lochia. Thus, all the prayers and fasts that she performed during the days without blood are invalid in retrospect.

☑ Allāh Most High will reward her for following His commandments, even if the prayers and fasts she performed are invalid in hindsight.

🔍 Observe what happens when bleeding returns in Diagram 12f.

Diagram 12f: Worship Performed After Bleeding Returns

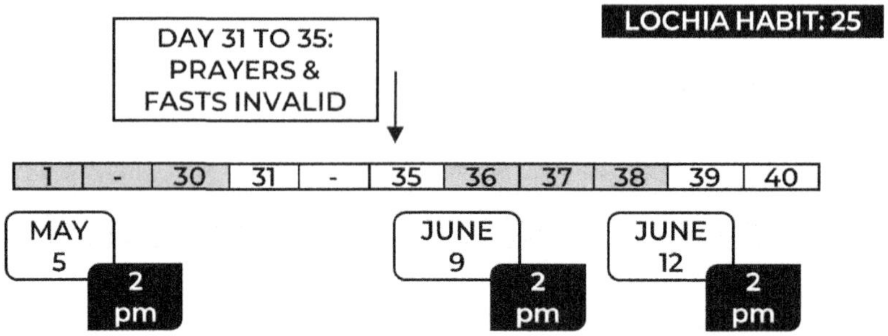

The prayers and fasts on Days 31 to 35 are invalid.

► She is not required to make up any of the prayers she performed on Days 31 to 35. The only exception is the performance of makeup prayers owed from previous years or vowed prayers since the debt to Allāh Most High was not lifted.

► She is required to make up any obligatory fasts performed on Days 31 to 35 as the fasts do not count in hindsight.

12.8 CHANGE IN THE HABIT

If the total bleeding does not exceed the lochia maximum of 960 hours for a woman with a lochia habit, then what she sees becomes her new habit.

This is upon the condition that a purity span of at least 15 complete days free of blood follows it and it ends outside the 40 days.

✅ A sound lochia only needs to be seen once for it to be taken as a habit.

🔍 Observe what her lochia habit becomes in Diagram 12g.

Diagram 12g: Change in Habit

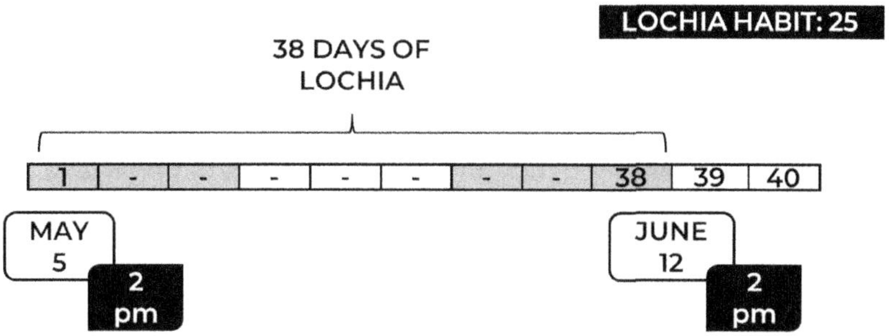

She sees 15 days free of blood after the bleeding stops at the completion of Day 38.

► Her lochia habit changes from 25 days to 38 compete days.

12.9 BLEEDING EXCEEDING THE LOCHIA MAXIMUM

When the lochia maximum of 960 hours is reached, it is obligatory to take a *ghusl* and begin praying, even if the bleeding continues. There can be no increase in the maximum time.

If the blood exceeds the lochia maximum of 960 hours, the woman must revise her situation.

➔ The details of what to do when bleeding exceeds the maximum are covered in Chapter 13.

POSSIBLE DAYS OF LOCHIA PROTOCOL

- After childbirth, a woman has 40 possible days (960 hours) to experience lochia.
- Whenever she sees blood during the possible days of lochia, she acts like a menstruating woman.
- Even if the bleeding exceeds her lochia habit, she continues to abide by the prohibitions.
- If the blood returns within the 40 days after having stopped, it takes the ruling of lochia.
- The gaps of purity during the 40 possible days of lochia are considered lochia in retrospect.
- A *ghusl* is obligatory when bleeding either stops within the 40 possible days or the lochia maximum of 40 complete days (960 hours) is reached.
- If the entire span of bleeding does not exceed the maximum of 960 hours, then what she sees becomes her new habit, as long as a purity span of at least 15 complete days free of blood follows it and it ends outside the 40 days.
- She cannot consider any bleeding beyond 40 complete days (960 hours) to be lochia. Once the maximum of 40 complete days (960 hours) is reached, lochia can be no more.

12.10 RULING FOR THE PURIFICATORY SHOWER (GHUSL)

A *ghusl* is obligatory to perform once blood stops during the possible days of lochia or the lochia maximum of 960 hours is reached.

> The *ghusl* is described in Sections 6.2 to 6.3.

12.11 GHUSL TIME & THE HABIT

With respect to the *ghusl* time and the habit:

❶ When bleeding ends before the lochia maximum of 960 hours, the *ghusl* time is **added** to the lochia habit.

❷ When bleeding ends at the lochia maximum of 960 hours, the *ghusl* time is **not** added to the lochia habit.

> ➔ When the *ghusl* time is added to the lochia habit, it affects many related rulings which are summarized in Table 6l.
>
> Observe a summary of this ruling in Chart 12h.

Chart 12h: Ghusl Time Added to the Habit

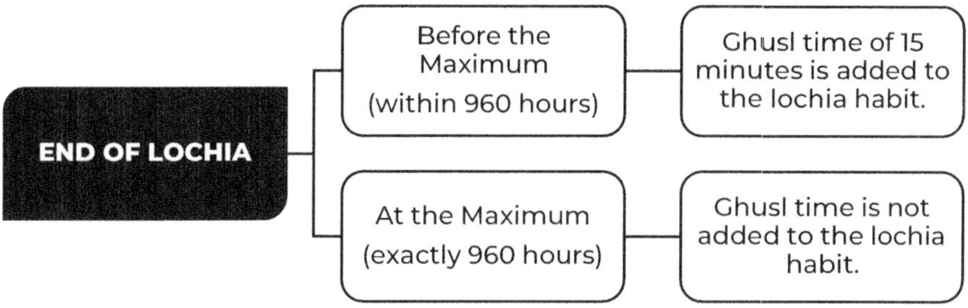
END OF LOCHIA
Before the Maximum (within 960 hours)
Ghusl time of 15 minutes is added to the lochia habit.
At the Maximum (exactly 960 hours)
Ghusl time is not added to the lochia habit.

12.12 LOCHIA BEGINNER & THE GHUSL TIME

Because a lochia beginner does not have a habit, if her bleeding stops before 40 days, she will follow the rulings related to a woman whose bleeding stops at/after the habit. The assumption is that her blood is sound, and the bleeding will not return after it stops.

However, it is advisable for her to take another *ghusl* at 40 days just in case the bleeding is not followed by a purity span of 15 days. This is similar to the concept of taking a precautionary *ghusl* when the bleeding stops before the habit. The precautionary *ghusl* is taken to preserve the validity of her prayers.

> ➔ The rulings related to bleeding stopping at or after the habit are summarized in Table 6l.

12.13 LOCHIA BEGINNER & THE HABIT

If the total bleeding does not exceed the lochia maximum of 960 hours, then what she sees becomes her lochia habit. This is upon the condition that a purity span of at least 15 complete days free of blood follows it, and the purity span ends outside the 40 days.

☑ She is no longer a lochia beginner.

> 🔍 Observe which days become her habit in Diagram 12i.

Diagram 12i: Lochia Beginner

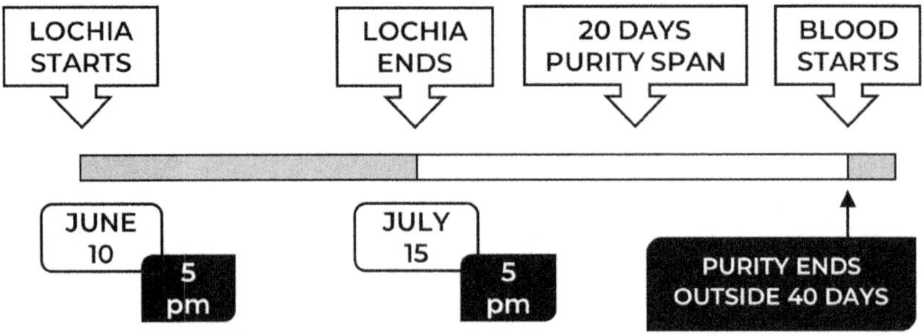

> A woman gives birth to her first baby on June 10th at 5 pm. She bleeds for 35 days. The blood is followed by 20 days of purity.

► Her possible days of lochia start when she gives birth on June 10th at 5 pm, and they end after 40 complete days (960 hours) on July 20th at 5 pm.

► When the blood stops at the completion of Day 35 (July 15th) at 5 pm she takes a *ghusl* and begins praying.

► Her lochia habit of 35 complete days is established. She is no longer a lochia beginner.

12.14 MENSTRUATION AFTER LOCHIA

After a woman's lochia ends, she must see a purity span of at least 15 complete days (360 hours) before any bleeding can be considered menstruation.

For many women, breastfeeding causes their hormones to fluctuate, and some may not see menstrual bleeding for an entire year after giving birth. Others experience abnormal bleeding and spotting.

If a woman is experiencing abnormal bleeding, her problem is resolved by using her menses and purity habits that she had from before her pregnancy.

It must be mentioned that the duration of her pregnancy does not become her purity habit, even if she did not see blood for that time. A purity habit is established with the days that occur between a menses and a menses or a lochia and a menses.

⚠ Pregnant women should store their calendar of menses dates in a secure place in case they need it after giving birth.

➔ The way the habits are used to resolve her issue is discussed in Section 13.6.

🔍 Observe the major differences between menstruation and lochia in Diagram 12j.

Table 12j: Differences Between Menstruation & Lochia

RULING	MENSES	LOCHIA
Minimum	3 complete days (72 hours)	No minimum
Maximum	10 complete days (240 hours)	40 complete days (960 hours)
Blood Stops Before Three Days	Make *wuḍū*ʾ	Take a *ghusl*
Precondition	Purity span of 15 days	Pregnancy
Separators	At least 15 complete days (360 hours) of purity need to separate between two menstruations	At least six months need to separate between two lochia
End of Post-Marital Waiting Period (*ʿidda*)	Completion of three menstruations	Giving birth

REVIEW QUESTIONS

1. How do the rulings related to the possible days of lochia differ from the rulings related to the possible days of menses?
2. What is the ruling for blood that exceeds the lochia habit within the possible days of lochia?
3. What is the ruling for blood that stops and starts within the possible days of lochia? What is the ruling for the worship performed in-between the two shows of blood?
4. What are the conditions for the bleeding after childbirth to become a woman's lochia habit?

Chapter 13

Blood Exceeding Forty Days

IN THIS CHAPTER

- ✧ Common misconceptions
- ✧ Possible days of lochia
- ✧ Rulings in retrospect
- ✧ Solving problems

Once bleeding exceeds 40 days, a woman cannot consider the excess blood to be lochia. However, there is a lot of confusion around this ruling. Thus, before explaining the rulings related to bleeding exceeding 40 days (960 hours), a few common misconceptions need to be busted.

Misconception #1: When bleeding exceeds 40 days (960 hours), a woman continues to refrain from praying because she is still bleeding.

> ➔ **Busted:** Once the lochia maximum is reached, a woman is obliged to take a *ghusl* and begin her obligatory worship – even if she is still bleeding. Lochia can be no more. This is the ruling regardless of whether the bleeding that exceeds the lochia maximum is spotting or a full flow.

Misconception #2: When bleeding exceeds 40 days (960 hours), a woman gives herself a habit of 40 days of lochia.

> ➔ **Busted:** This is only true for a lochia beginner, which is discussed in Section 13.3. For a woman with a lochia habit, when the bleeding exceeds 40 days, she must return to her lochia habit. She considers the days outside her lochia habit to be

abnormal uterine bleeding (*istiḥāḍa*). As discussed in Section 11.7, a woman with a habit cannot create a habit for herself. The habit is based upon what she experienced in the past.

Misconception #3: Any blood experienced after the 40 days is considered menstruation.

➔ **Busted:** A purity span of at least 15 complete days (360 hours) free of blood must separate between a lochia and a menses. When the bleeding exceeds 40 days, a woman must use her lochia, menses, and purity habits to determine when the expected time of menstruation begins.

13.1 RULINGS FOR POSSIBLE DAYS OF LOCHIA (PDL)

As for the rulings in the moment, the same principles discussed in Chapter 12 for the possible days of lochia apply. She follows the rulings for the possible days of lochia (PDL) because she cannot be certain that the bleeding will exceed the maximum until it happens.

Brief recap of the PDL rulings:

- Whenever a woman sees blood during the possible days of lochia, she considers it to be lochia.
- When the blood exceeds her lochia habit within the possible days of lochia, she continues to abide by the prohibitions.
- She must either wait for the blood to stop within the possible days of lochia or for the bleeding to reach the lochia maximum of 960 hours.

13.2 BLOOD REACHING THE MAXIMUM

When the lochia maximum of 960 hours is reached, she is obliged to take a *ghusl* and begin praying. There can be no increase in the maximum time.

13.3 RULING FOR A LOCHIA BEGINNER

When the lochia maximum is reached and the bleeding has not stopped, a lochia beginner is obliged to:

- ✧ Take a *ghusl* at 40 complete days (960 hours).
- ✧ Start praying.
- ✧ Make *wuḍū*ʾ for her prayers and not *ghusl*.
- ✧ Record her lochia habit as 40 complete days (960 hours).

☑ Her lochia habit of 40 complete days (960 hours) is established. She will use this habit for future births if necessary.

☑ She is no longer a lochia beginner.

> 🔍 Observe when the *ghusl* is taken in Diagram 13a.
>
> 🔍 Compare the difference in rulings for a lochia beginner and woman with a lochia habit in Table 13b.

Diagram 13a: Lochia Beginner

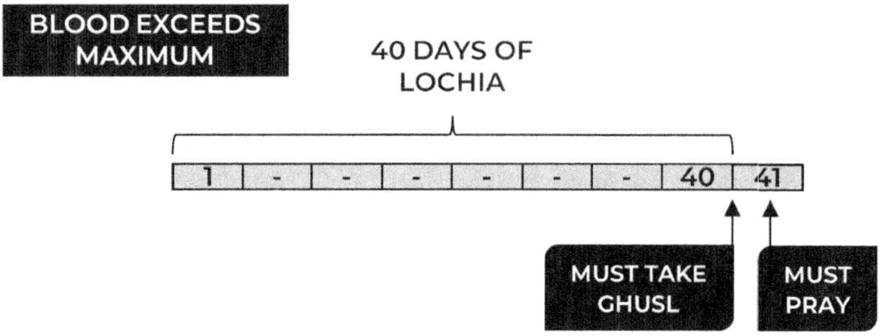

A woman gives birth to her first baby and the bleeding continues beyond 40 days.

► Even though she is still bleeding, she is obliged to take a *ghusl* at 960 hours and begin praying.

► She would not miss any prayers on Day 41 onwards because this bleeding is not lochia.

► She performs her prayers with *wuḍūʾ* and she does not take a *ghusl* for her prayers.

► If this situation occurred during *Ramaḍān*, she would begin fasting.

► She records her lochia habit as 40 complete days (960 hours).

Table 13b: Comparison Between a Beginner & Woman With a Habit

RULING	LOCHIA BEGINNER	WOMAN WITH A HABIT
Bleeding Does Not Exceed 960 Hours	Becomes her lochia habit. *	Becomes her lochia habit. *
Bleeding Exceeds 960 Hours	Given a lochia habit of 40 days (960 hours).	Returns to her lochia habit from a previous birth.

*Providing that a 15-day purity span that ends outside the 40 days follows it.

13.4 RULING FOR A WOMAN WITH A LOCHIA HABIT

When the lochia maximum is reached and the bleeding has not stopped, a woman with a lochia habit is obliged to:

- Take a *ghusl* at 40 complete days (960 hours).
- Start praying.

- ✧ Return to her lochia habit.
- ✧ Consider the blood seen outside the habit and beyond the maximum of 960 hours as abnormal bleeding.
- ✧ Make *wuḍū*ʾ for her prayers and not *ghusl*.
- ✧ Make up the days of missed prayers over her lochia habit.

Observe when the *ghusl* is taken in Diagram 13c.

Diagram 13c: Woman With a Lochia Habit

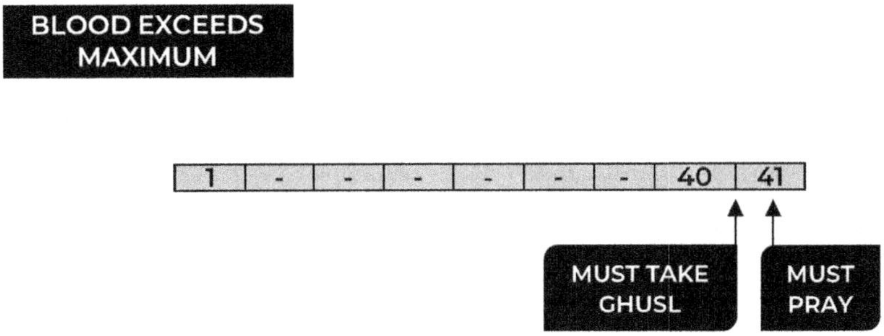

A woman has a lochia habit of 38 days. With her second baby, the bleeding continues beyond 40 days.

► Even though she is still bleeding, she is obliged to take a *ghusl* at 960 hours and begin praying.

► She would not miss any prayers on Day 41 onwards because this bleeding is not lochia.

► She performs her prayers with *wuḍū*ʾ and she does not take a *ghusl* for her prayers.

► If this situation occurred during *Ramaḍān*, she would begin fasting.

► Her lochia habit remains 38 days.

13.5 RETURNING TO THE LOCHIA HABIT

For a woman with a lochia habit, when her bleeding exceeds the maximum of 960 hours, her situation must be reevaluated using her lochia habit. The habit will determine which days are ruled as lochia or purity.

Observe which days are considered lochia in Diagram 13d.

Diagram 13d: Returning to Lochia Habit

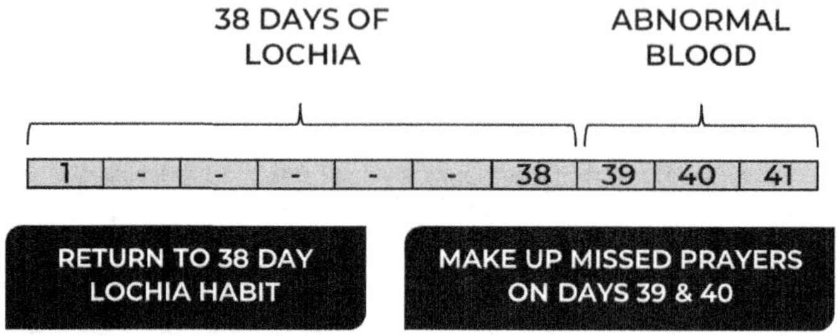

Building on the scenario in Diagram 13c, her situation will be reevaluated using her habit.

► According to her lochia habit, she will consider the first 38 days of bleeding to be lochia. This is the ruling regardless of whether the bleeding was spotting or a full flow.

► Days 39 and 40 of the bleeding are in excess of her 38-day lochia habit. In retrospect, they are no longer ruled as lochia and are deemed to be days of legal purity.

► She must make up the obligatory (*farḍ*) and *witr* prayers missed on days 39 and 40. She is not sinful for missing these prayers, but rather she owes their performance in retrospect.

► The rulings for performing worship during abnormal uterine bleeding (*istiḥāḍa*) apply to her, which are discussed in Chapter 17.

13.6 MENSTRUATION AFTER LOCHIA

A purity span of at least 15 complete days (360 hours) must separate between a woman's lochia and her next menses. When bleeding exceeds the lochia maximum, a woman will use her purity and menses habits from before pregnancy to determine when the expected time of menstruation will begin.

☑ This ruling applies to the lochia beginner and a woman with a lochia habit.

⚠ If she does not remember her habits, she estimates to the best of her ability and uses those dates as her habits.

🔍 Observe which days are considered menstruation in Diagram 13e.

Diagram 13e: Menstruation After Lochia

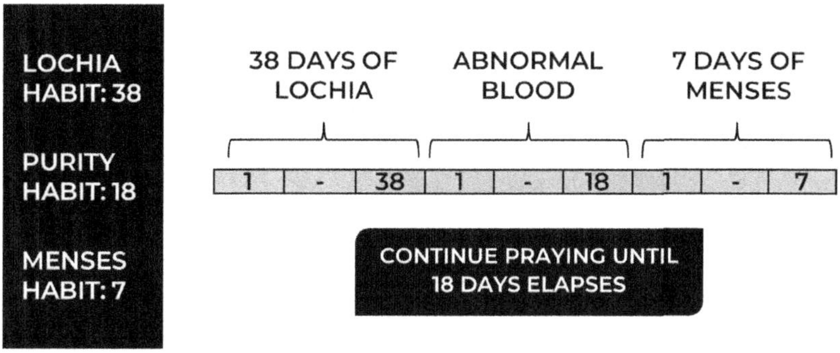

After her 38-day lochia habit, she continues to bleed for 25 days. Before pregnancy, her purity habit was 18 days, and her menses habit was 7 days.

► She is obliged to wait until 18 days elapses after her 38-day lochia habit before she can consider the bleeding to be menses.

► The 7 days following the 18-day purity habit are menses.

The scenarios given are basic and they are specifically designed to demonstrate certain points. In real life, when a woman experiences abnormal bleeding, determining which days are lochia or menstruation may not be as simple.

Women should double check their situation with a teacher. In addition, if they are able, they should dedicate the time and effort to study these rulings in detail.

REVIEW QUESTIONS

1. What does a lochia beginner do if her bleeding exceeds the maximum? What is her habit?
2. What does a woman with a lochia habit do if her bleeding exceeds the maximum? What is her habit?

Chapter 14

Miscarriages

IN THIS CHAPTER

- Types of miscarriages
- Ruling of blood before the miscarriage
- Ruling of blood after the miscarriage
- Burial rites

Miscarrying a child is a difficult test to bear in this world. Out of His mercy and love for His creation, Allāh Most High promises an immense reward for the woman who accepts her trial with patience: a ticket to Paradise.

> The Prophet ﷺ said, "By the One in whose hand is my soul, the miscarried fetus will carry its mother by its umbilical cord into Paradise, if she was seeking its reward."
>
> (*Aḥmad*, 22090; *ibn Mājah*, 1609)

Through the example of the Prophet ﷺ, believers learn how to practically deal with the loss of a child. He ﷺ lost three of his sons before they reached the age of two, and he ﷺ buried three of his adult daughters. He ﷺ lost six out of his seven children during his lifetime.

Sadness and grief are normal emotions to feel. When the Prophet Muḥammad ﷺ was burying his son Ibrāhīm رضي الله عنه, he stood over his son's grave weeping. One of the Companions رضي الله عنه questioned the Prophet's ﷺ crying. He ﷺ responded, "Verily, the eyes shed tears and the heart is grieved, but we will not say anything except what is pleasing to our Lord. We are saddened by your departure, O Ibrāhīm." (*Bukhārī*, 1303)

14.1 TYPES OF MISCARRIAGES

There are two types of miscarriages:

- The miscarriage of a developed fetus.
- The miscarriage of an undeveloped embryo.

The distinguishing factor between the two types of miscarriages is how far the baby developed.

14.2 DEFINITION OF A DEVELOPED FETUS

If what is miscarried possesses a discernible human feature, then it is a miscarriage of a developed fetus. Examples of a discernible human feature are a finger, a toe, or a nail.

> ☑ The baby does not need to be completely formed to be ruled as a developed fetus.

14.3 DEFINITION OF AN UNDEVELOPED EMBRYO

If what is miscarried has no discernible features, then it is a miscarriage of an undeveloped embryo. Examples of an undeveloped embryo are a form that resembles a chewed-up clump of flesh or a blood clot.

14.4 DEVELOPMENT BY NUMBER OF MONTHS OR WEEKS

Women often ask for a weekly time range to differentiate between the two types of miscarriages. The truth is that the scholars do not mention a time range.

Each woman's situation will differ, and for many miscarriages, the baby stopped developing at an earlier stage. For example, a woman could have been pregnant for three months, but the baby really stopped developing at 6 weeks. Even though she was pregnant for a full trimester, what she miscarries will be ruled as an undeveloped embryo.

Thus, a woman cannot judge which type of miscarriage she had based upon how many weeks she was pregnant or through the images of fetal development that she sees on the internet. Instead, she must understand how far along the baby developed by either seeing what she miscarried or asking her doctor.

In general, a miscarriage before eight weeks will be ruled as an undeveloped embryo, and a miscarriage after 120 days will be ruled as lochia. The uncertainty is usually in-between this time, from nine weeks to sixteen weeks.

14.5 BLOOD DURING PREGNANCY

As discussed in Sections 10.1 to 10.3, bleeding during pregnancy is considered abnormal uterine bleeding (*istiḥāḍa*). Therefore, a pregnant woman is still obliged to pray when she sees any blood.

However, because bleeding during pregnancy is not normal, she should keep track of the blood she sees. Depending on what she miscarries, the ruling can change in retrospect.

☑ Whenever a miscarriage occurs, a woman either maintains her pregnancy status or loses it.

SIGNS OF A MISCARRAIGE

Most miscarriages occur before the twelfth week of pregnancy, which is during the first trimester.

Signs and symptoms of a miscarriage might include:

- Vaginal spotting or bleeding.
- Pain or cramping in the abdomen or lower back.
- Fluid or tissue passing from the vagina.
- No longer feeling pregnancy symptoms.

If a pregnant woman experiences vaginal bleeding, it is vital that she contact her doctor immediately.

Nevertheless, she should stay hopeful and positive. Many women who have vaginal spotting or bleeding in their first trimester go on to have successful pregnancies.

14.6 MISCARRIAGE OF A DEVELOPED FETUS

With the miscarriage of a developed fetus, the woman's pregnancy status is maintained.

- ✧ Consequently, any blood she saw during her pregnancy is still ruled as abnormal bleeding. A pregnant woman cannot menstruate.
- ✧ After the exiting of the developed fetus, the vaginal blood is ruled as lochia, even if the child was not a fully formed human being.

> 🔍 Observe which days are considered lochia in Diagram 14a.

Diagram 14a: Miscarriage of a Developed Fetus

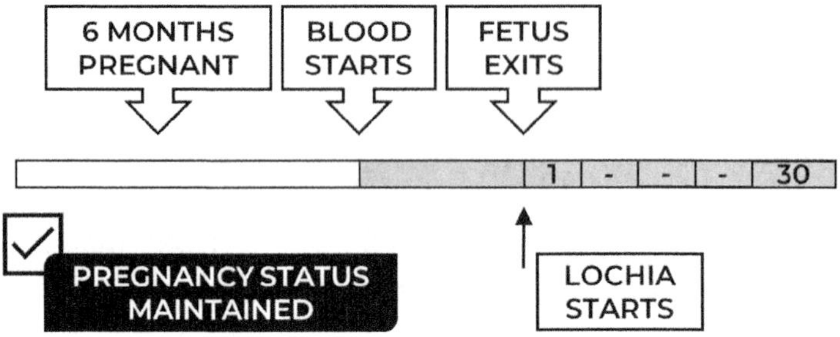

A woman is pregnant for 6 months. She bleeds for 10 days, and then she miscarries a developed fetus. She bleeds for 30 days thereafter.

► While she is pregnant, any blood seen is abnormal bleeding.

► When a woman miscarries a developed fetus, her pregnancy status is maintained.

► The 10 days of blood before the miscarriage is still ruled as abnormal bleeding.

► The vaginal blood seen after the exiting of the baby is considered lochia (*nifās*).

14.7 BURIAL RULINGS FOR A DEVELOPED FETUS

With respect to the burial, the fetus is not shrouded and there is no funeral prayer. The child is named, washed, wrapped in a clean cloth, and buried.

☑ Only a child who breathed in this world will have a funeral prayer (*janāza*) performed.

14.8 MISCARRIAGE & BURIAL OF A STILL BIRTH

A still birth is when a child is born dead. The vaginal blood after the exiting of the baby is always considered lochia (*nifās*). The burial rulings are the same as in Section 14.7 for a developed fetus.

☑ Only a child who breathed in this world will have a funeral prayer (*janāza*) performed.

> The Prophet ﷺ said, "When a servant's child dies, Allāh Most High asks His angels, 'Have you taken the life of the child of My slave?' They reply in the affirmative. He then asks, 'Have you taken the fruit of his heart?' They reply in the affirmative. Thereupon He asks, 'What has My slave said?' They say: 'He praised You and said: Verily, we belong to Allāh and to Him we shall return.' Allāh says: 'Build a house for My slave in Paradise and name it the House of Praise.'"
>
> (*Tirmidhī*, 1021)

14.9 MISCARRIAGE OF AN UNDEVELOPED EMBRYO

With the miscarriage of an undeveloped embryo, the woman's pregnancy status is lost.

- ✧ Consequently, any blood she saw during pregnancy is reevaluated using her menses and purity habits.

✧ Whatever blood fell into her time of menses is ruled as menstruation and whatever blood fell into her time of purity is ruled as abnormal bleeding (*istiḥāḍa*).

⚠ This is yet another reason why it is obligatory to record one's habits, as well as any bleeding seen during pregnancy.

🔍 Observe what happens with the miscarriage of an undeveloped embryo in Diagram 14b.

Diagram 14b: Miscarriage of an Undeveloped Embryo

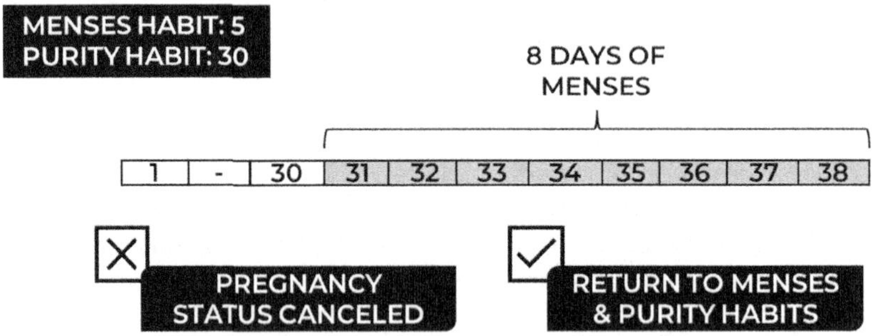

A woman has a purity habit of 30 days and a menses habit of 5 days. She becomes pregnant. After a month, on Day 31 she starts to bleed. On Day 36, she miscarries and bleeds for 3 days.

▶ While she is pregnant, the blood she sees on Days 31, 32, 33, 34, and 35 is abnormal bleeding because she is still pregnant.

▶ When she miscarries an undeveloped embryo on Day 36, her pregnancy status is lost.

▶ The blood after the miscarriage – as well as the blood before the miscarriage – will be reevaluated according to her habits.

► The 5 days of abnormal bleeding are deemed menses because it is within her menstrual place. The next 3 days after the miscarriage are also menses because it is within the possible days of menses.

► If a purity span of at least 15 complete days (360 hours) follows this bleeding, her menses habit changes to 8 complete days.

NEVER LOSE HOPE

Recite these supplications for righteous children.

رَبِّ لَا تَذَرْنِى فَرْدًا وَأَنتَ خَيرُ الْوٰرِثِينَ

Rabbi lā tadharnī fardan wa anta khayru'l wārithīn

"My Lord! Do not leave me childless, and You are the Best of Inheritors."

(*al-Anbiyā'*, 21:89)

رَبِّ هَبْ لِي مِنَ الصَّالِحِينَ

Rabbi hab lī minaṣ-ṣāliḥīn

"My Lord! Bless me with righteous offspring."

(*aṣ-Ṣaffāt*, 37:100)

رَبِّ هَبْ لِي مِن لَدُنْكَ ذُرِّيَّةً طَيِّبَةً إِنَّكَ سَمِيعُ الدُّعَاءِ

Rabbi hab lī mil ladunka dhurriyyatan ṭayyibatan innaka samīʿud-duʿā'

"My Lord, grant me from Yourself righteous offspring. Indeed, You are the Hearer of supplication."

(*Āli ʿImrān*, 3:38)

14.10 BURIAL RULINGS FOR AN UNDEVELOPED EMBRYO

With respect to the burial, the embryo is not shrouded and there is no funeral prayer (*janāza*).

The embryo, amniotic sack, umbilical cord, and placenta are wrapped in a cloth and buried. The embryo is not named or washed.

> 🔍 Compare the rulings between an undeveloped embryo and a developed fetus in Table 14c.

Table 14c: Summary of Miscarriage Rulings

MISCARRIAGE	UNDEVELOPED EMBRYO *(no discernible features)*	DEVELOPED FETUS *(discernible feature)*
Blood During Pregnancy	Abnormal bleeding	Abnormal bleeding
After Baby Exits – Pregnancy Status	Lost	Remains
After Baby Exits – Blood Before Exiting	Return to habits	Abnormal bleeding
After Baby Exits – Blood After Exiting	Return to habits	Lochia
Named & Washed	No	Yes
Shrouded & Funeral Prayer	No	No
Wrapped & Buried	Yes	Yes

14.11 POST-MARITAL WAITING PERIOD

If a woman is divorced while she is pregnant, her post-marital waiting period (ʿ*idda*) ends when she miscarries a developed fetus or has a still birth.

If she miscarries an undeveloped embryo, her post-marital waiting period (ʿ*idda*) ends with the completion of three menstrual cycles.

REVIEW QUESTIONS

1. What are the different types of miscarriages? Define each.
2. What is a discernible human feature? Give an example.
3. How do the rulings differ for each miscarriage?

PART FOUR:
Purity Rulings

Verily Allāh loves
those who always
turn to Him in
repentance and
those who purify
themselves

Qurʾān
2:222

Chapter 15

The Sound Purity

IN THIS CHAPTER

- Types of purity spans
- Conditions of a sound purity
- How to establish a purity habit
- Examples of an unsound purity

Purity is an essential part of a believer's life, and Islam encourages purification at all possible levels.

> The Prophet ﷺ said, "Purity is half of faith."
>
> (*Muslim*, 223)

The beloved Prophet ﷺ emphasized physical purification, such that believers are instructed to keep their bodies and clothes clean from filth.

He ﷺ urged spiritual purification, exhorting Muslims to purify their hearts from the filth of polytheism, arrogance, and hypocrisy.

He ﷺ taught ritual purification, which is a requirement for certain acts of worship to be accepted like the prayer.

Once a woman's menstruation or lochia finishes and she takes her *ghusl*, she is now in a state of ritual purity. She must start performing her prayers again and fasting if it is *Ramaḍān*.

However, the rulings related to purity from menstruation or lochia entail more than beginning to pray again. Just like there are definitions and conditions for menstruation and lochia, so too are there for a purity span.

15.1 DEFINITION OF PURITY

The term purity span (*ṭuhr*) generally refers to a duration that is not considered menstruation or lochia. Therefore, the prohibitions related to menstruation and lochia do not apply.

> ☑ During her purity span, a woman can pray, fast, read the Qurʾān, touch the Qurʾān, have sexual intercourse, and the like.

15.2 NEED FOR A PURITY SPAN BETWEEN BLOODS

There is a need for a woman to experience a purity span after her menstrual bleeding ends. Otherwise, she cannot consider the next show of blood to be menstruation. The same applies to the bleeding that follows lochia.

> ☑ Sound bloods cannot occur back-to-back. Rather, a duration of purity must separate between them.

15.3 PURITY SPAN MINIMUM

The purity span must meet the stipulated minimum.

- **Between a menstruation and a menstruation:** A minimal duration of 15 complete days (360 hours) free of blood must occur for the second bleeding to be ruled as menstruation.
- **Between a lochia and a menstruation:** A minimal duration of 15 complete days (360 hours) free of blood must occur for the second bleeding to be ruled as menstruation.
- **Between a lochia and a lochia:** A minimal duration of six months must occur for the second bleeding to be ruled as lochia, as discussed in Section 11.6.

> ⚠ Even if a purity span of 15 days follows the bleeding, it does not automatically mean that the next blood is menstruation. It depends on the woman's habits. These principles are detailed in Chapter 18.

15.4 PURITY SPAN MAXIMUM

As for the maximum duration of purity, there is none. A purity span can technically last a lifetime.

15.5 SOUND PURITY VS. UNSOUND PURITY

Depending on its characteristics, the purity span can be classified into one of two main categories: a sound purity (*aṭ-ṭuhr aṣ-ṣaḥīḥ*) or an unsound purity (*aṭ-ṭuhr al-fāsid*).

- The **sound purity** (*aṭ-ṭuhr aṣ-ṣaḥīḥ*) is the only purity span that can be taken as a habit. It must meet three specific conditions, which are explained in Sections 15.6 to 15.10.
- The **unsound purity** (*aṭ-ṭuhr al-fāsid*) can never be taken as a habit because it fails to meet at least one of the conditions for a sound purity, which is noted in Sections 15.12 to 15.15.

> Compare the difference between a sound purity and unsound purity in Chart 15a.

Chart 15a: Sound Purity vs. Unsound Purity

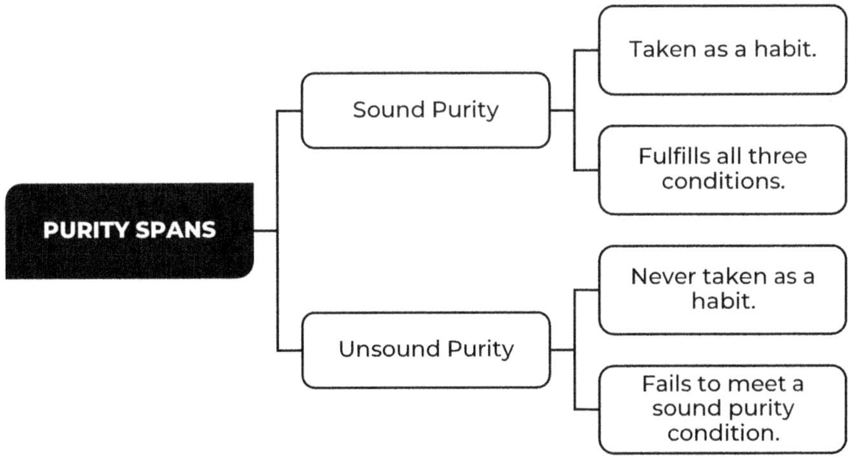
PURITY SPANS
Sound Purity
Taken as a habit.
Fulfills all three conditions.
Unsound Purity
Never taken as a habit.
Fails to meet a sound purity condition.

The purity habit is needed:

- To resolve a woman's situation whenever she experiences abnormal bleeding.
- To help a woman determine when she can stop praying if her bleeding starts before her expected time of menses, also known as early blood.

> ➔ Refer to Chapter 18 for the rulings related to the Early Blood Formula.

15.6 SOUND PURITY CONDITIONS

The sound purity (*aṭ-ṭuhr aṣ-ṣaḥīḥ*) has three conditions:

1. It lasts for a duration of at least 15 complete days (360 hours) or more.
2. It is free from blood during this entire span.
3. It occurs between two sound bloods.

☑ All three conditions must be met without exception.

15.7 FIRST CONDITION: AT LEAST 15 DAYS (360 HOURS) OR MORE

The purity span must reach a duration of at least 15 complete days (360 hours).

- A 'day' in the Sacred Law means a day and its night, which is 24 hours. Fifteen days of 24 hours equals 360 hours.
- The purity days will not be counted correctly if the 24-hour stipulation is overlooked.

⚠️ If the duration of purity is less than 15 complete days, the purity span is unsound, and it cannot be taken as a habit.

🔍 Compare how the days of purity are counted in Diagram 15b and Diagram 15c.

Diagram 15b: First Condition

JAN 1, 10 pm — ❌ **15 DAYS (360 HOUR) PURITY SPAN** — **JAN 15, 10 pm**

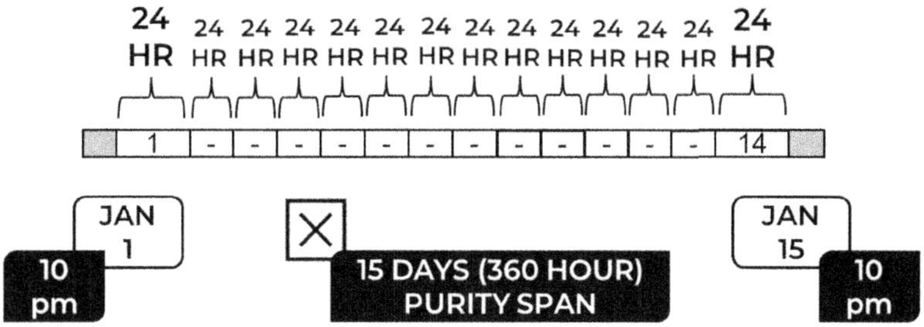

A woman's menstruation ends on January 1st at 10 pm and she begins bleeding again on January 15th at 10 pm.

▶ Outwardly, it looks like she saw 15 days of purity.

▶ If the days are counted by the hour, she has only seen 14 complete days, which does not fulfill the requirement for a sound purity.

Diagram 15c: First Condition

JAN 1, 10 pm — ✓ **15 DAYS (360 HOUR) PURITY SPAN** — **JAN 16, 10 pm**

Part Four: Purity Rulings | 227

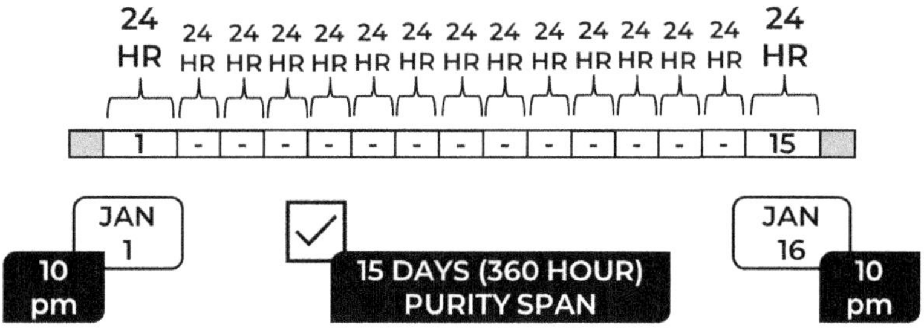

A woman's menstruation ends on January 1st at 10 pm and she begins bleeding again on January 16th at 10 pm.

▶ Outwardly, it looks like she saw 16 days of purity.

▶ If the days are counted by the hour, it equals 15 complete days (360 hours).

▶ Condition #1 for a sound purity is fulfilled.

15.8 SECOND CONDITION: FREE FROM BLOOD FOR THE ENTIRE SPAN

Blood cannot be present within any of the days of purity. From its beginning to its end, the purity span must be entirely free from all colored vaginal discharge, including the colors brown and fresh yellow.

⚠ If colored vaginal discharge is seen during any of its days, it makes the purity span unsound and it cannot be taken as a habit.

➔ The colors of blood are discussed in Chapter 3.

🔍 Observe which days are free from blood in Diagram 15d.

Diagram 15d: Second Condition

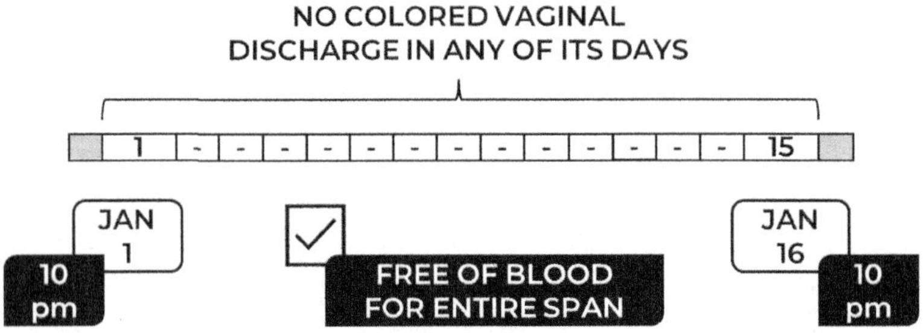

A woman's menstruation ends on January 1st at 10 pm and she begins bleeding again on January 16th at 10 pm.

► The purity span is from January 1st 10 pm to January 16th 10 pm.

► There is no occurrence of colored vaginal discharge during any of the days of purity.

► Condition #2 for a sound purity is fulfilled.

15.9 THIRD CONDITION: SITUATED BETWEEN TWO SOUND BLOODS

On each end of the purity, there must be a sound blood. This can happen in a few ways:

- ✧ The purity span occurs between a menses and a menses.
- ✧ The purity span occurs between a lochia and a menses.

⚠ If the purity span does not occur between two sound bloods, it makes the purity span unsound and it cannot be taken as a habit.

🔍 Observe which types of blood are on each end of the purity span in Diagram 15e.

Diagram 15e: Third Condition

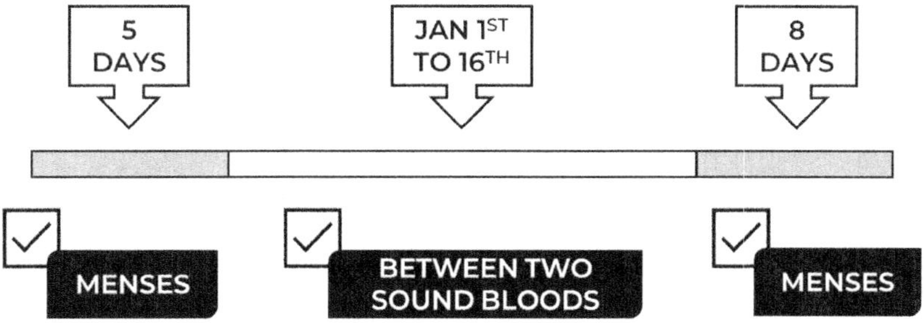

A woman's menstruation of 5 days ends on January 1st at 10 pm. She begins bleeding again on January 16th at 10 pm for 8 days.

► The purity span is from January 1st 10 pm to January 16th 10 pm.

► The blood preceding the purity span is ruled as 5 days of menstruation, and the blood following the purity span is ruled as 8 days of menstruation. Both are sound bloods.

► Condition #3 for a sound purity is fulfilled.

ESTABLISHING A PURITY HABIT

- Most recent sound purity a woman saw.
- Purity span is not less than 15 days (360 hours).
- Purity span is free from blood for the entire duration.
- Purity span occurs between a menses and a menses, or between a lochia and a menses.
- Only need to see it once to become a habit.
- Obliged to record it.

15.10 ESTABLISHING A PURITY HABIT

If a purity span abides by the definition and conditions of the sound purity (*aṭ-ṭuhr aṣ-ṣaḥīḥ*), it becomes a woman's purity habit.

- ✧ A sound purity only needs to be seen once for it to become a habit.
- ✧ The most recent sound purity will be used as her habit.

⚠ A woman cannot make up a habit for herself. Rather, she must physically see it occur within her life.

🔍 In Diagrams 15c to 15e, the purity span meets all three conditions for a sound purity. Therefore, it will become the purity habit.

15.11 RECORDING THE PURITY HABIT

It is obligatory upon every woman to record her purity habit.

During the purity span (*ṭuhr*), a woman should take note of the following:

- ✧ The number of purity days that she sees before her next bleeding begins.
- ✧ Any show of colored discharge, even if it is spotting or starts before her expected time of menstruation.
- ✧ Whether the purity span meets all the conditions for a sound purity and can be taken as a habit.

USE A MISWĀK

Use the *miswāk* to freshen the mouth.

SHOWER

Take a *ghusl* every Friday to clean the body.

CLIP NAILS

Trim fingernails and toenails once a week.

REMOVE HAIR

Remove armpit and pubic hair once a week.

PURITY HABITS FROM THE SUNNA

Based on the habits learned from the *sunna*, it is best to take a *ghusl*, clip one's nails, and remove armpit and pubic hair once a week, with preference given to Friday. If this is not possible, then these actions are performed every 15 days. It is sinful to leave them for more than 40 days. Any method used for hair removal is permissible, such as shaving, waxing, or creams, providing that it does not cause harm to the body. The *sunna* for removing hair under the arms is achieved by plucking, although shaving is acceptable too.

15.12 TYPES OF UNSOUND PURITY

Whenever a purity span fails to fulfill one of the sound purity's conditions, it is automatically classified as an unsound purity (*aṭ-ṭuhr al-fāsid*). An unsound purity cannot be taken as a habit.

There are three types of unsound purity. Their technical terms are:

- ✧ An incomplete purity (*aṭ-ṭuhr an-nāqiṣ*)
- ✧ An unsound complete purity (*aṭ-ṭuhr at-tāmm al-fāsid*)
- ✧ An intervening purity (*aṭ-ṭuhr al-mutakhallil*)

The consequences for seeing an unsound purity will be different for each type, and the rulings are dependent upon the woman's habits and unique situation.

> ➔ Sections 15.13 to 15.15 describe each type of unsound purity with a diagram.

15.13 INCOMPLETE PURITY

An incomplete purity (*aṭ-ṭuhr an-nāqiṣ*) is a purity span that is less than 15 complete days (360 hours).

☑ It is an unsound purity because it does not meet Condition #1 of a sound purity.

> ⚠ Whenever an unsound purity is experienced, a woman needs to reevaluate her situation using her habits.
>
> ➔ Section 20.19 demonstrates what can possibly occur when an incomplete purity is experienced.
>
> 🔍 Observe an example of an incomplete purity in Diagram 15f.

Diagram 15f: Incomplete Purity

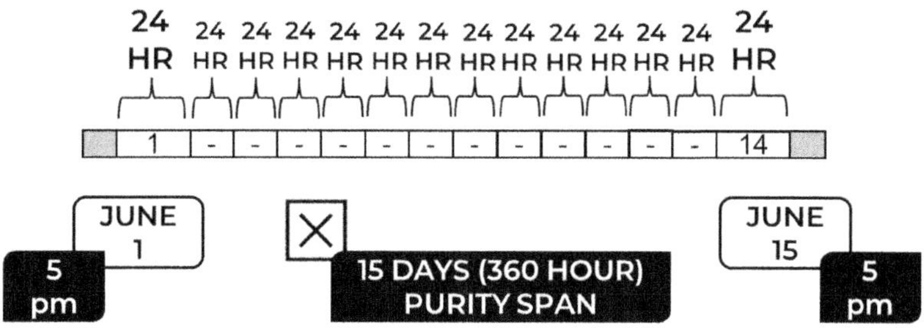

A woman's menstruation ends on June 1st at 5 pm and she begins bleeding again on June 15th at 5 pm.

► The purity span is from June 1st 5 pm to June 15th 5 pm.

► The purity span is less than 15 complete days (360 hours).

► The purity span is unsound.

15.14 UNSOUND COMPLETE PURITY

A complete purity (*aṭ-ṭuhr at-tāmm*) is a general term used for any purity span that is 15 complete days (360 hours) or more. A complete purity could be part of a sound purity span or an unsound purity span.

A **sound complete purity** is a purity span of 15 complete days (360 hours) or more that is free from blood for its entire duration, and it occurs between two sound bloods. An example of a sound complete purity was previously given in Diagram 15e.

An **unsound complete purity** (*aṭ-ṭuhr at-tāmm al-fāsid*) is a purity span of 15 complete days (360 hours) or more, but there is blood present in its beginning, middle, or end.

☑ It is an unsound purity because it does not meet Condition #2 of a sound purity.

⚠ Whenever an unsound purity is experienced, a woman needs to reevaluate her situation using her habits.

🔍 Observe an example of an unsound complete purity in Diagram 15g.

Diagram 15g: Unsound Complete Purity

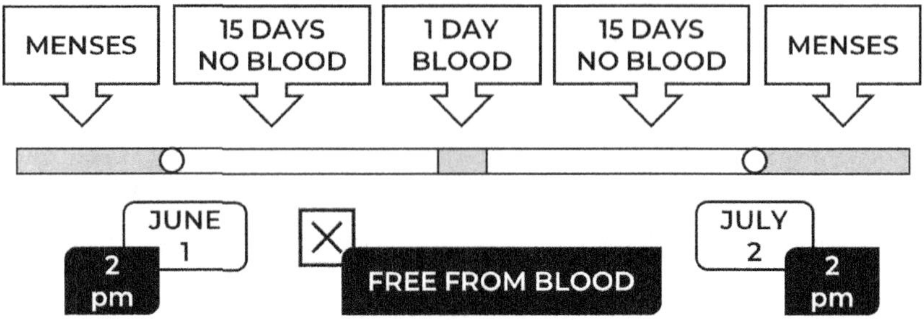

A woman's menstruation ends on June 1st at 2 pm. She begins bleeding again on June 16th at 2 pm. The blood lasts for a day, and it does not return until July 2nd at 2 pm.

► The entire purity span is from June 1st 2 pm to July 2nd 2 pm.

► The purity span is 31 days with one day of abnormal bleeding (*istiḥāḍa*) occurring on June 16th.

► The purity span is unsound.

For Diagram 15g, it is important to note that the duration from June 1st to June 16th is a complete purity of 15 days (360 hours). However, it is between a menses and one day of abnormal bleeding. According to Condition #3, a sound purity must be between two sound bloods, like a menses and a menses.

Similarly, the duration from June 17th to June July 2nd is a complete purity of 15 days (360 hours). However, it is between one day of abnormal bleeding and a menses. It does not meet Condition #3 of a sound purity.

Between the two menstruations, the purity span from June 1st to July 2nd is a complete purity of more than 15 days, but one day of blood occurs in the middle of it. The purity span is unsound, and the 31 days cannot be taken as a habit.

15.15 INTERVENING PURITY

An intervening purity (*aṭ-ṭuhr al-mutakhallil*) is a purity span between two shows of blood during the 10 possible days of menses or the 40 possible days of lochia that follow childbirth.

☑ It is an unsound purity because it does not meet Condition #3 of a sound purity.

⚠ Whenever an unsound purity is experienced, a woman needs to reevaluate her situation using her habits.

➔ Section 20.19 demonstrates what can possibly occur when an intervening purity is experienced.

Observe an example of an intervening purity in Diagram 15h.

Diagram 15h: Intervening Purity

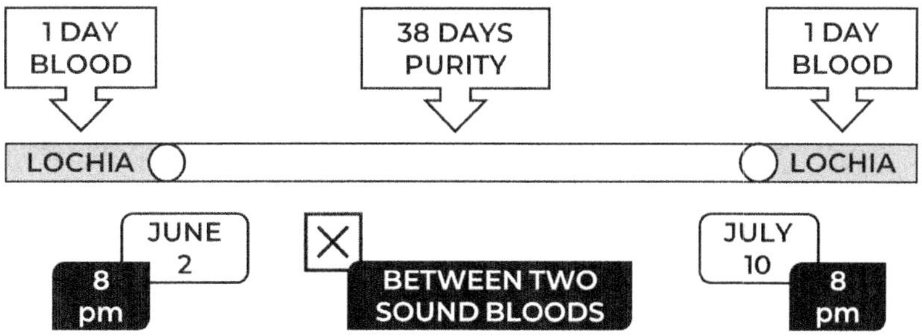

A woman's sees one day of blood on June 1st at 8 pm after giving birth and it stops on June 2nd at 8 pm. The blood returns on July 10th at 8 pm and lasts for one day.

▶ The possible days of lochia are from June 1st 8 pm to July 11th 8 pm.

▶ The purity span is from June 2nd 8 pm to July 10th 8 pm.

▶ The purity span is 38 days, but it is between two shows of blood during the 40 possible days of lochia. The entire purity span, along with the first and last day of blood, is ruled as one lochia.

▶ The purity span is unsound.

15.16 BLEEDING DURING PURITY

Any blood seen during a woman's purity span is unsound, and it cannot be taken as a menses or lochia habit. This blood is known as abnormal uterine bleeding (*istiḥāḍa*).

A woman must continue to perform her obligatory worship during this time, even though she is seeing blood.

➔ The rulings related to abnormal uterine bleeding (*istiḥāḍa*) are explained in Chapter 16.

🔍 View an example of unsound blood occurring during a purity span in Diagram 15g.

REVIEW QUESTIONS

1. What is a purity span?
2. How many days of purity must separate between a menses and a menses? A lochia and a menses?
3. What are the conditions of a sound purity?
4. What is the maximum time limit for a purity span?

Chapter 16

Abnormal Uterine Bleeding (*Istiḥāḍa*)

IN THIS CHAPTER

- ✧ Definition of abnormal uterine bleeding
- ✧ Examples of abnormal uterine bleeding
- ✧ Permitted actions
- ✧ Intimacy with abnormal bleeding

Umm Ḥabība رضي الله عنها was the sister of Zaynab bint Jaḥsh رضي الله عنها, the wife of the Prophet ﷺ. She was married to ʿAbdur Raḥmān ibn ʿAwf رضي الله عنه, one of the ten companions promised Paradise.

It is related that Umm Ḥabība رضي الله عنها experienced abnormal uterine bleeding (*istiḥāḍa*) for seven years. The Mother of the Believers ʿĀʾisha رضي الله عنها mentioned, "I saw her washtub full of blood." In another *ḥadīth*, ʿĀʾisha رضي الله عنها says Umm Ḥabība رضي الله عنها took a *ghusl* in her sister's washtub "...till the redness of the blood overcame the water." (*Muslim*, 334)

When Umm Ḥabība رضي الله عنها asked the Messenger of Allāh ﷺ about her bleeding, he ﷺ said to her:

> "Wait (and act like a menstruating woman) for the length of time that your menses used to prevent you. Thereafter, take a purificatory shower (*ghusl*) and pray."
>
> (*Muslim*, 334)

In several *aḥādīth*, the Prophet ﷺ conveys a similar message. He teaches women that when they experience abnormal bleeding, the bleeding that falls into the time of a woman's habit is menstruation, whereas any bleeding seen outside of that time is not menstruation. Moreover, during the days of abnormal bleeding, a woman must pray despite the presence of blood.

In another version, the Prophet ﷺ explained to Umm Ḥabība ؓ that abnormal bleeding "…is not menstruation, but rather it is bleeding from a (ruptured) vein (ʿirq)." (*Muslim*, 334) Scholars clarify that the meaning of the *ḥadīth* is that abnormal bleeding is not the sound bleeding that a woman sees when the uterine lining sheds as menstruation. Instead, it is from a different place in the vagina or due to another reason.

In an alternative report, it explicitly mentions that ʿAbdur Raḥmān ibn ʿAwf ؓ would have intercourse with Umm Ḥabība ؓ while she was experiencing abnormal bleeding. (*Abū Dāwūd*, 309) This is an additional proof that the prohibitions related to a menstruating woman do not apply.

Even some of the Prophet's wives experienced abnormal bleeding. ʿĀʾisha ؓ said:

> "One of the wives of Allāh's Messenger ﷺ joined him in the spiritual retreat (*ʿitikāf*) and she noticed blood and yellowish discharge. She put a dish under her when she prayed."
>
> (*Bukhārī*, 310)

Thus, abnormal uterine bleeding (*istiḥāḍa*) is something that any woman can experience, and women should not become stressed out when they see it.

However, some women will have more serious situations that may require medical attention. Nonetheless, this circumstance can be a means for obtaining reward if the woman with abnormal bleeding handles her struggle with the right attitude.

The female Companions ؓ confronted their trials with grace. They remained firm in their faith and did whatever it took to worship Allāh Most High in every situation He placed them, no matter how difficult.

16.1 DEFINITION OF ABNORMAL UTERINE BLEEDING

Abnormal uterine bleeding (*istiḥāḍa*) is any colored vaginal discharge that is not ruled as menstruation or lochia. It is unsound blood, and it can never be taken as a habit.

- It can be any color, whether it be red, brown, or fresh yellow.
- It can be spotting or a constant flow.
- It can be seen at any time within the month.

16.2 EXAMPLES OF ABNORMAL BLEEDING

Examples of abnormal uterine bleeding (*istiḥāḍa*) are:

- Blood seen by a girl who is less than 9 lunar years of age (approximately 8 solar years and 9 months).
- Blood that does not reach the menstrual minimum of 3 complete days (72 hours) within the possible days of menses. Refer to Chapters 4 and 5.
- Blood that exceeds 10 complete days (240 hours) for a menstrual beginner.
- Blood that exceeds the menses habit and 10 complete days (240 hours). Refer to Chapter 7.
- Blood seen during pregnancy. Refer to Chapter 10.
- Blood that exceeds 40 complete days (960 hours) for lochia beginners. Refer to Chapter 13.
- Blood that exceeds the lochia habit and 40 complete days (960 hours) for a woman with a habit. Refer to Chapter 13.
- Blood seen by a menopausal woman who is at least 55 lunar years (approximately 53 solar years and 4 months) that is not black, red, or like her premenopausal period. Refer to Chapter 19.

16.3 ALL FORMS OF WORSHIP PERMITTED

The prohibitions that apply to a woman in a state of menstruation and lochia do not apply to a woman who is experiencing abnormal bleeding. Rather, she is required to carry out her obligatory worship despite the presence of blood.

- She is required to pray her obligatory (*farḍ*) and *witr* prayers. All prayers must be performed with *wuḍūʾ*.
- She must fast if it is *Ramaḍān*.
- She is permitted to pray *sunna/nafl* prayers, fast *sunna/nafl* fasts, recite the Qurʾān, directly touch the Qurʾān with *wuḍūʾ*, enter a mosque, and perform *ṭawāf* with *wuḍūʾ*.

16.4 PRAYING WHILE BLEEDING

A woman is only obliged to make *wuḍūʾ* when abnormal bleeding exits and not *ghusl*. The blood is filthy (*najis*) and its presence on the clothes or body could affect the validity of her prayers.

> ➔ The detailed rulings related to how to pray with abnormal bleeding are discussed in Chapter 17.

16.5 PRAYING WITH BLOOD ON CLOTHES

If a woman prays with a spot of blood on her clothes or body that is the size of a *dirham* (about five centimeters in diameter), it is slightly disliked (*makrūh tanzīhān*). Thus, it is recommended to remove the blood before praying – although the prayer is valid if it is not removed.

If a woman prays with more than this amount on her clothes or body, and she has the means to remove it, the prayer is not valid.

> ➔ An exception may apply for a woman who is following the Excused Person's Rulings. See Section 17.13.

16.6 HOW TO REMOVE BLOOD FROM CLOTHES

To purify clothes soiled with blood, the soiled area must be washed with water until the body of the blood is removed. If this is achieved through one washing under running water, it is sufficient.

- Using soap is not a condition.
- Stains that remain after the washing are excused.

Using a washing machine:

Washing machines can be used to clean clothes soiled with blood. However, it is best to remove the body of blood first. To do so, one washes the soiled area under running water before mixing the garment with other clothes in the washing machine.

If one did not purify the clothes beforehand and washed all the clothes together in a washing machine, then if they come out free of any traces of filth, one can assume that they are ritually pure. However, contemporary scholars state that it is still best to wash the clothes in three cycles of water.

16.7 INTIMACY DURING ABNORMAL BLEEDING

It is permissible to engage in sexual intercourse during abnormal bleeding no matter how heavy the flow.

Sex with abnormal bleeding:

If a woman's flow is very heavy, it may feel strange and contradictory to engage in sexual intimacy. Therefore, a woman in this situation must bear in mind that her aim should be to keep her marriage happy for the sake of Allāh Most High. An active sex life is a fundamental component of a good marriage.

Consequently, she should update her husband about her abnormal bleeding issues and discuss with him what the ideal solution is for their sex life, especially if it is a recurring situation.

He may not be bothered by the bleeding, and this could ease her concerns. Conversely, they may agree to resort to other methods of intimacy, like foreplay and the like. Potentially, he could wear a condom if there are concerns about hygiene.

What is important is that the couple unite upon how to handle this issue, and they do not allow it to become a reason for marital discord.

16.8 COMPARISON TO MENSTRUATION & LOCHIA

During the days of menstruation and lochia, a woman is not permitted to engage in certain actions. However, these prohibitions do not apply to abnormal uterine bleeding (*istiḥāḍa*).

> Compare the rulings concerning the three types of blood that a woman can experience in Table 16a.

Table 16a: Comparison Between Different Types of Blood

ACTION	MENSES & LOCHIA	ABNORMAL BLEEDING
Obligatory Prayers	Unlawful	Obligatory with *wuḍūʾ*
Obligatory Fasts	Unlawful	Obligatory
***Sunna / Nafl* Prayers**	Unlawful	Permissible with *wuḍūʾ*
***Sunna / Nafl* Fasts**	Unlawful	Permissible
Touching the Qurʾān	Unlawful	Permissible with *wuḍūʾ*
Reciting the Qurʾān	Unlawful	Permissible
Entering the Mosque	Unlawful	Permissible
Making *Ṭawāf*	Unlawful	Permissible with *wuḍūʾ*
Marital Relations	Unlawful	Permissible
Divorce	Unlawful	Permissible

MAKING SENSE OF ABNORMAL BLEEDING

Medically, vaginal bleeding is considered abnormal when:

- Bleeding is heavy such that it interferes with a woman's life.
- Bleeding or spotting occurs between periods.
- Bleeding occurs during or after sex.
- Periods are irregular or missed.

Recurring abnormal uterine bleeding can be indicative of an underlying hormonal imbalance or a more serious issue. Therefore, a woman in this situation should seek help from a qualified doctor or specialist concerning how to interpret her abnormal bleeding.

Questions to ask a doctor:

- What is the likely cause of my abnormal bleeding?
- Is it due to fibroids, endometriosis, polycystic ovary syndrome (PCOS), or a thyroid imbalance?
- Is my condition serious?
- Am I at risk for any other health problems?
- Will I be able to conceive?
- Based on the cause, what treatment options do you recommend?
- Are there natural ways to heal my issue without the use of medication?

See Section 20.20 for a comprehensive list of possible reasons for abnormal bleeding, as well as treatment options.

REVIEW QUESTIONS

1. Does abnormal uterine bleeding prevent the performance of a woman's obligatory prayers and fasts?
2. What other actions can a woman engage in while seeing abnormal uterine bleeding?
3. Is it permissible to pray with clothing that is soiled with blood?
4. How is clothing that is soiled with blood purified?

Chapter 17

Praying While Bleeding

IN THIS CHAPTER

- Praying with spotting
- Praying with a constant flow
- Blocking blood from exiting
- Excused person's rulings

Allāh Most High says:

﴿ وَجَٰهِدُواْ فِى ٱللَّهِ حَقَّ جِهَادِهِۦ هُوَ ٱجْتَبَىٰكُمْ وَمَا جَعَلَ عَلَيْكُمْ فِى ٱلدِّينِ مِنْ حَرَجٍ ﴾

> Strive for (seeking the pleasure of) Allāh, a striving that is owed to Him. He has chosen you and did not impose any hardship on you in the religion. (*al-Ḥajj*, 22:78)

A possible meaning for striving in this verse is to endeavor to worship Allāh Most High in the way that He deserves to be worshiped and to obey Him in the manner that He deserves to be obeyed. He has chosen who will believe in Him, and with that belief comes responsibilities.

In the same instance, Allāh Most High comforts His creation. He affirms that He has not made anything in the Sacred Law or the religion of Islam a hardship. Allāh Most High wants ease for His servants.

He has allowed the shortening of prayers during travel, the ability to substitute *wuḍūʾ* and *ghusl* for *tayammum*, and the dispensation for a sick or traveling person to not fast.

Likewise, for a woman experiencing abnormal bleeding, certain rulings may be relaxed due to her situation. Constant abnormal bleeding can be uncomfortable and challenging. However, Allāh

Most High provides a way for her to practice her religion and continue to pray with the Excused Person's Rulings despite her circumstance.

Ḥamna bint Jaḥsh ﵂ experienced a situation of excessive abnormal bleeding. ʿImrān ibn Ṭalḥa ﵁ relates that his mother, Ḥamna ﵂, said:

> "I had blood flow that was plentiful and severe. So, I went to the Prophet ﷺ to ask and inform him about it. I found him ﷺ in the house of my sister, Zaynab bint Jaḥsh ﵂. I said, 'O Messenger of Allāh! I suffer from excessive and severe blood flow. So, what do you command me to do concerning it? It is preventing me from praying and fasting.' He ﷺ said: 'Insert a *kursuf* for it will block the blood flow.' Ḥamna ﵂ responded, 'It is more than that.' He ﷺ said, 'Tighten it to your body like a belt.' Ḥamna ﵂ responded, 'It is more than that.' He ﷺ said, 'Use a cloth.' Ḥamna ﵂ responded, 'It is more than that. Indeed, I am bleeding heavily.'"
>
> (*Tirmidhī*, 128; *Aḥmad*, 27475; *ibn Mājah*, 627)

Ḥamna's ﵂ bleeding was copious, to the extent that she thought it should prevent her from praying and fasting. In *Tirmidhī*'s version, the story continues with the Prophet ﷺ affirming that her abnormal bleeding is not menstruation, but it is a "...kick from the devil."

Scholars explain that what is meant by a kick is that the devil will come to women during this time and try to confuse them. He will make them doubt their habit and convince them that the blood is menstruation so that they leave their worship.

Therefore, women with abnormal bleeding must be mindful of the devil's plotting and take care to not fall prey to his tricks.

17.1 RULING OF PRAYING WITH ABNORMAL BLEEDING

Women experiencing abnormal vaginal bleeding (*istiḥāḍa*) are obliged to pray.

Every woman's abnormal bleeding situation will be unique. Some women may see occasional spotting, while others may see a constant flow of blood.

Therefore, the rulings related to how a woman will pray are dependent upon two factors:

- Whether the blood continues to exit her vagina while she is making *wuḍū'* or praying the obligatory prayer.

- Whether she possesses the ability to stop the blood flow for this duration.

17.2 PRAYING WITH SPOTTING

Spotting in this context means that the bleeding is not a constant flow. Rather, the exiting of vaginal blood happens occasionally. A woman could see sporadic bleeding within the prayer time, or the day, or the month.

Because the bleeding is light and not constant, a woman who experiences the spotting of blood should be able to:

- Wipe away the blood.
- Wash her front private part.
- Make *wuḍū'*.
- Pray the obligatory prayer of the time without any bleeding exiting.

If this is the case – that she can complete her *wuḍū'* and pray the obligatory prayer without blood exiting – then what she has done is sufficient for her prayer to count.

There is no need for her to resort to the Excused Person's Rulings, make *wuḍū'* for every prayer time, and the like. Every time she makes *wuḍū'*, she keeps the status of ritual purity – unless blood exits her vagina or another *wuḍū'* nullifier occurs.

☑ She is treated as a normal person with the rulings related to ritual purity and the prayer.

17.3 PRAYING WITH A CONSTANT FLOW

A constant flow of blood means that a woman does not have the ability to make *wuḍūʾ* and pray the obligatory prayer of the current time without vaginal blood exiting. If this is the case, then the rulings will differ for a virgin and a non-virgin.

◆ Women who are virgins will always use the Excused Person's Rulings, providing that they fulfill the conditions for establishing the excuse. Refer to Section 17.8.

◆ Women who are non-virgins must first try to block the blood flow from exiting the vagina.

- ⋄ Blocking the blood for non-virgins is mandatory according to many scholars.
- ⋄ There are certain women who may be exempt from this ruling, and their cases are mentioned in Section 17.6 Exceptions to Blocking.

17.4 BLOCKING BLOOD FLOW

Any manageable action that can be taken to stop the blood flow for the sake of the prayer's validity must be attempted.

The Prophet ﷺ advised Ḥamna bint Jaḥsh ؓ to block her abnormal bleeding with a *kursuf*, and when that was not possible, he ﷺ continued to suggest ways for her to minimize the blood flow.

Past scholars also wrote about stuffing (*ḥashū*') to stop blood from exiting the vagina when a woman experiences abnormal bleeding.

In today's times, this can easily be achieved with the use of tampons, moon cups, tissue, or similar materials. Based on her body and circumstance, a woman should choose what is feasible for her situation.

The goal is to stop the blood from exiting to maintain ritual purity while she makes *wuḍūʾ* and prays. She is only required to block for the duration of her *wuḍūʾ* and prayer, and she is not obliged to keep anything inserted in her vagina for the entire day – unless she finds it easier.

If she can successfully complete her *wuḍūʾ* and obligatory prayer without bleeding exiting the vagina, then this is sufficient for her prayer to count. Every time she makes *wuḍūʾ*, she keeps the status of ritual purity – unless blood exits from her vagina or a different *wuḍūʾ* nullifier occurs.

☑ She is treated as a normal person with the rulings related to ritual purity and the prayer.

How-to block blood:

A non-virgin woman with *istiḥāḍa* should first wash her front private part and dry herself. Then she inserts a tampon, moon cup, or tissue to prevent the flow from exiting. Refer to Diagram 17a to see where a tampon or a mooncup is worn inside the vaginal canal.

There are different levels of absorbency for tampons, such as light, normal, and super. A woman should choose whichever absorbency works best for her situation. Choosing the right size will ensure better protection from leakage.

It may be helpful to research tips on how to insert tampons or mooncups, as doing it the wrong way may cause unnecessary discomfort. For example, a tampon should be pushed towards the woman's back because the vaginal canal is slanted, and it should not be pushed upward towards the sky. It helps to sit on a toilet or to squat when inserting. It is also best to insert a tampon while the vaginal canal is wet with blood and not dry.

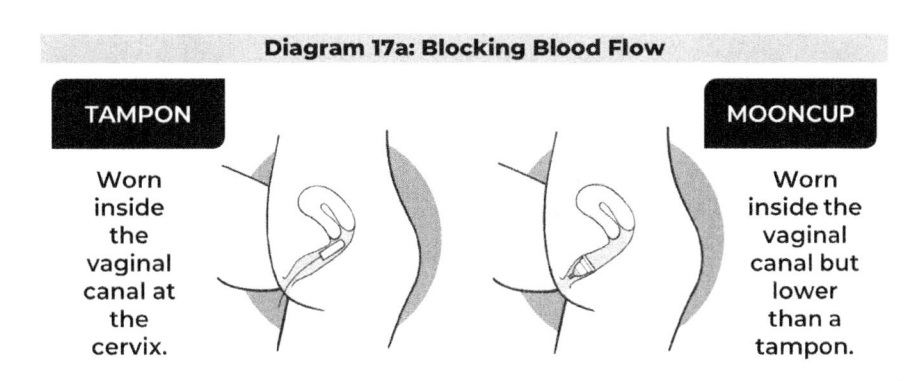

Diagram 17a: Blocking Blood Flow

TAMPON

Worn inside the vaginal canal at the cervix.

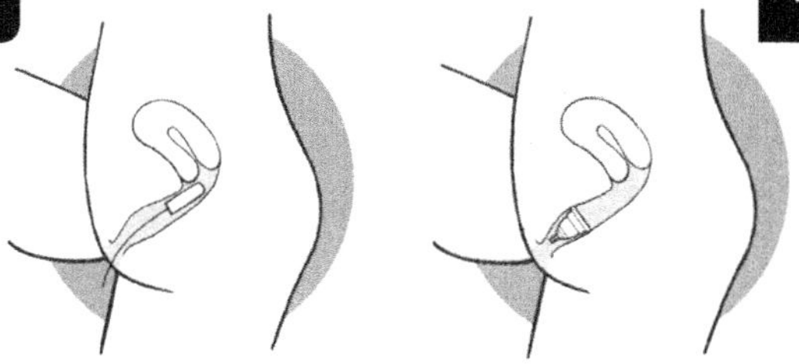

MOONCUP

Worn inside the vaginal canal but lower than a tampon.

17.5 BLOOD LEAKING AFTER BLOCKING

If blood exits while she makes *wuḍūʾ* or prays, her *wuḍūʾ* is nullified and the prayer is not valid. Additionally, any blood that leaks down the string of a tampon and exits the vagina nullifies *wuḍūʾ*.

If despite taking the means to block, a woman's flow is very heavy such that the bleeding cannot be stopped from exiting during her entire *wuḍūʾ* and the obligatory prayer, then she will resort to the Excused Person's Rulings.

> ➔ The rulings related to the Excused Person's Rulings are discussed in Sections 17.7 to 17.13.

TOXIC SHOCK SYNDROME (TSS)

Toxic shock syndrome is a rare but serious medical condition caused by a bacterial infection. It has been linked to prolonged usage of super absorbency tampons and other intra-vaginal devices.

Symptoms of TSS can vary from person to person, but they include sudden fever, vomiting, and dizziness. If a woman suspects that she has TSS, she must remove her tampon immediately and contact a doctor.

To prevent TSS, she should wash her hands before inserting a tampon, change her tampon every few hours, and use the lowest level of absorbency needed for her situation.

17.6 EXCEPTIONS TO BLOCKING

The following scenarios are examples of when a woman is not required to block her vaginal blood from exiting. Instead, she must resort to the Excused Person's Rulings for praying.

◆ A virgin girl or woman. Some scholars believe that it is sinful for a virgin to insert anything inside of the vagina. This has nothing to do with breaking her virginity. The argument revolves around potentially and purposely inflicting harm upon her by breaking her hymen or causing unnecessary discomfort because she is not sexually active. Consequently, she will automatically resort to the Excused Person's Rulings.

◆ For a non-virgin, if blocking the blood flow is deemed harmful or causes undue hardship, then she will resort to the Excused Person's Rulings. Being 'harmful' or causing 'undue hardship' is determined through clear signs, a past experience, or the opinion of an upright, expert Muslim doctor.

For example, if a pregnant woman experiences vaginal bleeding, the blood is ruled as abnormal bleeding and she must continue to pray. However, it is not normal to bleed during pregnancy, and a doctor will most likely advise her against inserting anything into her vagina for fear of harming the baby.

◆ According to the laws of fasting, inserting an object into the vagina such that it completely disappears into the vagina breaks the fast.

As such, a non-virgin woman cannot insert a mooncup into the vagina while she is fasting. The mooncup is inserted entirely into the vaginal canal and no part of it remains outside of the body. Refer to Diagram 17a for an illustration.

Similarly, inserting anything wet into the vagina breaks the fast – even if the object does not completely disappear inside the vagina. See Section 10.5 about the ruling for vaginal exams.

Thus, a non-virgin woman experiencing abnormal bleeding should dry her private parts properly and only insert dry materials to block the flow, while taking care to leave part of the object outside of the body. Tampons can be an option if she leaves the string hanging outside of the vaginal hole as shown in Diagram 17a.

If this is not possible, then she would use the Excused Person's Rulings during the fasting day and block her bleeding from *Maghrib* to *Fajr*.

> ➔ The Excused Person's Rulings are taught in Sections 17.7 to 17.13.

17.7 EXCUSED PERSON'S RULINGS

The Excused Person's Rulings are used by anyone whose *wuḍū*ʾ continues to break due to the reoccurrence of a *wuḍū*ʾ nullifier for an entire prescribed prayer time. An example would be abnormal bleeding that is a constant flow.

For a woman with normal ritual purity, whenever blood exits the vagina, her *wuḍū*ʾ breaks. However, for the excused person, this is not the case. She is granted a special status which permits ease in practicing specific rulings related to ritual purity.

With the excused person status, a woman with abnormal bleeding can make *wuḍū*ʾ, and even if the bleeding continues to flow from her vagina, her *wuḍū*ʾ remains valid.

She can perform regular acts of worship – such as praying, making *ṭawāf*, and touching the Qurʾān – without being obliged to renew her *wuḍū*ʾ within the same prayer time.

However, the Excused Person's Rulings do not necessarily apply to every woman who is experiencing abnormal bleeding. The matter returns to the amount of blood she is seeing and if she can establish the excuse based on the conditions stated by scholars.

17.8 ESTABLISHING THE EXCUSED PERSON STATUS

There are two conditions that must be met to establish the excused person status:

1. The vaginal bleeding is constant, which means that a woman cannot make *wuḍū*ʾ and pray the obligatory prayer without the excuse occurring.

2. This circumstance lasts for an entire prescribed prayer time.

'*Constant*' means that the vaginal bleeding is flowing to the extent that it is impossible for her to make *wuḍū*ʾ and pray her obligatory prayer without vaginal blood exiting.

'*Lasts for an entire prescribed prayer time*' means that from the very beginning of a prescribed prayer time to its end, the vaginal bleeding is present.

- ✧ The prescribed prayer time refers to the five obligatory prayer times: *Fajr*, *Ẓuhr*, *ʿĀṣr*, *Maghrib*, or *ʿIshāʾ*.

- ✧ For example, *Fajr* enters at 5 am and exits at 6:30 am. The excuse would need to be active for the entire prescribed prayer time – meaning from the entrance of *Fajr* at 5 am all the way until it exits at 6:30 am.

☑ The time between the exiting of the *Fajr* prayer time to the entering of *Ẓuhr* prayer time is not a prescribed prayer time, and it would not count towards establishing the excuse.

17.9 MAINTAINING THE EXCUSED PERSON STATUS

After establishing the excused status, a woman is now classed as an excused person. She only needs to see vaginal bleeding occur at least once in every subsequent prayer time to maintain this status.

Thus, to establish the excused person status, the vaginal bleeding must be ongoing for an entire prayer time – from its beginning to its end.

Thereafter, it becomes easier. She only needs to see vaginal bleeding at least once in every subsequent prayer time.

☑ There is no condition for the bleeding to remain constant.

17.10 FORMS OF WORSHIP PERMITTED

While she maintains the excused person status, she can pray her obligatory (*farḍ*) and *sunna* prayers, even though vaginal bleeding exits during her *wuḍūʾ* or her prayers.

☑ The same applies to touching the Qurʾān, making *ṭawāf*, and all acts of worship that require ritual purity.

However, this is only if the *wuḍūʾ* was made for the excuse. Making *wuḍūʾ* for the excuse means that a woman saw vaginal bleeding, and this is the reason that she is performing *wuḍūʾ*.

17.11 WUḌŪʾ NULLIFIERS FOR THE EXCUSED PERSON

The *wuḍūʾ* of an excused person is not nullified by the reoccurrence of vaginal bleeding within the same prayer time.

Instead, the *wuḍūʾ* made for the excuse is nullified when:

- ✧ The prayer time exits. Therefore, the excused person must make a new *wuḍūʾ* within each prayer time.
- ✧ Other *wuḍūʾ* nullifiers occur that are unrelated to vaginal bleeding, like passing wind, bleeding from a cut, flowing pus, urinating, defecating, or sleeping.
- ✧ The excuse becomes active after it was inactive. For example, when *wuḍūʾ* was made, the blood was not present. When the vaginal bleeding returns, this *wuḍūʾ* is nullified.

Chart 17b: Excused Person Status

ESTABLISH EXCUSED STATUS	• Vaginal bleeding is constant, such that she cannot make *wuḍūʾ* and pray the obligatory prayer without the excuse occurring. This inability to keep *wuḍūʾ* lasts for an entire prescribed prayer time.
MAINTAIN EXCUSED STATUS	• The vaginal bleeding occurs at least once in every subsequent prayer time.
LOSE EXCUSED STATUS	• The vaginal bleeding does not occur for an entire prescribed prayer time.

17.12 LOSING THE EXCUSED PERSON STATUS

The excused person status is lost whenever the vaginal bleeding does not occur for an entire prescribed prayer time.

Losing the excused person status means that the woman is no longer able to resort to its rulings. If she needs to use the rulings again, she must first repeat the entire process for establishing the excuse, which is explained in Section 17.8.

> Compare the rulings for the Excused Person Status in Chart 17b.

17.13 EXCUSED PERSON PRAYING WITH BLOOD ON CLOTHES

As mentioned in Section 16.5, if a woman prays with blood on her clothes or body that is more than the size of a *dirham* and she has the means to remove it, then the prayer is not valid. However, the excused person may be exempt from removing the blood before praying.

If an excused person's clothing is already soiled with blood that is more than the size of a *dirham* and she believes that:

- By the time she finishes praying, new blood will not soil her clothing again; then the existing blood must be removed, and she is not permitted to pray before removing it.

- By the time she finishes praying, more than a *dirham* of blood will soil her clothing again; then the blood does not need to be removed and she is permitted to pray in her clothing.

For example, a woman established the excuse for abnormal vaginal bleeding (*istiḥāḍa*). Her blood flow is very heavy, and her underwear is soiled with blood that is more than the size of a *dirham*.

Based on her reasoned judgment, she believes that by the time she finishes making *wuḍūʾ* and praying the obligatory prayer, this amount of blood will exit again. She is not obliged to purify her clothing from the blood before praying.

☑ Alternatively, she can change her clothing before praying if she has access to another clean garment.

➔ The rulings related to removing blood from clothing are discussed in Section 16.6.

REVIEW QUESTIONS

1. How can a woman pray with abnormal bleeding?
2. What is the difference between praying with blood that is spotting and praying with blood that is a constant flow?
3. What are the conditions for establishing, maintaining, and losing the excuse?

Chapter 18

Early Blood Formula

IN THIS CHAPTER

- ✧ Definition of early blood
- ✧ Bleeding begins before 15 days of purity
- ✧ Bleeding begins after 15 days of purity
- ✧ Exceptions to the rulings

A common question that women ask is:

> *"I saw blood before the days of my purity habit finished. Is this early blood menstruation?"*

There are two possible scenarios:

- ✧ Early blood begins **before** a purity span of 15 complete days.
- ✧ Early blood begins **after** a purity span of 15 complete days.

18.1 BLOOD STARTS BEFORE A PURITY SPAN OF 15 DAYS

If bleeding begins before a purity span of 15 complete days (360 hours), a woman cannot consider the early blood to be menses. Instead, she must reevaluate her situation by returning to her habits before considering any blood to be menstruation.

Some women count 15 days from the end of their previous menses, and they stop praying thereafter. Unless a woman's purity habit is 15 complete days, she cannot stop praying after Day 15. Rather, she will consider the blood to be abnormal bleeding (*istiḥāḍa*).

> Observe when she stops praying in Diagram 18a.

Diagram 18a: Blood Starts Before a 15 Day Purity

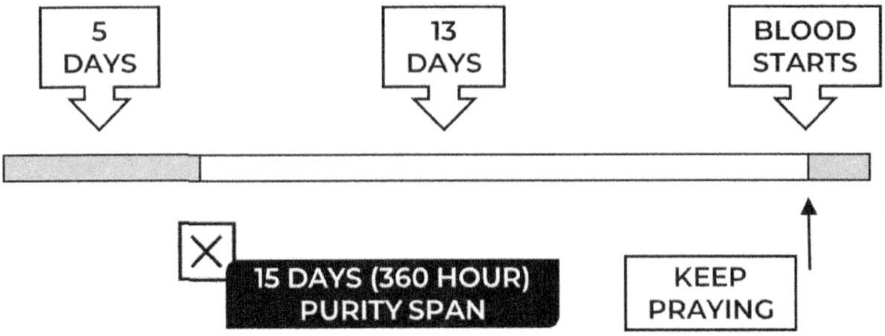

A woman has a menses habit of 5 days and purity habit of 20 days. The next month, she sees 5 days of blood in accordance with her menses habit. It is followed by 13 days of no bleeding, and then early blood begins.

▶ The bleeding begins before a purity span of 15 complete days.

▶ She considers the early blood to be abnormal bleeding.

▶ She reevaluates her situation by returning to her menses and purity habits.

▶ She continues to pray until her purity habit of 20 days elapses, counting from the time her previous menses ended.

▶ Thereafter, if blood is seen in her menstrual place, she considers it to be menstruation.

Chart 18b: When Early Blood Is Seen

18.2 BLOOD STARTS AFTER A PURITY SPAN OF 15 DAYS

When bleeding begins after a purity span of 15 complete days (360 hours), according to the *Ḥanafī madhhab* the Early Blood Formula is used to determine if the bleeding should be considered menstruation.

Early blood can be indicative that a woman's cycle this month will not act like it usually would. It is quite possible that she may bleed over 10 days due to the early blood. If that occurs, then she will return to her menses and purity habits.

◆ The Early Blood Formula revolves around securing the habit in place and number. In principle, any time blood is seen within the menstrual place it will always be ruled as menstruation, providing that it reaches the menstrual minimum of 3 days (72 hours).

For this reason, the Early Blood Formula guides a woman by using her habits so that she does not haphazardly miss her prayers and fasts when bleeding starts earlier than expected.

◆ The Early Blood Formula is a ruling in the moment, which means that it is used as a daily guideline to help women know if they should continue to pray or not. Depending on what happens, the ruling could change in retrospect.

Observe when the blood comes early in Diagram 18c.

Diagram 18c: Blood Starts After a 15 Day Purity

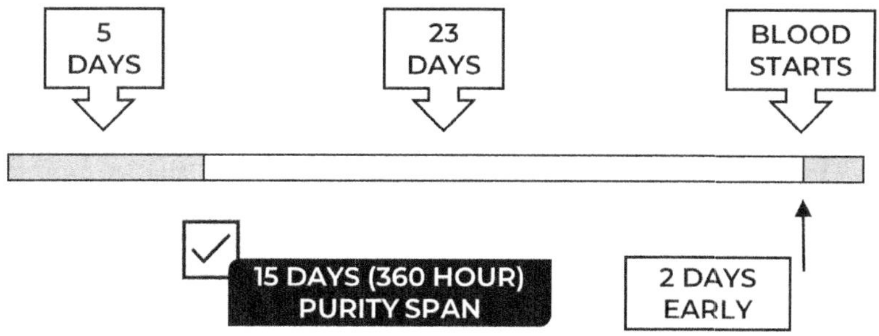

A woman has a menses habit of 5 days and purity habit of 25 days. She sees 5 days of blood in accordance with her menses habit. It is followed by 23 days of no bleeding, and then bleeding begins.

▶ The bleeding begins after a purity span of 15 complete days.

▶ The bleeding starts two days before her purity habit of 25 days elapses.

The question is: Does she consider the second bleeding to be menstruation or abnormal bleeding? The answer relies on a simple math calculation.

18.3 EARLY BLOOD FORMULA

The Early Blood Formula is applied by hypothetically adding the remaining days of the purity habit to the number of days of the menses habit. If the resulting number equals:

- **Less than 10 or exactly 10 complete days** (240 hours), the woman stops her worship and treats the early blood as menstrual blood.
- **More than 10 complete days**, the woman treats the early blood as abnormal bleeding (*istiḥāḍa*) until the completion of her purity habit. Therefore, she continues to pray and fast.

☑ Using this formula requires a woman to know her habits, which is another reason why women must take care to record their dates of bleeding.

⚠ Depending on what happens, the ruling could change in retrospect.

🔍 Observe a summary of the Early Blood Formula in Chart 18d.

Chart 18d: Early Blood Formula

EARLY BLOOD FORMULA
Less Than / Exactly 10 Complete Days
Early blood is considered menses.
Exceeds 10 Complete Days
Early blood is considered abnormal bleeding.

> 🔍 Compare the different ways the Early Blood Formula is applied in Diagrams 18e and 18f.

Diagram 18e: Early Blood Formula

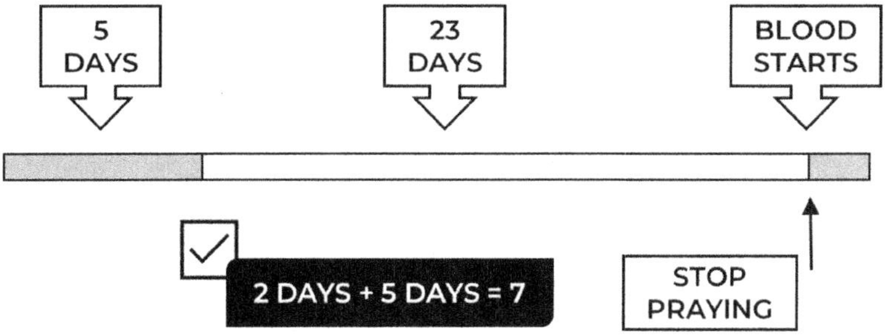
5 DAYS
23 DAYS
BLOOD STARTS
2 DAYS + 5 DAYS = 7
STOP PRAYING

> Building on the situation in Diagram 18c, the bleeding begins after a purity span of 15 complete days; consequently, the Early Blood Formula is applied.
>
> ► The bleeding starts two days before her purity habit of 25 days elapses.
>
> ► Two days remaining of her purity habit plus five days of her menses habit does not exceed 10 days.
>
> ► She considers the early blood to be menstruation.

► Her ten possible days of menses starts on Day 24 with the early blood.

However, if the bleeding started a week earlier, the ruling would not be the same, like what is shown in Diagram 18f.

Diagram 18f: Early Blood Formula

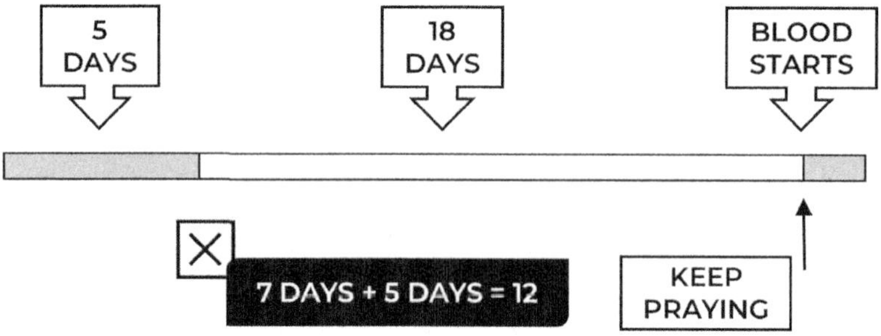

A woman has a menses habit of 5 days and purity habit of 25 days. She sees 5 days of blood in accordance with her menses habit. It is followed by 18 days of no bleeding, and then her bleeding begins earlier than expected.

► The bleeding begins after a purity span of 15 complete days. The Early Blood Formula is applied.

► The bleeding starts 7 days before her purity habit of 25 days elapses.

► Seven days remaining of her purity habit plus five days of her menses habit exceeds 10 days.

► She considers the 7 days of early blood to be abnormal blood, and she must continue to pray.

► Once her purity habit of 25 days elapses, if blood is seen, she considers it to be menstrual bleeding, and she acts like a menstruating woman. If the blood ends earlier than expected, she should take a *ghusl* just in case the rulings change in retrospect.

18.4 RULINGS IN RETROSPECT

It is worth mentioning that the ruling in the moment can change in retrospect.

◆ For early blood treated as menstruation, if the total bleeding exceeds the menstrual maximum, then her situation must be reevaluated using her purity and menses habits.

- ✧ In retrospect, the early blood will be ruled as abnormal bleeding.
- ✧ Only what she saw in accordance with her menses habit will be menstruation.

◆ For early blood treated as abnormal bleeding, if the total bleeding does not exceed 10 complete days and a purity span of 15 complete days (360 hours) follows it, then her situation must be reevaluated.

- ✧ In retrospect, the entire duration of blood will be ruled as menstruation.
- ✧ Her new menses habit is established.

> 🔍 Observe what happens to the early blood that was treated as menses in 18e after the bleeding exceeds 10 days in Diagram 18g.

Diagram 18g: Rulings in Retrospect

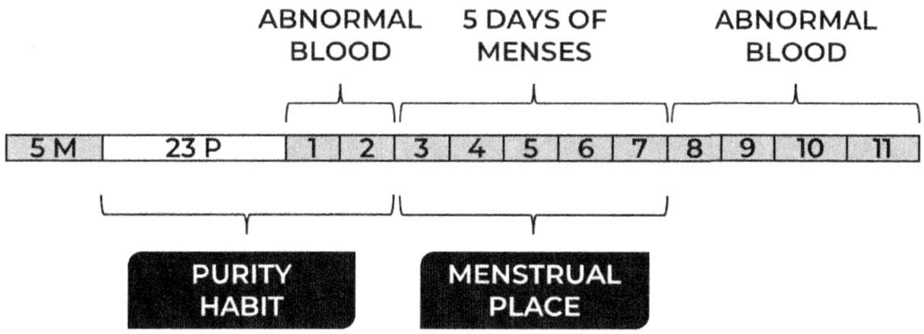

Building on the situation in Diagram 18e, the total bleeding exceeds 10 days (240 hours). Her menses and purity habits are used to determine which days are ruled as menstruation.

▶ In retrospect, the two days of early blood are ruled as abnormal bleeding. They are now considered legal purity and complete her 25-day purity span in accordance with her habit.

▶ The five days of blood in her menstrual place is menstruation in accordance with her habit.

▶ In retrospect, the remaining days of blood that she considered to be menstruation are ruled as abnormal bleeding.

▶ She must make up any obligatory (*farḍ*) and *witr* prayers missed on the days that are ruled as abnormal bleeding, but she is not sinful for missing them.

▶ She would not miss any prayers for the bleeding seen on Day 11 onwards because this bleeding is not menstruation.

18.5 LONG PURITY EXCEPTION

An exception to the Early Blood Formula is when a woman has a long purity habit. If she sees early blood after a purity span of 15 complete days, it may be considered menstruation.

The long purity exception is:

- ✧ If the remaining days of her purity habit are at least 18 days, the early blood will be treated as menstruation.

Why is 18 days the minimum requirement for this exception? Because a minimal menstruation of 3 days and a minimal purity span of 15 days could possibly occur within it.

This 15-day purity span would separate between the bloods, and consequently, there is no chance that the early blood will be added to her usual habit.

☑ A woman who experiences erratic fluctuations in her cycle, such that her purities alternate between long and short durations, may need to make use of the long purity exception.

Observe when she stops praying in Diagram 18h.

Diagram 18h: Long Purity Exception

A woman has a menses habit of 3 days and a purity habit of 40 days.

After seeing 3 days of menstrual blood, she sees 20 days of purity, and then her bleeding begins earlier than expected.

► The early blood comes 20 days before her purity habit of 40 days elapses. The exception to the Early Blood Formula applies.

► The early blood is deemed to be menstruation because at least 18 days remain from her 40-day purity habit.

REVIEW QUESTIONS

1. What does a woman do if her bleeding starts before 15 days of purity elapses?
2. What is the Early Blood Formula? When is it used?
3. What does a woman do if the resulting number equals less than 10 or exactly 10 complete days? What about if it equals more than 10 complete days?
4. Can the ruling of menstruation or abnormal bleeding change in retrospect?

PART FIVE:
Concluding Topics

Indeed Allāh
loves those
who excel in
doing good

Qur'ān
5:13

Chapter 19

Menopause

IN THIS CHAPTER

- Medical definition of menopause
- Sacred law definition of menopause
- Exceptions to the ruling
- Blood stopping before menopausal age

Menopause is the end of menstruation. It is a natural biological process that all women are destined to experience. Once a woman reaches menopause, she will no longer be able to have children. Marking the end of her childbearing years can be bittersweet and possibly painful.

Moreover, women may find themselves contemplating deeply about their lives and their purpose. They may even feel frustrated that they are not able to carry out and complete the same tasks that they could when they were younger.

The Mother of the Believers Sawdah bint Zamʿa ﵂ was the first wife of the Prophet ﷺ after Lady Khadīja's demise ﵂. She was a widow with children when he ﷺ married her. Based on the accounts of her life, it is obvious that she was extremely righteous, simple in character, and dedicated to the directives of the Prophet ﷺ.

In her later years, Lady Sawdah ﵂ was overcome by weakness and inactivity. During the Final Pilgrimage, on the night of Muzdalifa, she made a request from the Prophet ﷺ to leave earlier than everyone else.

Due to her physical condition, she believed that it would be difficult for her to walk at the same pace as them. The Prophet ﷺ granted her permission to leave before *Fajr*. (*Bukhārī*, 1680) Through this dispensation, every year on *ḥajj* the weak and disabled among the Muslims are allowed the same ease and mercy.

Within the last years of his life ﷺ, she graciously gave her turn during the week to Lady ʿĀʾisha ﵂ in an effort to gain the pleasure of the Prophet ﷺ because she knew that the Prophet ﷺ possessed a deep love for her. (*Bukhārī*, 2688)

Lady ʿĀʾisha ﵂ was very fond of Lady Sawdah ﵂ and greatly admired her carefree disposition, simplicity of speech, and purity of heart. She once said, "I have never met a woman that I wished to be like most in character other than Sawdah bint Zamʿa, who was strong-minded." (*Muslim*, 1463)

Lady Sawdah ﵂ teaches believing women that old age and what comes with it is inevitable, but this biological change should not hold one back from doing what it takes to please Allāh Most High. In the end, what matters the most is the quality of a person's heart and how much they aimed to live their life for Allāh Most High.

19.1 MENOPAUSE ACCORDING TO DOCTORS

Medically, menopause is when a woman does not experience menstruation for 12 months. It usually occurs between 45 and 55 years of age. Before reaching menopause, periods usually start to become less frequent over a few months or years before they stop altogether. Sometimes they can stop suddenly.

19.2 MENOPAUSE ACCORDING TO ḤANAFĪ SCHOLARS

The age of menopause is 55 lunar years (approximately 53 solar years and 4 months) according to the *Ḥanafī madhhab*.

- ✧ If a woman reaches the age of menopause and her menstrual cycles have stopped, she is deemed to be a menopausal woman.
- ✧ Before this age, if her menstrual cycles stopped, she will not be considered a menopausal woman because there is no maximum time limit for experiencing purity.

> ⚠ This classification will impact how she performs her post-marital waiting period if she was divorced. Refer to Sections 19.6 and 19.7.

19.3 BLEEDING AFTER 55 LUNAR YEARS

As a general principle, any colored vaginal discharge that exits after 55 lunar years is not menstruation. Instead, the discharge is considered abnormal uterine bleeding (*istiḥāḍa*).

However, an exception to this principle is if the discharge is black, red, or like her pre-menopausal period. In such a case, the bleeding could be ruled as menstruation.

> ➔ The details related to the colors black, red, brown, and lighter discharges are explained in Sections 19.4 and 19.5.

? What if the red blood starts due to hormone replace therapy (HRT)?

Hormone replacement therapy (HRT) is a treatment given to relieve the symptoms of menopause. It replaces hormones that are at a lower level. If the red blood a menopausal woman sees is a result of hormone replacement therapy (HRT), then it is menses, providing that it reaches 72 hours. However, she should consult a doctor and scholar about her situation.

19.4 BLACK OR RED BLOOD

The colors black and red are obvious colors of blood. When a woman over the age of 55 lunar years sees it, she will consider the blood to be menstruation.

✔ This is upon the condition that the blood reaches the menstrual minimum of 3 days (72 hours), and it abides by the other conditions of menstruation mentioned in Chapter 4.

> View an example of red blood ruled as menses in Diagram 19a.

Diagram 19a: Black or Red Blood

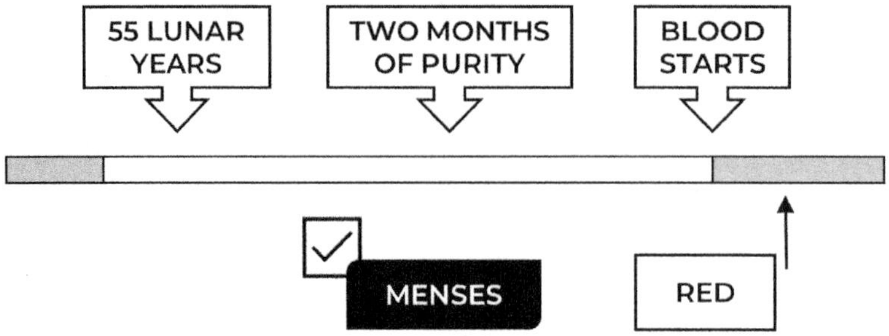

A 55 lunar year-old woman sees 4 days of red blood after a purity span of two months.

► The blood is red.

► The blood reaches the menstrual minimum of 3 complete days (72 hours), and it comes after a 15-day purity span.

► This blood is considered menstruation despite it occurring after 55 lunar years.

19.5 LIKE HER PREMENOPAUSAL PERIOD

The premenopausal period refers to the colors of blood that a woman used to see during her menstruation before she reached menopause.

If a woman over the age of 55 lunar years sees the other colors of blood – such as brown and yellow – it is only ruled as menstruation if the colors occur like her premenopausal bleeding. Otherwise, the blood is considered abnormal uterine bleeding (*istiḥāḍa*).

☑ This is upon the condition that the blood reaches the menstrual minimum of 3 days (72 hours), and it abides by the other conditions of menstruation mentioned in Chapter 4.

Compare the situations in Diagrams 19b and 19c.

Diagram 19b: Like Her Premenopausal Period

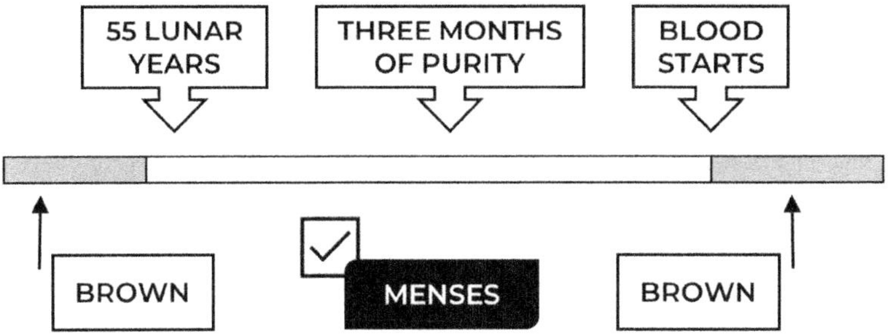

A 55 lunar year-old woman used to see only brown blood as menstruation before menopause. After she reaches 55 years of age, she sees a purity span of three months and then 7 days of brown blood.

► She used to see only brown blood during her menstruation before menopause.

► The brown blood after menopause reaches the menstrual minimum of 3 complete days (72 hours), and it comes after a 15-day purity span.

► The brown blood is considered menstruation despite it occurring after 55 lunar years.

Diagram 19c: Like Her Premenopausal Period

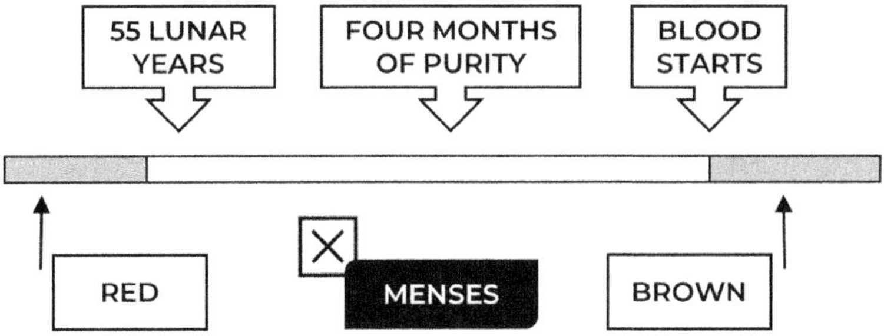

A 55 lunar year-old woman used to see only red blood as menstruation before menopause. After she reaches 55 years of age, she sees a purity span of four months and then 6 days of brown blood.

► She used to see only red blood during her menstruation before menopause.

► The brown blood after menopause is not considered menstruation, even though it reaches 3 days.

POINTS TO REMEMBER

- The age of menopause is 55 lunar years.
- Any colored discharge seen by a menopausal woman is considered abnormal bleeding.
- The exception to the rule is if the blood is red, black, or like her premenopausal period.
- Black and red are always considered colors of menstrual blood.
- As for the other colors, the consideration is that they occur like her premenopausal period.
- The blood must reach 3 complete days (72 hours) and abide by the other conditions of menstruation.

19.6 POST-MARITAL WAITING PERIOD

If a menopausal woman is divorced, she must complete her post-marital waiting period (*ʿidda*) by months and not by menstrual periods.

The duration of her post-marital waiting period is three full months. Once three full months elapses from the time the divorce is issued, her post-marital waiting period is finished.

- ✧ If her menstruation suddenly returns during her 3-month waiting period, then she must restart her post-marital waiting period and complete it with three menstrual periods. Thereafter, she is free to marry.

- ✧ If her menstruation suddenly returns after her 3-month waiting period is finished, she does not need to redo her post-marital waiting period and she is free to marry. However, if she is divorced by her new husband, her waiting period must be completed with three menstrual periods.

> ﴾ As for your women past the age of menstruation, if you are in doubt, their waiting period is three months, and those who have not menstruated as well. ﴿
>
> (*aṭ-Ṭalāq*, 65:4)

19.7 EARLY MENOPAUSE

If a woman stops experiencing menstruation but she is younger than 55 lunar years, then she is not ruled as a menopausal woman according to the *Ḥanafī madhhab*.

- ✧ If she is divorced, she must complete her post-marital waiting period (*ʿidda*) with the completion of three menstrual periods.

- ✧ If she takes medication to bring on bleeding so that she can complete her post-marital waiting period, the blood will be classified as menses, even if it is only brown or yellow.

> ⚠ If the medication does not work and she will remain in her *ʿidda* for an extended period, she should contact a scholar and seek a dispensation from another *madhhab*.

REASONS FOR BLEEDING AFTER MENOPAUSE

Sudden vaginal bleeding after menopause is not normal, and it should be evaluated by a doctor. Postmenopausal vaginal bleeding can be caused by:

- Endometrial or vaginal atrophy (lining of the uterus or vagina is thin and dry)
- Hormone replacement therapy (HRT)
- Uterine cancer or endometrial cancer
- Endometrial hyperplasia (lining of the uterus becomes too thick)
- Uterine polyps (growths in the uterus)
- Cervical cancer

The cause of bleeding may be entirely harmless, or it could result from something serious; so, it is important for women in this situation to see a doctor promptly.

REVIEW QUESTIONS

1. What is menopause? Is there a difference in the definition given by doctors and scholars?
2. Can a menopausal woman experience menstruation? What are the conditions?
3. What is the length of the post-marital waiting period for a menopausal woman?

Chapter 20

Most Popular Questions

20.1 I went to the bathroom and saw blood, but I do not know when it came out. When do I consider my menses to have started?

Menstruation begins when colored discharge exits the vagina during the expected time of menses. If a woman finds colored discharge on her underwear and she is unsure when it exited, then she considers the start time to be when she first sees the blood. (Ibn ʿĀbidīn, *Manhāl al-Wāridīn*)

However, if it is possible for her to estimate when it exited, like maybe she felt wetness in her underwear and she believes it was from blood, then she would consider her start time at that point.

20.2 If I wake up at *Fajr* and do not see blood, do I make up the ʿ*Īsha*ʾ prayer?

Yes. From a legal perspective, menstruation ends when a woman last saw blood. Thus, she takes a *ghusl*, makes up the ʿ*Īsha*ʾ and *witr* prayers, and then prays *Fajr*. (Ibn ʿĀbidīn, *Radd al-Muḥtār*)

20.3 How do I know if I am really seeing yellow discharge?

The best thing to do is to use a *kursuf* to determine the colors of blood. The way to use the *kursuf* along with its related rulings are discussed in Chapter 8.

However, women should not become excessive about checking their colors of discharge. It is not a form of worship, and it can lead to baseless misgivings.

When it reached the daughter of Zayd ibn Thābit (Allāh have mercy on her) that some women were asking for lanterns in the middle of the night to check for purity, she criticized them for this and said, "Women never used to do this." (*Muwaṭṭa*ʾ, 86)

Scholars explain that she reproached these women because they were waking up in the depths of the night to look at their discharge when there was no need.

If one is unsure if they are seeing yellow discharge, it is advisable to ask a female relative, friend, or teacher to judge what is seen on the *kursuf.*

20.4 I heard that the colors yellow and turbid are not menses. Is that true?

The female Companion Umm ʿAṭīya ﷺ said:

> "We used to never consider turbid or yellow after purity to be of significance."
>
> (*Abū Dāwūd*, 307)

A similar *ḥadīth* is found in *Ṣaḥīḥ al-Bukhārī* without the words 'after purity.' (*Bukhārī*, 326)

The way many scholars interpret this statement is that after the possible days of menses have passed, if the colors yellow or turbid are seen during a woman's purity span, they are not ruled as menses. As for seeing these colors during the time of menses, they are ruled as menstrual blood. (Ibn Ḥajar, *Fatḥ al-Bārī;* as-Sahāranfūrī, *Badhl al-Majhūd*)

Interestingly, Imām Bukhārī (Allāh have mercy on him) titled the chapter heading as "The Chapter on Yellow and Turbid Outside the Days of Menstruation."

Moreover, the Mother of Believers ʿĀʾisha ﷺ taught the female Companions ﷺ that yellow is a color of menstrual blood. In a *ḥadīth* found in the *Muwaṭṭaʾ* of Imām Mālik, the maid servant of the Mother of Believers ʿĀʾisha ﷺ said:

> "Women used to send small boxes to ʿĀʾisha, the Mother of the Believers, that had a piece of cotton cloth (*kursuf*) contained in

> them in which there was a yellow discharge upon it from menstrual blood. They would ask her about the prayer. She would say to them, 'Do not be hasty (to take a *ghusl*) until you see a white discharge.'" By that she meant purity from menses.
>
> (*Muwaṭṭa'*, 85)

'Ā'isha ☙ instructed the female Companions ☙ to not rush to take a *ghusl*, but rather they should wait until the yellow-colored discharge ends. What is understood from this *ḥadīth* is that a woman's menstruation is not finished until she is free from all colored vaginal discharge.

20.5 Can I remove body hair during menstruation?

Yes, it is permissible to remove body hair and cut one's nails during menstruation and lochia. However, if a person is in a state of sexual impurity (*janāba*), it is disliked. (*al-Fatāwā al-Hindīya*)

20.6 Are marital relations permitted when bleeding stops before three days during the possible days of menses?

When blood stops before 72 hours during the possible days of menses, in retrospect it is ruled as abnormal uterine bleeding (*istiḥāḍa*). The woman must make *wuḍū'* and begin praying.

As for sexual intercourse, out of precaution couples should avoid it. Whenever blood stops before the habit, the bleeding may return, and those days will be ruled as menses in retrospect. (Ibn ʿĀbidīn, *Radd al-Muḥtār*)

20.7 Can I delay taking my *ghusl* after my bleeding ends? What if I know that the bleeding will return?

Delaying the *ghusl* within the prayer time can be obligatory or recommended depending on the woman's habit. Refer to Table 61 for the rulings. As for delaying the *ghusl* beyond the prayer time after bleeding has stopped, it is not permissible.

Once it is established that the bleeding has stopped and there is no chance of it returning, it is obligatory to take a *ghusl*. Women must use their personal judgement about this matter. Cycles tend to fluctuate in number, especially as women age or near menopause, and sometimes women's cycles are not consistent enough to know what to expect.

Therefore, the best thing to do is to use the *kursuf* to check if the discharge has ended. It helps women to stop second guessing themselves and taking multiple showers. Refer to Sections 8.7 and 8.8 for its related rulings.

20.8 My menses is going to end while I am in an airplane. What do I do?

If a woman's menstruation stops while she is on an airplane, she will make *tayammum* to exit a state of major ritual impurity. She then makes *wuḍūʾ* for her prayers.

A woman who thinks that her menses may end on the airplane should take care to travel with a little Ziploc bag of sand, dirt, or a rock to use for *tayammum*.

20.9 I am spotting during *ʿumra* or after inserting an IUD. Is it menstruation?

A common mistake that women make is that they assume that spotting, light bleeding, or irregular bleeding cannot be ruled as menstruation.

In the *Ḥanafī madhhab*, the rulings are not dependent upon the qualities or heaviness of the blood. There is no condition for menstrual bleeding to be continuous either. Rather, the rulings revolve around the habits.

Thus, when a woman is experiencing abnormal bleeding, the only way to know when her menstruation starts is by using her purity and menses habits.

A woman who does not remember her habits should try her hardest to remember when the last time was that she saw a normal menstrual cycle and how long it lasted. Even if she is not absolutely certain, a reasoned guess is sufficient.

If this is not possible, then she can take medication to regulate her bleeding and establish a habit for the future.

20.10 Where did the concept of the habit come from? Why not consider colors and flow?

The *Ḥanafī madhhab* does not rely upon the strengths of colors or qualities of blood (*tamyīz*) like other schools of law (*madhāhib*). The reason for this difference of opinion is based upon how the scholars interpreted certain *aḥādīth*.

The wife of the Prophet ﷺ ʿĀʾisha ؓ said:

> "Fāṭima bint Abī Ḥubaysh ؓ came to the Prophet ﷺ and said, 'O Messenger of Allāh, indeed I am a woman who experiences abnormal bleeding such that I never see any purity. Do I leave praying?' The Prophet ﷺ responded, 'No. Verily that is from a (ruptured) vein, and it is not menstruation. Leave the prayer for the number of days (*qadr al-ayyām*) you used to menstruate, then take a purificatory shower (*ghusl*) and pray.'"
>
> (*Bukhārī*, 325)

The Arabic phrase '*qadr al-ayyām*' means the number of days or the time of the month that the woman in question would usually menstruate. This is her habit. Thus, when a woman experiences abnormal bleeding, the way to resolve her problem is to return to her habit.

There are numerous *aḥādīth* that convey a similar meaning in other *ḥadīth* works. Based on these *aḥādīth*, the Ḥanafī scholars explain how to establish a habit and use it so that a woman with abnormal bleeding knows when she should pray or not pray.

20.11 Can I take medication to delay my period in *Ramaḍān*?

Yes, it is permissible to take medication to stop or delay the oncoming of your menstruation during *Ramaḍān*. However, there are a few considerations that a woman must be aware of.

Firstly, many women take medication innocently thinking that they can easily manipulate their cycles, but they end up interfering with their natural hormonal system. This can result in unexpected breakthrough bleeding and spotting, which inevitably causes a lot of stress for a woman.

Secondly, the confusion can be made worse for those who may not know the rulings related to distinguishing what is menstrual blood and what is non-menstrual blood.

Thus, if a woman desires to take medication to manipulate her menstrual cycle, she needs to be aware that the medication may not help her in the way that she is expecting.

She also needs to record any spotting or colored discharge she sees, and she should have access to a teacher to ask her questions if problems occur.

20.12 If I wake up for *suḥūr* and do not see blood, do I intend to fast *Ramaḍān* if I haven't taken a *ghusl*?

If the menstrual maximum of 240 hours was reached before *Fajr* entered, then a woman must intend to fast *Ramaḍān* even if she takes the *ghusl* after *Fajr*. Once the maximum time has been reached, menstruation can be no more.

If the bleeding stopped before the menstrual maximum of 240 hours, and there is hypothetically enough time to complete the *ghusl* and say the opening *takbīr* of the prayer before *Fajr* enters (approximately 15 minutes in normal circumstances), then one makes the intention to fast at *Fajr*.

The fast is valid because one is deemed to be ritually pure from menstruation when *Fajr* enters, even if taking the *ghusl* is delayed until after that time. If one was unable to pray the *ʿĪshaʾ* and *witr* prayers before *Fajr* entered, they must be made up.

Otherwise, if from the time the blood stopped, she does not hypothetically have enough time to complete the *ghusl* and say the opening *takbīr* of the prayer before *Fajr* enters, the fast is not valid and she does not owe the *ʿĪshaʾ* and *witr* prayers. She imitates a fasting person for that day and makes up the fast after *Ramaḍān* is over in a time when she is able.

> ➔ These rulings are summarized in Table 6l in Chapter 6.

20.13 Can I take medication to delay my period for *ḥajj* or *ʿumra*?

It is permitted to take medication to delay the menstrual period for *ḥajj* or *ʿumra*. Two medications are commonly used by women: birth control pills or Primolut N.

Even if a woman takes medication, if she begins to bleed and it falls within her time of menses, the blood is ruled as menses – including spotting or a light flow. Thus, she should give ample time for her body to become used to the medicine so that this does not occur.

If a woman chooses to take birth control pills, she should start taking the pills months before she travels. By doing so, she can manipulate her cycle so that the dates for her expected time of menses are moved forward. The hope is that her expected time of menses will not fall within the actual days of *ḥajj* or *ʿumra*, and any bleeding seen will be ruled as abnormal blood.

If a woman does not want to take birth control that early, then she can take Primolut N (Norethisterone 5g tablets) before leaving her home country. She continues to take the pills while on *ḥajj* or *ʿumra*. In most cases, when the medication is stopped, withdrawal bleeding will occur approximately two to three days later.

It is best to consult a doctor about when one should start taking this medication, as well as what is the recommended dose, because each person's situation will be unique.

> ➔ Refer to Chapter 9 for the rulings related to *ḥajj* and *ʿumra*.

20.14 What if my menses starts before I do the *ṭawāf* and will only finish after my group leaves?

If a woman's menstruation starts before she can make the obligatory *ṭawāf*, she must wait until her menstruation finishes before performing the *ṭawāf*, even if it entails extending her trip.

If this is not possible, she should take medication to stop the flow immediately. She should inquire from a pharmacist what is the safest maximum dosage that she can take to stop her blood flow.

However, if all avenues have been explored and it is not possible to do any of them, as an absolute final resort, contemporary scholars say that she can make *ṭawāf* to remove herself from a state of *iḥrām* and offer the penalty for doing *ṭawāf* in a state of menses. She must also repent for doing a *ṭawāf* in a state of major ritual impurity.

Women should plan ahead as best as they can so that they do not find themselves in this situation. Likewise, travel agencies should leave ample time for women to stay in Makkah to perform their *ṭawāf* in case they menstruate unexpectedly.

20.15 Can a married women wear a tampon?

According to our research and the opinions of some contemporary scholars, yes, she can.

To begin, there is no direct prohibition from the Prophet ﷺ about this matter. In fact, there is a *ḥadīth* that the Prophet ﷺ told the female Companion Ḥamna bint Jaḥsh ﵂ to use a *kursuf* to stop her abnormal bleeding so that she could pray.

Some commentators of this *ḥadīth* mention that what is understood by the Prophet's ﷺ instruction is that she must place the *kursuf* inside her vagina to block the bleeding from exiting. (Mullā ʿAlī al-Qārī, *Mirqāt al-Mafātīḥ*; al-Dehlawī, *Lamaʿāt al-Tanqīḥ*; al-Nawawī, *Al-Minhāj;* as-Sahāranfūrī, *Badhl al-Majhūd*)

However, there is a position related in *al-Muḥīṭ al-Burhānī* and *Manhal al-Wāridīn* that it is disliked to insert a *kursuf* completely inside the vagina because it resembles masturbation. This may have been the understanding or concerns of scholars at that time. It does not necessarily mean that a tampon holds the same ruling.

Tampons are generally worn when a woman experiences a heavy flow. They are the size of half a finger and slightly expand when the blood is absorbed. The concern that it would lead to masturbation, especially for a married woman, may not be relevant.

Thus, if a married woman wears a tampon during menstruation, or to block her blood while experiencing abnormal bleeding, it is permissible. However, she should be aware of the rulings related to breaking her fast mentioned in Section 17.6.

> ➔ The rulings related to tampons are discussed in Chapter 8 and Chapter 17.

20.16 What is the ruling for bleeding after sex?

From a medical perspective, bleeding after sex is not considered normal. If it is occurring often, a woman should ask her doctor why she is experiencing bleeding after sex.

As for the ruling, there is no one-size-fits-all answer. In general, if the bleeding occurs within the ten possible days of menses, it is more precautionary to consider the blood to be menstruation.

However, if a doctor confirms otherwise then she can follow her doctor's opinion in this matter. For example, the doctor who examines her may confirm that she has a polyp on her outer cervix, which becomes irritated during intercourse and bleeds. In such a circumstance, the blood seen after sex would not be considered menstruation because it is not originating from the uterus.

20.17 What is the ruling for bleeding after vaginal exams?

Bleeding due to a confirmed vaginal injury is not menstruation. Therefore, if a woman undergoes a vaginal exam and she is told by her doctor that the bleeding that follows is due to an injury, then it will not be considered menstruation.

For example, it is possible for the cervix to become irritated during a pap smear when the practitioner collects the cell sample, which can cause light bleeding for a few hours after the procedure. This bleeding is not from inside the uterus, but rather it is from the doctor scraping the outer cervix.

However, more invasive procedures like surgery or examinations of the uterus may have a different ruling, and a woman should contact a scholar to inquire about her situation.

20.18 Is withdrawal blood from birth control and Primolut N considered menses?

Withdrawal bleeding is the blood that is seen after a woman stops taking birth control or similar type medications. The drop in hormone levels causes bleeding to occur.

Withdrawal bleeding is considered menses if it falls within the time of menstruation. Doctors generally say that withdrawal bleeding is not menstruation, but what they mean is that it is not the natural blood that occurs due to ovulation.

However, the legal definition of menstruation is not dependent upon ovulation. Rather, menstruation is blood that originates from the uterus. (Ibn ʿĀbidīn, *Manhāl al-Wāridīn*)

20.19 What is legal blood? Why am I being told that I menstruated when I did not see any blood on those days?

Legal blood (*ad-dam al-ḥukmī*) is an interval that the Sacred Law considers to be blood, even though there was no actual blood seen.

This may sound strange. There was no blood but then there is blood? Yes.

An easy way to demonstrate the concept of legal blood is with blood returning within the possible days of menstruation.

For example, a woman sees 5 days of menstrual bleeding. When it stops on day 5, she takes a *ghusl* and begins praying. On day 8, the blood returns.

In retrospect, days 6 and 7 are ruled as menstruation. The span free of blood on days 6 and 7 is an intervening purity (15.15). It connects the days together, and the span of purity is now called legal blood.

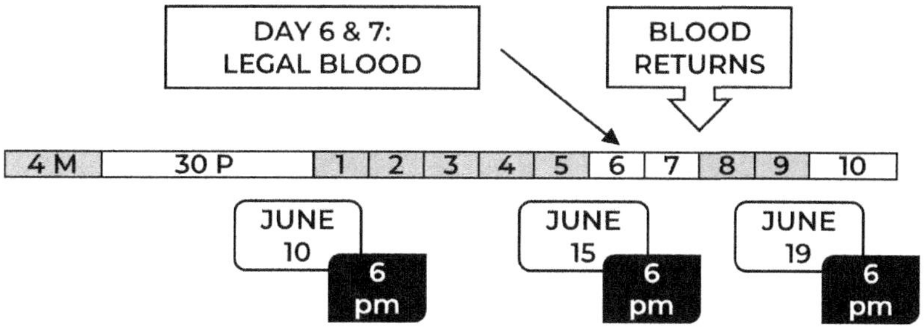

The same concept applies when a woman sees an incomplete purity (*aṭ-ṭuhr an-nāqiṣ*), which is a purity span that is less than 15 days (15.13). The span free of blood is called legal blood.

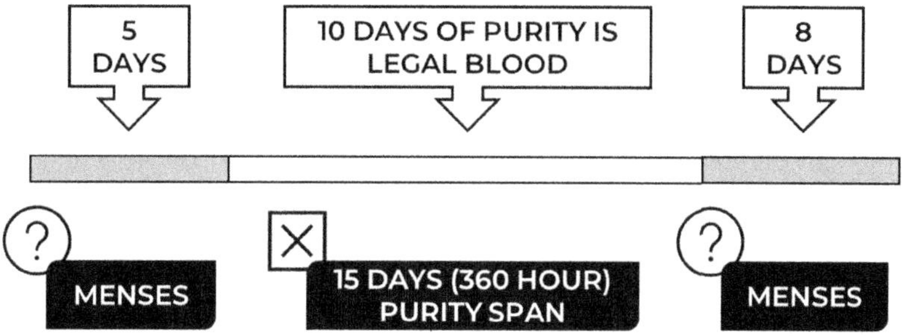

Both the intervening purity and incomplete purity do not separate between shows of blood. Rather, the entire duration of purity along with the shows of actual blood connect. All together they are ruled as continuous bleeding.

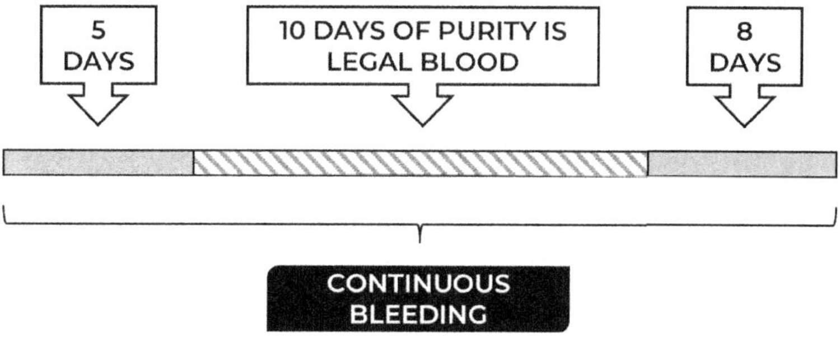

As such, if a woman returns to her habits because of abnormal bleeding, it may be that the time ruled as menstruation falls into the days that are legal blood whereas the time ruled as abnormal bleeding are the days when she experienced actual blood flow.

Treating an incomplete purity like continuous blood flow is a transmitted opinion (*riwāya*) from Imām Abū Ḥanīfa and it is the position of Imām Abū Yūsuf, a senior student of Imām Abū Ḥanīfa. Past scholars chose to use this position because it made problem solving quicker and easier. However, practically speaking, it can be difficult for a woman to live out the consequences of this ruling if she experiences spotting often.

Imām Muḥammad, another senior student of Imām Abū Ḥanīfa, said differently. He did not believe that menstruation could start or end without seeing actual blood (*ad-dam al-haqīqī*). Thus, it is best to consult a scholar to see if his position can be applied to make one's situation easier.

The differences of opinion are a mercy, and scholars note in their works that ease in these matters must be a priority for those helping women. (al-Indarpatī, *al-Fatāwā at-Tātārkhānīya*)

20.20 Why am I experiencing abnormal bleeding?

The following are a few suggestions for why abnormal bleeding can occur. It is best to consult a doctor about one's specific symptoms for a more precise understanding.

Stress and lifestyle changes: Disruptions to a woman's normal daily routine can impact the regularity of her menstrual cycle. For example, gaining or losing weight, dieting, changing exercise routines, undergoing stressful exams, and traveling can be a cause for menstrual irregularities.

Birth control / IUD: Going on or off birth control pills can affect a woman's menstruation. Some women may experience irregular periods or miss periods for up to six months after stopping birth control pills. Other forms of birth control, such as IUDs, can cause period irregularities like lighter or heavier flows.

Hormonal imbalances: An excess of the hormone estrogen can cause irregular bleeding or spotting, often due to the lining of the uterus growing too thick. Hormonal imbalances are common amongst teenagers, women nearing menopause (perimenopause), and women with thyroid issues.

Polycystic ovary syndrome (PCOS): Polycystic ovary syndrome occurs when the ovaries release abnormal amounts of androgens (male hormones), causing cysts to form. These ovarian cysts cause hormonal changes that can prevent ovulation and menstruation from occurring.

Women with PCOS may experience irregular periods or they may stop menstruating completely. Other symptoms include:

- Difficulty getting pregnant or infertility.
- Excessive body hair.
- Acne or oily skin.
- Weight gain, especially around the abdomen.
- Trouble losing weight.
- Male-pattern baldness or thinning hair.
- Dark skin patches on the back of the neck, under the armpits or under the breasts.

Uterine polyps or fibroids: Uterine polyps are small growths of endometrium tissue, whereas fibroids are growths made up of muscle tissue. Both are usually benign (noncancerous) and can cause heavy bleeding. Fibroids can also cause chronic and severe pain.

Endometriosis: Endometriosis occurs when the endometrial tissue that lines the uterus begins to grow outside the uterus, sometimes growing on the ovaries, fallopian tubes, intestines, or other digestive organs. This condition can cause painful bleeding, cramps, and painful intercourse.

Medications: Blood thinners (anticoagulants), anti-inflammatory drugs, hormone medications, or steroids can affect menstrual bleeding.

Pregnancy: Implantation bleeding happens when the fertilized egg attaches itself to the lining of the uterus. Spotting or a light flow of pink or brown bleeding may occur. Implantation bleeding typically occurs about ten to fourteen days after conception. Implantation bleeding is common and usually not a sign of a problem.

Pregnancy complications: Sparse spotting during the first trimester is often no cause for concern, but a doctor should still be consulted. Bleeding heavily during pregnancy may be a sign that a woman is experiencing a miscarriage or an ectopic pregnancy. An ectopic pregnancy is when a fertilized egg implants itself outside of the womb, usually in one of the fallopian tubes.

Endometrial hyperplasia: This is when the lining of the uterus becomes unusually thick because of having too many cells or abnormal cells. It can cause excessive bleeding.

Cancer: Abnormal bleeding can also be a sign of cancer of the uterus, cervix, vagina, or ovaries – especially after menopause.

HEALING ABNORMAL BLEEDING

To diagnose a woman with a potential cause for abnormal bleeding, a doctor will most likely do all or some of the following:

- Perform a physical exam like a pelvic ultrasound.
- Request a pap smear.
- Request a pregnancy test.
- Request a blood test.
- Request a thyroid test or hormone levels test.
- Consider investigative procedures like a hysteroscopy.

Once a reason has been identified, medications may be prescribed to help reduce or regulate the bleeding, like birth control pills.

Alternatively, many women choose to embark on their own healing journey and resolve their abnormal bleeding through natural means.

Natural healing methods can consist of:

- Altering dietary choices.
- Treating vitamin deficiencies.
- Engaging in daily exercise.
- Getting womb, pelvic, or body massages.
- Taking homeopathy remedies.
- Practicing stress reduction exercises.
- Undergoing trauma treatment.

Each woman's situation is unique, and every woman must choose the options that are best for her circumstance.

APPENDIX

...I will never deny
any of you
—male or female—
the reward of your
deeds. Both are
equal in reward...

Qurʾān
3:195

MENSES IN A NUTSHELL

Definition

- Blood: Originates from the uterus and exits the vagina.
- Minimum age: 9 lunar years old (8 solar years and 9 months).
- Cannot be from pregnancy, childbirth, an illness, or an injury.

Colors Of Blood

- Possible colors: Black, red, brown, turbid, yellow, green.
- White discharge mixed with color takes the ruling of blood.

Length

- Minimum: 3 complete days (72 hours)
- Maximum: 10 complete days (240 hours)
- Can be spotting or a full flow.

Minimum Purity

- Between menses & menses: 15 complete days (360 hours)
- Between lochia & menses: 15 complete days (360 hours)

Possible Days Of Menses

- From the onset of bleeding in a woman's expected time of menses, she has 10 possible days (240 hours) to menstruate.
- Whenever she sees blood during the possible days of menses, she acts like a menstruating woman, and all prohibitions apply.
- Even if the blood exceeds her menses habit, she continues to act like a menstruating woman.
- If the blood returns within the 10 days after having stopped, it takes the ruling of menses.
- The gaps of purity during the 10 possible days of menses are considered menstruation in retrospect.
- A *ghusl* is obligatory when menstrual bleeding either stops within the 10 possible days or the menstrual maximum of 10 complete days (240 hours) is reached.

Blood Stopping

- Sign that the bleeding has stopped: Seeing white discharge, clear discharge, or no discharge.
- The *kursuf* can be used to determine if the bleeding ended.

Bleeding Stops Before / At 240 Hours

- If the blood reaches 3 days (72 hours) and stops thereafter, she is obliged to:
  - Take a *ghusl.*
  - Start praying.
  - Follow the rulings in Table 6I.

Establishing Habit

- The entire duration is ruled as menses providing that:
  - The menstrual minimum of 3 days (72 hours) is met.
  - The menstrual maximum of 10 days (240 hours) is not exceeded.
  - A purity span of at least 15 days (360 hours) free of blood follows the blood.
- The most recent sound menses becomes her menses habit.
- It is obligatory to record the menses habit.

Bleeding Exceeding Maximum

- Any bleeding beyond 10 days (240 hours) is not menses. The woman must:
  - Take a *ghusl* at 10 days (240 hours).
  - Start praying.
  - Return to her menstrual and purity habits.

Pregnant Women

- She cannot menstruate but records the bleeding just in case a miscarriage occurs.

Menopausal Women

- Age of menopause: 55 lunar years (53 solar years, 4 months).
- Any colored discharge seen thereafter is abnormal bleeding.
- Exceptions: Black, red, or blood that is like her pre-menopausal period and it reaches 3 days (72 hours).

LOCHIA IN A NUTSHELL

Definition

- Blood: Originates from the uterus and exits the vagina.
- When: Following the delivery of most of the baby.
- Twins: Lochia starts after the exiting of the first child.
- Blood during labor: Not lochia.
- Blood from c-section incision: Not lochia.

Colors Of Blood

- Possible Colors: Black, red, brown, turbid, yellow, green.
- White discharge mixed with color takes the ruling of blood.

Length

- Minimum: None
- Maximum: 40 complete days (960 hours)
- Can be spotting or a full flow.

Minimum Purity

- Between lochia & menses: 15 complete days (360 hours)
- Between lochia & lochia: 6 months

Possible Days Of Lochia

- After childbirth, a woman has 40 possible days (960 hours) to experience lochia.
- Whenever she sees blood during the possible days of lochia, the prohibitions for a menstruating woman apply.
- Even if the bleeding exceeds her lochia habit, she continues to abide by the prohibitions.
- If the blood returns within the 40 days after having stopped, it takes the ruling of lochia.
- The gaps of purity during the 40 possible days of lochia are considered lochia in retrospect.
- A *ghusl* is obligatory when bleeding either stops within the 40 possible days or the lochia maximum of 40 complete days (960 hours) is reached.

Blood Stopping

- ✧ Sign that the bleeding has stopped: Seeing white discharge, clear discharge, or no discharge.
- ✧ The *kursuf* can be used to determine if the bleeding ended.

Bleeding Stops Before / At 960 Hours

- ✧ If the blood stops before / at 960 hours, she is obliged to:
  - Take a *ghusl*.
  - Start praying.
  - Follow the rulings in Table 6l.

Establishing Habit

- ✧ The entire duration is ruled as lochia providing that:
  - The blood does not exceed 40 days (960 hours).
  - A purity span of at least 15 days (360 hours) free of blood follows it.
  - The purity span ends outside the 40 days.
- ✧ The most recent sound lochia becomes her lochia habit.
- ✧ It is obligatory to record the lochia habit.

Bleeding Exceeding Maximum

- ✧ Any bleeding beyond 40 days (960 hours) is not lochia. The woman must:
  - Take a *ghusl* at 40 days (960 hours).
  - Start praying.
- ✧ Woman with a habit: Return to her lochia habit.
- ✧ Lochia beginner: 40-day (960 hours) habit is established.

Menses After Lochia

- ✧ Use purity and menses habits from before pregnancy to know the expected time of menses.

Miscarriages

- ✧ Developed fetus: Pregnancy status is maintained. The blood after the fetus exits is lochia.
- ✧ Undeveloped embryo: Pregnancy status is canceled. Return to menses and purity habits.

PURITY IN A NUTSHELL

Definition

- The duration that is not considered menses or lochia.

Minimum Purity Span

- Between menses & menses: 15 complete days (360 hours)
- Between lochia & menses: 15 complete days (360 hours)
- Between lochia & lochia: 6 months

Maximum Purity Span

- None

Types Of Purity

- Sound: Fulfills 3 conditions and taken as habit.
- Unsound: Missing a condition and never taken as habit.

Sound Purity Conditions

- Three conditions:
    - It is not less than 15 complete days (360 hours).
    - It is free from blood for the entire duration.
    - It occurs between two sound bloods.

Establishing Habit

- All 3 conditions met: Becomes the purity habit.
- The most recent sound purity becomes her purity habit.
- It is obligatory to record the purity habit.

Blood During Purity Span

- Unsound blood (*istiḥāḍa*) and never taken as habit.
- Breaks *wuḍūʾ* upon exiting and is filthy (*najis*).
- Prohibitions of menstruation do not apply.
- Must still pray and fast.
- Sexual intercourse is permitted.

Praying With Blood

- ✧ Spotting: If the blood does not exit during *wuḍū*ʾ or prayer, the prayer is valid.
- ✧ Heavy flow:
    - Virgins: Use excused person's rulings.
    - Non-virgins: Try to block; otherwise use excused person's rulings.

GLOSSARY OF TERMS

A

Abnormal uterine bleeding (*istiḥāḍa*): Any blood that is not considered menstruation or lochia.

At the maximum: Menstrual bleeding that stops exactly at 240 hours or lochia bleeding that stops exactly at 960 hours.

B

Before the maximum: Menstrual bleeding that stops before 240 hours or lochia bleeding that stops before 960 hours.

- ✧ *Before the habit*: Less than the habit in number.
- ✧ *At the habit*: Exact number of the habit.
- ✧ *After the habit*: More than the habit in number.

Beginner (*mubtadaʾa*):

- ✧ *Menstruation*: A girl who is experiencing the first menstrual period of her life.
- ✧ *Lochia*: A woman who is having her first lochia either through giving birth or a miscarriage of a developed fetus.

Blood (*dam*): Any vaginal discharge that is not completely white or clear.

Blood starts (*ẓuhūr ad-dam*): Colored vaginal discharge exits from the vagina or appears at the edge of the vaginal opening.

Blood stops (*inqiṭāʿ ad-dam*): Clear discharge, white discharge, or no discharge is seen on the *kursuf* upon its immediate removal.

C

Cesarean delivery (C-section): A surgical procedure used to deliver a baby through incisions in the abdomen and the uterus.

Complete purity (*aṭ-ṭuhr at-tāmm*): A purity span of at least 15 complete days (360 hours) or more. It could be part of a sound purity span or an unsound purity span.

Connects: The purity span does not separate between two shows of blood. The entire duration is ruled as continuous blood flow. Commonly mentioned when speaking about an incomplete purity or an intervening purity.

D

Developed fetus (*mustabīn al-khalq*): Contains at least one discernible human feature, such as a finger, foot, or toenail. The fetus does not need to be completely formed.

Disliked (*makrūh*): It could mean that the action is prohibitively disliked or slightly disliked.

- Prohibitively disliked (*makrūh taḥrīmān*): One is firmly commanded to leave the action, and it is sinful to do it. Unlike the unlawful (*ḥarām*), it may be established through a speculative text or its meaning is open for interpretation.
- Slightly disliked (*makrūh tanzīhān*): One is encouraged to leave the action. It is not sinful to do it, but one is rewarded for leaving it.

E

Early blood: Blood that starts before the expected time of menstruation based on a woman's purity habit.

Excuse (*ʿudhr*): A constant ablution nullifier, such as abnormal vaginal bleeding, urinary incontinence, or blood from a cut.

Excused person (*maʿdhūr* or *ṣāḥib al-ʿudhr*): A person who established the excused person status.

Excused person status (*ḥukm al-maʿdhūr*): A status established by someone experiencing a constant ablution nullifier. The ablution made due to this status is not nullified by the reoccurrence of the excuse within the same prayer time.

F

Fasting day: The time that the fast is performed, which is from the entrance of the *Fajr* prayer time to the entrance of the *Maghrib* prayer time.

Filth (*Najis / Najāsa*): Physical filth or impurity, like blood, urine, feces, semen, and vomit.

Fresh discharge: Discharge that is seen upon the immediate removal of a properly placed *kursuf*.

Fresh yellow: Discharge that exits the vagina as yellow.

G

***Ghusl*:** Purificatory shower that removes the state of ritual impurity.

Legally, it means to rinse the nose, the mouth, and the entire body with water at least once. Water must reach every part of the outer body that is possible to rinse without undue hardship.

***Ghusl* time:** Amount of time it takes to get undressed, perform the obligatory actions of the *ghusl*, dry oneself, get dressed, face the *qibla*, and say 'Allāh' from '*Allāhu Akbar*.' Approximately 15 minutes.

H

Habit (*ʿāda*): Any bleeding or purity span that fulfills the definitions and conditions for a sound menstruation, a sound lochia, or a sound purity. The last (most recent) sound blood and/or sound purity that a woman saw will be used as the habit.

- **Habit In Place** (*makān/zamān*): The expected time that menstruation is supposed to occur according to a woman's purity habit. It could also refer to the place in the month that her menstruation is expected to occur, like in the beginning, middle, or end of the month.

- **Habit In Number** (*ʿadad*): The expected amount of days that a woman will menstruate according to her menses habit.

Ḥanafī madhhab: One of the four traditional Sunni schools of Islamic law.

Its eponym is the 8th-century Kufan scholar, Abū Ḥanīfa an-Nuʿmān ibn Thābit, whose legal views were preserved primarily by his two most important disciples, Imām Abū Yūsuf and Imām Muḥammad ibn al-Ḥasan ash-Shaybānī. Allāh have mercy on them.

I

Impermissible (*ḥarām*): Unlawful, such that a person is sinful for doing the action and rewarded for avoiding it. It is based upon decisively established texts, and its meaning is not open for interpretation.

Incomplete purity (*aṭ-ṭuhr an-nāqiṣ*): A purity span that is less than 15 complete days (360 hours).

Internal *kursuf*: Tampons, mooncups, or any material inserted inside the vaginal canal.

Intervening purity (*aṭ-ṭuhr al-mutakhallil*): A purity span between two shows of blood during the 10 possible days of menses or the 40 possible days of lochia that follow childbirth.

Invalid: Does not legally count, such that a person is not considered to have fulfilled the right due to Allāh.

ʿItikāf: Spiritual retreat commonly done during the last ten nights of *Ramaḍān*.

J

Janāba: Sexual impurity, which is a state of ritual impurity that occurs after engaging in sexual intercourse or ejaculating.

K

Kaffāra: Expiation or atonement for committing an unlawful act, like purposely breaking a *Ramaḍān* fast without a lawful excuse.

Kursuf: Cotton cloth placed at the opening of vagina, properly secured between the labia minora (inner lips).

L

Legal blood (*ad-dam al-ḥukmī*): An interval that the Sacred Law considers to take the ruling of blood despite there being no actual blood.

Legal purity (*aṭ-ṭuhr al-ḥukmī*): A duration of blood that the Sacred Law considers to be purity (i.e. another term for *istiḥāḍa*).

Lochia (*nifās*): The normal, healthy blood that a pregnant woman expels after childbirth or after the miscarriage of a developed fetus. Legally, it is blood that originates from the uterus and comes through the vagina after the exiting of most of the baby.

M

Major ritual impurity (*al-ḥadath al-akbar*): A state that necessitates the purificatory shower (*ghusl*), such as after engaging in sexual intercourse or ejaculating.

Mandatory (*wājib*): An act that one is required to perform. The one who leaves it is sinful. Unlike the unlawful, it could have been established through a speculative text or its meaning is open for interpretation.

Menopausal woman (*iyās*): A woman who has reached 55 lunar years (approximately 53 solar years and 4 months).

Menopause: When a woman is considered to no longer experience menstruation.

Menstrual blood / menstruation (*ḥayḍ*): The normal, healthy blood that a woman expels monthly when she does not get pregnant. Legally, it is blood that originates from the uterus and comes through the vagina of a female who is at least 9 lunar years old. It is not blood due to an illness, pregnancy, or childbirth.

Menstrual place / habit in place (*makān*): The expected time that menstruation is supposed to occur according to a woman's purity habit. It could also refer to the place in the month that her menstruation is expected to occur, like in the beginning, middle, or end of the month.

Minimal purity: At least 15 complete days free of colored discharge between a menses and a menses or between a lochia and a menses.

Minor ritual impurity (*al-ḥadath al-aṣghar*): A state that necessitates ablution (*wuḍūʾ*), like after sleeping, urinating, or flatulence.

Mooncup / menstrual cup: A small, foldable, reusable device made from silicone, rubber or plastic that collects, rather than absorbs, the menstrual blood when inserted into the vagina.

N

Najis / Najāsa: Physical filth or impurity, like blood, urine, feces, semen, and vomit.

Non-virgin: A person who previously engaged in sexual intercourse.

Normal vaginal discharge (*ruṭūbat ʾl-farj*): Completely white or clear vaginal discharge.

O

Obligatory (*farḍ*): An act that one is required to perform. The one who leaves it is sinful. It is based upon decisively established texts, and its meaning is not open for interpretation.

P

Pads: An absorbent item worn by women in their underwear to catch blood when menstruating. Also known as a sanitary pad, sanitary towel, sanitary napkin, or feminine napkin.

Panty liners: A thin absorbent pad worn by women in their underwear to absorb light menstrual flow or vaginal discharge.

Permissible / lawful (*mubāḥ*): An act that entails neither reward nor punishment in the Hereafter.

Pilgrim sanctity (*iḥrām*): The sacred state that is a prerequisite for performing *ḥajj* or *ʿumra*. A person enters into a state of *iḥrām* by making the intention for *ḥajj* or *ʿumra*, while chanting the *talbiya*.

Possible days of lochia: A range of time in which a woman could possibly experience lochia. It starts from the time most of the baby exits up to the completion of 40 complete days (960 hours).

Possible days of menstruation: A range of time in which a woman could possibly menstruate. It lasts up to 10 complete days (240 hours). The possible days can potentially start when blood is seen after a purity span of least 15 complete days (360 hours) free of blood, but it is more precisely determined using a woman's purity habit.

Post-marital waiting period (*ʿidda*): The period that follows a woman's divorce or the death of her husband.

Precautionary *ghusl*: A *ghusl* that is taken in specific situations for the purpose of preserving the validity of a woman's prayers if her bleeding is not followed by a purity span of at least 15 days (360 hours).

Preferred prayer time (*al-waqt al-mustaḥabb*): It is from the entering of the *ʿAṣr* prayer time to the start of the prohibitively disliked time, which is when the sun can be looked at with ease.

Pregnancy status: The Sacred Law confirms a woman's pregnancy.

Pregnant woman (*ḥāmil*): Any woman who is pregnant.

Premenopausal period: The colors of blood that a woman used to see during her menstruation before she reached menopause.

Prohibitions: Acts which are unlawful to engage in during menstruation or lochia.

Prohibitively disliked (*makrūh taḥrīmān*): One is firmly commanded to leave the action, and it is sinful to do it. Unlike the unlawful, it could have been established through a speculative text or its meaning is open for interpretation.

Purity (*ṭuhr*): The state free of menstruation or lochia.

Purity span (*ṭuhr*): A duration of time that must separate between a menstruation and menstruation, or a lochia and menstruation, or a lochia and a lochia.

R

Real blood (*ad-dam al-ḥaqīqī*): Blood that can be physically seen with the eye.

Recommended (*mustaḥabb*): One is rewarded for performing it, but there is no sin or blame for leaving it.

Ritual impurity: An intangible state of impurity that prevents the performance of certain acts of worship like the prayer.

- ✧ Major ritual impurity requires *ghusl* due to sexual impurity or the cessation of menses / lochia.
- ✧ Minor ritual purity requires *wuḍūʾ* due to experiencing a *wuḍūʾ* nullifier.

Ritual purity: The state achieved after performing *wuḍūʾ* or *ghusl*.

Ruling in the moment: The daily guideline of how a menstruating woman or a woman in a state of lochia must act.

Ruling in retrospect: The retroactive answer once enough information about a woman's situation is acquired.

S

Sacred Law (*sharīʿah*): Religious rulings and laws based on the Qurʾān, *Sunna*, scholarly consensus (*ijmāʿ*), or legal analogy (*qiyās*).

Separates (*al-fāṣil bayna ad-damayn*): The purity span separates between two shows of blood, and each blood is ruled individually.

Slightly disliked (*makrūh tanzīhān*): One is lightly commanded to leave the action, although it is not sinful to do it. One is rewarded for leaving it.

Spotting: Vaginal bleeding that is not constant.

Sound blood (*ad-dam aṣ-ṣaḥīḥ*): Menstruation and lochia

Sound purity (*aṭ-ṭuhr aṣ-ṣaḥīḥ*): A purity span that fulfills three conditions: 1) It lasts for at least 15 complete days or more; 2) It is free from blood during this entire span; and 3) It is situated between two sound bloods.

***Sunna*:** The way of the Prophet Muhammad ﷺ.

- When using it to refer to a source of law, it includes the Prophet's ﷺ statements, actions, and tacit approval.
- When using it to refer to a ruling for an action, it means that which the Prophet ﷺ or the Companions ﷺ did most of the time. One is rewarded for acting upon the *sunna*. Leaving it without an excuse is blameworthy and not sinful.

T

Tampon: A plug of soft material inserted into the vagina to absorb menstrual blood.

***Ṭawāf*:** Circumambulation around the Kaʿba.

***Tayammum*:** Dry ablution is a substitute for *wuḍūʾ* and *ghusl*.

U

Undeveloped embryo (*ghayr mustabīn al-khalq*): No discernible human feature was formed.

Unlawful (*ḥarām*): Impermissible to do, such that a person is sinful for doing the action and rewarded for avoiding it. It is based upon decisively established texts, and its meaning is not open for interpretation.

Unsound blood (*ad-dam al-fāsid*): Any blood other than menstruation or lochia (i.e. *istiḥāḍa*).

Unsound complete purity (*aṭ-ṭuhr at-tāmm al-fāsid*): A purity span of 15 complete days (360 hours) or more, but there is blood present in its beginning, middle, or end.

Unsound purity (*aṭ-ṭuhr al-fāsid*): A purity span that does not meet one of the sound purity's conditions, such as an incomplete purity, an unsound complete purity, or an intervening purity.

V

Valid: Legally counts, such that a person is considered to have fulfilled the right due to Allāh.

Virgin: A person who never engaged in sexual intercourse.

Voluntary (*nafl*): Not obligatory to perform, but one is rewarded for doing it.

W

Woman with a habit (*muʿtāda*):

- *Menstruation*: A woman with a previous sound menstrual period and/or sound purity.
- *Lochia*: A woman that has previously experienced lochia through giving birth or the miscarriage of a developed fetus.

***Wuḍūʾ*:** Ablution for ritual purification, which must be done before performing the ritual prayer.

***Wuḍūʾ* nullifier:** That which breaks the state of ritual impurity, such as urinating, defecating, vaginal bleeding, blood flowing from a cut, vomiting a mouthful, sleeping, and the like.

BIBLIOGRAPHY

Fiqh

ʿĀbidīn, ʿAlāʾ ad-Dīn. *Al-Hadīya al-ʿAlāʾīya*

al-Indarpatī, ʿĀlim ibn al-ʿAlāʾ. *Al-Fatāwā at-Tātārkhānīya*

al-Kāsānī, ʿAlāʾ ad-Dīn Abū Bakr. *Badāʾiʿ aṣ-Ṣanāʾiʿ fī Tartīb Al-Sharāʾiʿ*

al-Marghīnānī, Burhān ad-Dīn Abī al-Ḥasan Alī ibn Abī Bakr. *Al-Hidāya* with commentary by al-ʿAlāma ʿAbdil Ḥayy al-Laknawī

al-Mawṣilī, ʿAbdullāh ibn Maḥmūd. *Al-Ikhtiyār li Taʿlīl al-Mukhtār*

al-Maydānī, ʿAbd al-Ghanī al-Ghunaymī. *Al-Lubāb fī Sharḥ al-Kitāb*

al-Qārī, Mullā ʿAlī ibn Sulṭān Muḥammad. *Fatḥ Bāb al-ʿInāya bi Sharḥ Kitāb al-Nuqāya*

al-Shaybānī, Muḥammad ibn al-Ḥasan. *al-Aṣl*

al-Shurunbulālī, Ḥasan ibn ʿAmmār. *Marāqī al-Falāh Sharḥ Nūr al-Iyḍāh*

al-Ṭaḥṭāwī, Aḥmad ibn Muhammad. *Ḥāshiyat al-Ṭaḥṭāwi ʿalā Marāqī al-Falāh*

Burhanpuri, Nizam along with a group of scholars. *Al-Fatāwā al-Hindīya*

Ibn ʿĀbidīn, Muḥammad Amīn. *Manhāl al-Wāridīn min Bihār al-Fayḍ ʿala Dhukhr al-Mutaʾahhilīn fī Masāʾil al-Ḥayḍ*

- *Radd al-Muḥtār ʿalā al-Durr al-Mukhtār*

Ibn Māza, Burhān ad-Dīn Mahmūd ibn Aḥmad. *Al-Muḥīṭ al-Burhānī fī al-Fiqh al-Nuʿmānī*

Shaykhī Zādah, ʿAbdur Raḥmān ibn Muḥammad. *Majmaʿ al-Anhur fī Sharḥ Multaqā al-Abḥur*

Hadith

al-Aṣbaḥī, Mālik ibn Anas ibn Mālik. *Muwaṭṭa᾿ al-Imām Mālik* (Narration of Imām Muḥammad ibn al-Ḥasan al-Shaybānī)

al-ʿAsqalānī, Aḥmad ibn Ḥajar. *Fatḥ al-Bārī bi Sharḥ Ṣaḥīḥ al-Bukhārī*

- *Bulūgh al-Marām min Adillat al-Aḥkām*

al-ʿAynī, Abū Muḥammad Maḥmūd ibn Aḥmad ibn Mūsā. *ʿUmdat al-Qārī Sharḥ Ṣaḥīḥ al-Bukhārī*

al-Bukhārī, Abū ʿAbdillāh Muḥammad ibn Ismāʿaīl. *Al-Jāmiʿ al-Musnad aṣ-Ṣaḥīḥ*

al-Dehlawī, ʿAbdul-Ḥaqq. *Lamaʿāt al-Tanqīḥ fī Sharḥ Mishkāt al-Maṣābīḥ*

al-Nasāʾī, Abū ʿAbd Al-Raḥmān Aḥmad ibn Shuʿayb al-Khurāsānī. *Sunan an-Nasāʾī*

al-Nawawī, Abū Zakariyyā Yaḥyā ibn Sharaf. *Al-Minhāj Sharḥ Ṣaḥīḥ Muslim ibn al-Ḥajjāj*

al-Qārī, Mullā ʿAlī ibn Sulṭān Muḥammad. *Mirqāt al-Mafātīḥ Sharḥ Mishkāt al-Maṣābīḥ*

al-Qazwīnī, Abū ʿAbdillāh Muḥammad ibn Yazīd Ibn Mājah. *Sunan Ibn Mājah*

al-Sahāranfūrī, Khalīl Aḥmad. *Badhl al-Majhūd fī Ḥall Sunan Abī Dāwūd*

al-Tahānawī, Ẓafar Aḥmad Al-ʿUthmānī. *ʿIlāʾ as-Sunan*

al-Ṭabarānī, Sulaymān ibn Aḥmad al-Lakhamī al-Shāmī. *Al-Muʿjam al-Kabīr*

al-Tirmidhī, Muḥammad ibn ʿĪsā ibn Sawra. *Sunan at-Tirmidhī*

al-Zaylaʿī, Jamāl al-Dīn. *Naṣb al-Rāya*

Tafsir

al-Jaṣāṣ, Aḥmad ibn ʿAlī Abū Bakr al-Rāzī. *Aḥkām al-Qurʾān*

al-Qurṭubī, Abū ʿAbdillāh Muḥammad ibn Aḥmad ibn Abī Bakr. *Al-Jāmiʿ li-Aḥkām al-Qurʾān*

al-Ṭabarānī, Sulaymān ibn Aḥmad al-Lakhamī al-Shāmī. *Al-Tafsir al-Kabīr*

Medical

Cleveland Clinic. (2021, November, 11). *Abnormal Uterine Bleeding.* https://my.clevelandclinic.org/health/diseases/15428-uterine-bleeding-abnormal-uterine-bleeding

Cleveland Clinic. (2021, July, 6). *Bloody Show.* https://my.clevelandclinic.org/health/symptoms/21605-bloody-show

Cleveland Clinic. (2021, November, 11). *Heavy Menstrual Bleeding.* https://my.clevelandclinic.org/health/diseases/17734-menorrhagia-heavy-menstrual-bleeding

Cleveland Clinic. (2022, May, 11). *Lochia.* https://my.clevelandclinic.org/health/symptoms/22485-lochia

Cleveland Clinic. (2019, August, 25). *Normal Menstruation.* https://my.clevelandclinic.org/health/articles/10132-normal-menstruation

Cleveland Clinic. (2021, May, 26). *Postmenopausal Bleeding.* https://my.clevelandclinic.org/health/diseases/21549-postmenopausal-bleeding

Cleveland Clinic. (2021, November, 30). *Vaginitis.* https://my.clevelandclinic.org/health/diseases/9131-vaginitis

Healthline. (2019, May, 1). *Everything You Need To Know About a Miscarriage.* https://www.healthline.com/health/miscarriage

Medical News Today. (2017, May, 26) *Is Postmenopausal Bleeding Normal?* https://www.medicalnewstoday.com/articles/317624

Medical News Today. (2019, February, 4) *What Is Bloody Show?* https://www.medicalnewstoday.com/articles/324358

Medical News Today. (2019, May, 9) *What To Know About Premenstrual Syndrome.* https://www.medicalnewstoday.com/articles/325314

National Health Service. (2021, June, 9). *PMS – Premenstrual Syndrome.* https://www.nhs.uk/conditions/pre-menstrual-syndrome/

National Health Service. (2019, September, 27). *Toxic Shock Syndrome.* https://www.nhs.uk/conditions/toxic-shock-syndrome/

National Health Service. (2021, January, 25). *Vaginitis.* https://www.nhs.uk/conditions/vaginal-discharge/

Office on Women's Health. (2021, February, 2). *Premenstrual Syndrome.* https://www.womenshealth.gov/menstrual-cycle/premenstrual-syndrome

WebMD. (2020, August, 17) *Vaginitis.* https://www.webmd.com/women/guide/sexual-health-vaginal-infections

Printed in Great Britain
by Amazon

40330168R00178